IMPRIMIS
A Fiftieth Anniversary Collection

Hillsdale College Press

Hillsdale College Press
33 East College Street
Hillsdale, Michigan 49242
www.hillsdale.edu

Printed and bound by Sheridan Books, Chelsea, Michigan
Cover design by Shanna Cote

IMPRIMIS *A Fiftieth Anniversary Collection*

Library of Congress Control Number: 2021924739
ISBN: 978-1-941946-03-9

First printing 2022

Third printing 2025

Contents

ECONOMICS

CULTURE

NATIONAL DEFENSE

THE CONSTITUTION

Foreword

In 1972, Hillsdale College began mailing *Imprimis*, free of charge, to a few thousand alumni and friends. Under a policy inviting anyone who wished to subscribe for free or enter free subscriptions for others, circulation grew to 335,000 over its first two decades. Ten years later, in 2002, it exceeded one million. At the 40-year mark, it had reached 2.6 million.

Imprimis is now a half-century old, and its circulation stands at over 6.2 million.

Why does Hillsdale College send *Imprimis* to increasing millions of American households and businesses at such great cost? There are two main answers to this question, each connected to the College's unique history.

The first is connected to Hillsdale's recent history. In the 1970s, the federal government sought to force the College to "count by race" in admissions and hiring. This was galling to a college that had opened its doors to blacks and women long before the Civil War. In addition to galling, it was wrong. Racial quotas violate the principle of equal rights that forms the basis of justice and concord in a free society. Furthermore, interfering with a private college's internal affairs violated the principle of limited government that is at the heart of American constitutionalism.

Hillsdale refused to comply. And as the battle wound its way through the courts, the College—which had never itself accepted federal taxpayer funds—was forced to go even further to maintain its independence. It was forced to tell its students and their parents that they could no longer accept federal grants or loans. Then, to stay competitive, Hillsdale had to replace that financial aid for its students and their parents with private contributions. To do this it needed a lot of friends, and *Imprimis* proved to be an effective vehicle for making them.

The second reason for publishing *Imprimis* is connected to the College's older history. Hillsdale's Articles of Association, dating to 1844, commit the College to provide "sound learning" of the kind needed to perpetuate the "inestimable blessings" of "civil and religious liberty." This idea of duty to the nation has remained strong at Hillsdale, even as other colleges and universities have fallen prey to the mind-numbing doctrines of moral and cultural relativism and the oppression of "political correctness."

Maintaining the College's independence, then, is inseparable from defending the Constitution and the principles of liberty that underlie it. This means promoting the ideas of limited government, free enterprise, individual rights, personal responsibility, and strong national defense. In promoting these ideas nationwide through *Imprimis*—as in all its work—Hillsdale College is carrying out its original mission.

As *Imprimis* heads into its sixth decade, Americans are divided politically— not in the ordinary way, over what policies should be pursued to preserve and improve our beloved country, but over the extraordinary question of whether our country deserves our love.

In line with Hillsdale's old and noble mission, *Imprimis* will continue to cultivate, through reasoned argument, the love that is due America.

Douglas A. Jeffrey
Vice President for External Affairs and Editor of *Imprimis*
Hillsdale College

POLITICS

Do We Need Our Country Anymore?

Larry P. Arnn

December 2018

As we reach the end of this turbulent year, the uproar of the hour is against the nation-state, and not for the first time. "World leaders" are now accustomed to call for the subordination of the nation to the good of the globe. This call is amplified by the media and intellectual elites, who march in lockstep. If the call is right, the peoples of the world will enter a new age of global peace, prosperity, and cooperation. If it is wrong, the free nations of the world will lose the remnants of democratic accountability that have kept them free.

The occasion for the latest outburst of transnationalist enthusiasm was a grim anniversary, the 100th Armistice Day, the annual remembrance of November 11, 1918, the end of the First World War. The losses in Europe in that war were staggering: 8.5 million soldiers were killed, including 900,000 from the British Empire and Commonwealth and 1.36 million French. By comparison, the number of British military killed in the Second World War, a much costlier war overall in terms of life and treasure, was just under 400,000; that of French military killed, France's army having been defeated quickly, 210,000. Such horrors had never been seen, and their scars are still visible all over Europe: lists of the dead on the walls of colleges, statues in town squares, national gatherings of solemn dignity.

Modern eyes see these wars as the result of the nation-state and proof that nationalism cannot be sustained. But this is precisely a half-truth. It leaves out the distinction that matters more than any: what *kind* of nations do we mean?

With world leaders gathered in Paris in what was to be an atmosphere of unity, President Macron of France was the keynote speaker at the Armistice Day ceremony, and his speech made a sensation in the press. He delivered it standing before the Arc de Triomphe, a monument to the Revolutionary and Napoleonic Wars that formed modern France. Beneath the Arc is the Tomb of the Unknown Soldier from World War I. As much as any place on earth, it is hallowed civic ground—a curious place to launch an attack upon the civic.

Nationalism, Macron argued, is the cause of war. Nationalism is the reason so many died in the twentieth century. The cure is to rid ourselves of nationalism. Macron spoke beautifully of the sacrifices of the soldiers who perished in World War I, of the misery in which they fought, of the lives they might have had. But as he mourned and honored them, he also conscripted them into the cause of transnationalism, for which he says they fought.

Here is the key passage that made the news:

> In those dark hours, that vision of France as a generous nation, of France as a project, of France promoting universal values, was the exact opposite of the egotism of a people who look after only their interests, because patriotism is the exact opposite of nationalism: nationalism is a betrayal of it.

What can it possibly mean to say that patriotism is the opposite of nationalism? Think of the meaning of the words. "Nation" comes from the Latin word *natus*, which means "birth" or "to be born." In its root, nation is the place where one is born. *Natus* is also the root of the word "nature," which means how and what a thing comes to be and therefore what it is. Nature and nation are connected terms. One might say it is the nature of man to have a nation. The classical philosophers, and for that matter the greatest French philosophers, say that very thing. Take Montesquieu, who like many of the best thinkers sought for a law or standard of behavior among nations that would avoid perpetual war. He did not propose, however, that the nation should pass away. To the contrary, he wrote: "Laws should be so appropriate to the people for whom they are made that it is very unlikely that the laws of one nation can suit another."

"Patriotism" is also an interesting word. It comes from the Latin root *pater*. The *pater* is the father, thus for example "paternity" and "patriarchy." The related Latin word *patria* means "fatherland." One is born to a mother and a father. One's nation is the land of one's mother and father. Of course, this is not the only way one can have a nation, but it is the usual way or the natural way.

So for Macron to say that patriotism is the opposite of nationalism is just a bit of silly wordplay. Did he mean that for a person to love his father he must despise the place where his father and mother brought him to life? In the distant past our fathers founded our nation. Are we to love them and despise their work? Are we to imagine that the patriotic founders of nations, and nations' patriotic defenders in war, despised their nations, and that we can emulate them only by doing the same?

Macron distorts the meaning of nationalism in order to condemn it. He calls it the "egotism of a people who look after only their interests." *Only* is a cheat word: who claims that any nation, or for that matter any individual, should look after *only* its own interest? Even Donald Trump, who is hardly acceptable in the polite company of "world leaders" and who Macron was setting himself against in his attack on nationalism, says the opposite frequently. To have a moral duty to look after one's children is not to have a duty to look after *only* them: that duty must come first, but it entails others.

———

According to Macron, "the spirit of revenge and the economic and moral crisis [following World War I] fueled the rise of nationalism and totalitarianism." This in turn produced World War II. This is true, but only part of the truth. The whole truth reveals that nationalism is both stubborn and, rightly conceived, necessary to many things, including the *prevention* of war. Nationalism is older than the people of France or of any country. It did not only result from the First World War, it also caused that war. But just as much, it caused the defeat of the aggressors. It is in fact the highest expression of human nature in community.

France had reason to provoke the First World War, but it did not. France had been defeated by Germany in the Franco-Prussian War, launched by Germany to help unite German provinces into one nation. France was stripped of two provinces. Modern Germany was drawn up in the Palace of Versailles, the home of Louis XIV. The establishment of modern Germany was therefore also a humiliation of France. Despite this, France did not begin the next war. Neither did Belgium or Luxembourg, both places that had suffered at the hands of Germany and would do so again. It was the Germans who were again the aggressors.

From this history we learn that it is not the nation-state, but the *kinds* of nation-states that matter. From the birth of political philosophy in ancient Athens, it has been understood in the West that the difference between good and bad regimes, just as between lives lived well and lives lived badly, is all-important.

This difference between good and bad regimes was at stake in the First World War as much as in any war in history. The war began with an act of raw aggression: the Germans with their allies the Austrians launched an attack in August 1914 upon Belgium and France in the north and Serbia in the south. The trouble had started in Serbia, where the heir to the Austrian throne was assassinated. Germany supported Austria by attacking two nations that had nothing to do with the trouble in Serbia and lay in the opposite direction.

The German plan for victory in 1914 was almost as ambitious as that of Hitler in 1939. It was drawn up by scholar and diplomat Kurt Riezler for German Prime Minister Bethmann-Hollweg, and its aims were draconian. France would cede northern territory, pay a war indemnity of ten billion German marks, and pay off all of Germany's existing national debt, making the French economy dependent upon the German. France would demolish its northern forts, and Belgium and Luxembourg would be annexed or become vassal states. The Belgian port of Antwerp would be annexed. In the east, Poland would be placed under German sovereignty "for all time."

This might be called the first modern plan for the international governance of Europe. And when it was overcome, it was not overcome by principles alone. Britain and France were devoted to the idea of the rights of man, but here in this war they chiefly saved the rights of the small powers—not to mention their own—through a mighty effort.

If France had lost the First World War, its people might have suffered earlier much of what they suffered after its defeat in the Second World War. French citizens were rounded up and shot, and French officials were compelled by threats to their families to participate in this. Following the surrender of France to Nazi Germany in 1940, of course, French officials were also compelled to help round up Jews for transport to the death camps. This might have been the fate of the French people for decades if not for the sacrifices of others—Russians, British, and Americans especially—to liberate them.

Macron's account of the two World Wars as a proof against nationalism includes a quote from the greatest Frenchman of his time, George Clemenceau, who served as the prime minister of France during the later years of World War I. In his victory speech of November 11, 1918, Clemenceau said that France had fought "for what is right and for freedom, [and] would always and forever be a soldier of ideals." Clemenceau surely believed this, but it is not all he believed.

At the outbreak of the war in 1914, issuing a call to arms, Clemenceau said:

It is for the Latin cause, for the independence of nationalities in Europe, that we are going to fight, for the greatest ideas that have honored the thought of mankind, ideas that have come to us from Athens and Rome and of which we have made the crowning work of that civilization which the Germany of Arminius pretends to monopolize, like those barbarians who melted into ingots the marvels of ancient art after the pillaging of Rome in order to make savage ornaments out of them.

The "Latin cause" is the cause of Rome, of which France is one of the first and chief successors. Arminius was a commander of the Germanic tribes who destroyed many Roman legions. According to Clemenceau, the lessons that come from Rome and Athens concern "mankind" and give rise to a civilization that inspires many nations. One precept of that civilization is the "independence of nationalities," and for that, he said, "we are going to fight."

It seems then that Clemenceau believed both in the nation-state and in the rights of man. We can find in Winston Churchill, who knew and adored Clemenceau, the clearest explanation of how the nation-state and the rights of man can be reconciled and why they must be reconciled.

In 1938, as Hitler loomed, Churchill gave the commencement address at the University of Bristol, of which he is still its longest serving chancellor. His speech presented a microcosm of his thinking of a lifetime. He began: "There are few words which are used more loosely than the word 'Civilization.' What does it mean? It means a society based upon the opinion of civilians."

To our ears that definition might seem too narrow. Doesn't civilization include painting and poetry? What about prosperity, technology, and progress? What we must understand is that Churchill begins not with a narrow but a *literal* definition. The word "civilization" is cognate with the word for *citizen*—that is, with the word for the member of a nation. When we speak of the civilization of Europe, we are speaking perforce of the nations that make up Europe.

To base a society "upon the opinions of civilians" is a decisive step. Civilians are to be distinguished not only from foreigners, but also from the military. The military is necessarily the strongest force, if one means physical force, in a nation. Relative to the military, civilians are weak. Societies ruled by force are always ruled by, or in alliance with, the military. Civilization, a society based upon "the opinions of civilians," is a society that has found a way to induce the strong to serve the common good and therefore to protect the weak.

Churchill continued: "The central principle of Civilization is the subordination of the ruling authority to the settled customs of the people and to their will as expressed through the Constitution." There must be "a people," and they must have "customs" and a "Constitution." Customs are what we develop as a people when we live together in common life. Customs vary from people to people, but they are called savage when a people are ruled by force. Civilization, on the other hand, "continually [grows] freedom, comfort, and culture." Civilization affords "a wider and less harassed life . . . to the masses of the people." It cherishes "the traditions of the past." The "inheritance bequeathed to us by former wise or valiant men becomes a rich estate to be enjoyed and used by all."

Civilization also requires a constitution, which establishes "parliaments where laws are made, and independent courts of justice in which over long periods those laws are maintained." In the myriad places where Churchill speaks of constitutionalism, a favorite theme, he adds that the people must have the right and power

> by constitutional action, by free unfettered elections, with secret ballot, to choose or change the character or form of government under which they dwell; that freedom of speech and thought should reign; that courts of justice, independent of the executive, unbiased by any party, should administer laws which have received the broad assent of large majorities or are consecrated by time and custom.

Churchill calls these things the "title deeds of freedom which should lie in every cottage home." And by "every" he means in every nation.

Churchill often points out that "parliament" means government by talking. To parley is to talk. The alternative to government by talking is government by force. It is not practical in any way to believe that a world-state, made up of people who cannot speak to each other, who do not live in the same way or have the same customs, could be anything but a despotism. The city, writes Aristotle, grows from our capacity for reason and speech. And so it must be.

In the European Union, to cite an example of a transnational form of government, the peoples of the member states cannot speak to each other, at least not in their familiar language, except through intermediaries. Any British subject can speak with any other, and the French can speak with the French, but those peoples cannot by themselves exercise decisive influence on the politics and policy of the European Union. On this theme one might read Václav Klaus, the former president of the Czech Republic. He lived some of his life under Nazi domination and most of it under Soviet domination in the Warsaw Pact. He helped lead his country to freedom, and he rejoiced and still rejoices that at last he has a country, in which fellow citizens are able to talk and make decisions together. And he is loath to surrender Czech sovereignty to the EU.

———

At the same time Churchill believed in the nation as the first element of civilization, he was also one of the inventors of the European Union. He had believed in collective security for decades. In 1946 he gave a speech in Zürich in which he called for a "United States of Europe." This speech is one of the building blocks of European unity, and he is counted as one of its heroes today. Churchill however kept a clear distinction between the collective institutions formed by nations and the nations themselves. In December 1948 he said:

> We are not seeking in the European movement...to usurp the functions of Government. I have tried to make this plain, again and again, to the heads of the Government. We ask for a European assembly without executive power. We hope that sentiment and culture, the forgetting of old feuds, the lowering and melting down of barriers of all kinds between countries, the growing sense of being "a good European"—we hope that all these will be the final, eventual and irresistible solvents of the difficulties which now condemn Europe to misery. The structure of constitutions, the settlement of economic problems, the military aspects—these belong to governments. We do not trespass upon their sphere.

Churchill spent much of his life trying to avoid the horrors of modern war and trying to erect structures to prevent them. But he did not seek to overturn the laws of nature or the sovereignty of nations. These cannot be rightfully overturned, and only disaster can come from the attempt.

Toward the end of his Armistice Day speech, President Macron called upon the political leaders of the world, on behalf of their peoples, to "take the United Nations' oath to place peace higher than anything." Higher than freedom? Higher than justice? Higher than the lives of our children? Must we abandon "Give me liberty or give me death"? For the sake of peace, should the French have surrendered in 1914 or 1939?

This radical statement of Macron gets near the heart of the movement toward transnationalism. The evils of the world, especially war, require that *anything* is justified to remove those evils—including the subordination of the nation-state, the only kind of community that can effectively represent the people.

President Trump, much derided everywhere as unfashionable, particularly in Europe, often speaks about the importance of the nation and the duty of government to serve the will and the interest of its citizens. This idea is unacceptable in our supposedly enlightened age. But Trump is often clear that he wishes well to other nations and thinks that respect for nationhood is key to good relations. Speaking at the United Nations in September, he said: "We believe that when nations respect the rights of their neighbors, and defend the interests of their people, they can better work together to secure the blessings of safety, prosperity, and peace."

On this point Trump and Churchill are agreed, and Macron is wrong. To have consent of the governed, there must be a people to give consent. Indeed, that is the first principle derived from human nature in the Declaration of Independence, and it is essential to distinguishing good government from bad.

The 2016 Election and the Demise of Journalistic Standards

Michael Goodwin

May/June 2017

I've been a journalist for a long time. Long enough to know that it wasn't always like this. There was a time not so long ago when journalists were trusted and admired. We were generally seen as trying to report the news in a fair and straightforward manner. Today, all that has changed. For that, we can blame the 2016 election or, more accurately, how some news organizations chose to cover it. Among the many firsts, last year's election gave us the gobsmacking revelation that most of the mainstream media puts both thumbs on the scale—that most of what you read, watch, and listen to is distorted by intentional bias and hostility. I have never seen anything like it. Not even close.

It's not exactly breaking news that most journalists lean left. I used to do that myself. I grew up at *The New York Times*, so I'm familiar with the species. For most of the media, bias grew out of the social revolution of the 1960s and '70s. Fueled by the civil rights and anti-Vietnam War movements, the media jumped on the anti-authority bandwagon writ large. The deal was sealed with Watergate, when journalism was viewed as more trusted than government—and far more exciting and glamorous. Think Robert Redford in *All the President's Men*. Ever since, young people became journalists because they wanted to be the next Woodward and Bernstein, find a Deep Throat, and bring down a president. Of course, most of them only wanted to bring down a Republican president. That's because liberalism is baked into the journalism cake.

During the years I spent teaching at the Columbia University School of Journalism, I often found myself telling my students that the job of the reporter was "to comfort the afflicted and afflict the comfortable." I'm not even sure where I first heard that line, but it still captures the way most journalists think about what they do. Translate the first part of that compassionate-sounding idea into the daily decisions about what makes news, and it is easy to fall into the habit of thinking that every person afflicted by something is entitled to help. Or, as liberals like to say, "Government is what we do together." From there, it's a short drive to the conclusion that for every problem there must be a government solution.

The rest of that journalistic ethos—"afflict the comfortable"—leads to the knee-jerk support of endless taxation. Somebody has to pay for that government intervention the media loves to demand. In the same vein, and for the same reason, the average reporter will support every conceivable regulation as a way to equalize conditions for the poor. He will also give sympathetic coverage to groups like Occupy Wall Street and Black Lives Matter.

A New Dimension

I knew all of this about the media mindset going into the 2016 presidential campaign. But I was still shocked at what happened. This was not naïve liberalism run amok. This was a whole new approach to politics. No one in modern times had seen anything like it. As with grief, there were several stages. In the beginning, Donald Trump's candidacy was treated as an outlandish publicity stunt, as though he wasn't a serious candidate and should be treated as a circus act. But television executives quickly made a surprising discovery: the more they put Trump on the air, the higher their ratings climbed. Ratings are money. So news shows started devoting hours and hours simply to pointing the cameras at Trump and letting them run.

As his rallies grew, the coverage grew, which made for an odd dynamic. The candidate nobody in the media took seriously was attracting the most people to his events and getting the most news coverage. Newspapers got in on the game too. Trump, unlike most of his opponents, was always available to the press, and could be counted on to say something outrageous or controversial that made a headline. He made news by being a spectacle.

Despite the mockery of journalists and late-night comics, something extraordinary was happening. Trump was dominating a campaign none of the smart money thought he could win. And then, suddenly, he was winning. Only when the crowded Republican field began to thin and Trump kept racking up primary and caucus victories did the media's tone grow more serious.

One study estimated that Trump had received so much free airtime that if he had had to buy it, the price would have been $2 billion. The realization that they had helped Trump's rise seemed to make many executives, producers, and journalists furious. By the time he secured the nomination and the general election rolled around, they were gunning for him. Only two people now had a chance to be president, and the overwhelming media consensus was that it could not be Donald Trump. They would make sure of that. The coverage of him grew so vicious and one-sided that last August I wrote a column on the unprecedented bias. Under the headline "American Journalism Is Collapsing Before Our Eyes," I wrote that the so-called cream of the media crop was "engaged in a naked display of partisanship" designed to bury Trump and elect Hillary Clinton.

The evidence was on the front page, the back page, the culture pages, even the sports pages. It was at the top of the broadcast and at the bottom of the broadcast. Day in, day out, in every media market in America, Trump was savaged like no other candidate in memory. We were watching the total collapse of standards, with fairness and balance tossed overboard. Every story was an opinion masquerading as news, and every opinion ran in the same direction—toward Clinton and away from Trump.

For the most part, I blame *The New York Times* and *The Washington Post* for causing this breakdown. The two leading liberal newspapers were trying to top each other in their demonization of Trump and his supporters. They set the tone, and most of the rest of the media followed like lemmings.

On one level, tougher scrutiny of Trump was clearly defensible. He had a controversial career and lifestyle, and he was seeking the presidency as his first job in government. He also provided lots of fuel with some of his outrageous words and deeds during the campaign. But from the beginning there was also a second element to the lopsided coverage. *The New York Times* has not endorsed a Republican for president since Dwight Eisenhower in 1956, meaning it would back a dead raccoon if it had a "D" after its name. Think of it—George McGovern over Richard Nixon? Jimmy Carter over Ronald Reagan? Walter Mondale over Reagan? Any Democrat would do. And *The Washington Post*, which only started making editorial endorsements in the 1970s, has never once endorsed a Republican for president.

But again, I want to emphasize that 2016 had those predictable elements plus a whole new dimension. This time, the papers dropped the pretense of fairness and jumped headlong into the tank for one candidate over the other. The *Times* media reporter began a story this way:

> If you're a working journalist and you believe that Donald J. Trump is a demagogue playing to the nation's worst racist and nationalist tendencies, that he cozies up to anti-American dictators and that he would be dangerous with control of the United States nuclear codes, how the heck are you supposed to cover him?

I read that paragraph and I thought to myself, well, that's actually an easy question. If you feel that way about Trump, normal journalistic ethics would dictate that you shouldn't cover him. You cannot be fair. And you shouldn't be covering Hillary Clinton either, because you've already decided who should be president. Go cover sports or entertainment. Yet the *Times* media reporter rationalized the obvious bias he had just acknowledged, citing the view that Clinton was "normal" and Trump was not.

I found the whole concept appalling. What happened to fairness? What happened to standards? I'll tell you what happened to them. The *Times* top editor, Dean Baquet, eliminated them. In an interview last October with the Nieman Foundation for Journalism at Harvard, Baquet admitted that the piece by his media reporter had nailed his own thinking. Trump "challenged our language," he said, and Trump "will have changed journalism." Of the daily struggle for fairness, Baquet had this to say: "I think that Trump has ended that struggle.... We now say stuff. We fact check him. We write it more powerfully that [what he says is] false."

Baquet was being too modest. Trump was challenging, sure, but it was Baquet who changed journalism. He's the one who decided that the standards of fairness and nonpartisanship could be abandoned without consequence.

With that decision, Baquet also changed the basic news story formula. To the age-old elements of who, what, when, where, and why, he added the reporter's opinion. Now the floodgates were open, and virtually every so-called news article reflected a clear bias against Trump. Stories, photos, headlines, placement in the paper—all the tools that writers and editors have—were summoned to the battle. The goal was to pick the next president.

Thus began the spate of stories, which continues today, in which the *Times* routinely calls Trump a liar in its news pages and headlines. Again, the contrast with the past is striking. The *Times* never called Barack Obama a liar, despite such obvious opportunities as "you can keep your doctor" and "the Benghazi attack was caused by an internet video." Indeed, the *Times* and *The Washington Post*, along with most of the White House press corps, spent eight years cheerleading the Obama administration, seeing not a smidgen of corruption or dishonesty. They have been tougher on Hillary Clinton during her long career. But they still never called her a liar, despite such doozies as "I set up my own computer server so I would only need one device," "I turned over all the government emails," and "I never sent or received classified emails." All those were lies, but not to the national media. Only statements by Trump were fair game.

As we know now, most of the media totally missed Trump's appeal to millions upon millions of Americans. The prejudice against him blinded those news organizations to what was happening in the country. Even more incredibly, I believe the bias and hostility directed at Trump backfired. The feeling that the election was, in part, a referendum on the media, gave some voters an extra incentive to vote for Trump. A vote for him was a vote against the media and against Washington. Not incidentally, Trump used that sentiment to his advantage, often revving up his crowds with attacks on reporters. He still does.

If I haven't made it clear, let me do so now. The behavior of much of the media, but especially *The New York Times*, was a disgrace. I don't believe it ever will recover the public trust it squandered.

The *Times*' previous reputation for having the highest standards was legitimate. Those standards were developed over decades to force reporters and editors to be fair and to gain public trust. The commitment to fairness made *The New York Times* the flagship of American journalism. But standards are like laws in the sense that they are designed to guide your behavior in good times and in bad. Consistent adherence to them was the source of the *Times*' credibility. And eliminating them has made the paper less than ordinary. Its only standards now are double standards.

I say this with great sadness. I was blessed to grow up at the *Times*, getting a clerical job right out of college and working my way onto the reporting staff, where I worked for a decade. It was the formative experience of my career where I learned most of what I know about reporting and writing. Alas, it was a different newspaper then. Abe Rosenthal was the editor in those days, and long before we'd ever heard the phrase "zero tolerance," that's what Abe practiced toward conflicts of interest and reporters' opinions. He set the rules and everybody knew it.

Here is a true story about how Abe Rosenthal resolved a conflict of interest. A young woman was hired by the *Times* from one of the Philadelphia newspapers. But soon after she arrived in New York, a story broke in Philly that she had had a romantic affair with a political figure she had covered, and that she had accepted a fur coat and other expensive gifts from him. When he saw the story, Abe called the woman into his office and asked her if it were true. When she said yes, he told her to clean out her desk—that she was finished at the *Times* and would never work there again. As word spread through the newsroom, some reporters took the woman's side and rushed in to tell Abe that firing her was too harsh. He listened for about 30 seconds, raised his hand for silence, and said (this is slightly bowdlerized): "I don't care if you have a romantic affair with an elephant on your personal time, but then you can't cover the circus for the paper." Case closed. The conflict of interest policy was clear, absolute, and unforgettable.

As for reporters' opinions, Abe had a similar approach. He didn't want them in the news pages. And if you put them in, he took them out. They belonged in the opinion pages only, which were managed separately. Abe said he knew reporters tended to lean left and would find ways to sneak their views into the stories. So he saw his job as steering the paper slightly to the right. "That way," he said, "the paper would end up in the middle." He was well known for this attitude, which he summed up as "keeping the paper straight." He even said he wanted his epitaph to read, "He kept the paper straight." Like most people, I thought this was a joke. But after I related all this in a column last year, his widow contacted me and said it wasn't a joke—that, in fact, Abe's tombstone reads, "He kept the paper straight." She sent me a picture to prove it. I published that picture of his tombstone alongside a column where I excoriated the *Times* for its election coverage. Sadly, the *Times*' high standards were buried with Abe Rosenthal.

Looking to the Future

Which brings us to the crucial questions. Can the American media be fixed? And is there anything that we as individuals can do to make a difference? The short answer to the first question is "No, it can't be fixed." The 2016 election was the media's Humpty Dumpty moment. It fell off the wall, shattered into a million pieces, and can't be put back together again. In case there is any doubt, 2017 is confirming that the standards are still dead. The orgy of visceral Trump-bashing continues unabated.

But the future of journalism isn't all gloom and doom. In fact, if we accept the new reality of widespread bias and seize the potential it offers, there is room for optimism. Consider this—the election showed the country is roughly divided 50-50 between people who will vote for a Democrat and people who will vote for a Republican. But our national media is more like 80-20 in favor of Democrats. While the media should, in theory, broadly reflect the public, it doesn't. Too much of the media acts like a special interest group. Detached from the greater good, it exists to promote its own interest and the political party with which it is aligned.

Ronald Reagan's optimism is often expressed in a story that is surely apocryphal, but irresistible. He is said to have come across a barn full of horse manure and remarked cheerfully that there must be a pony in it somewhere. I suggest we look at the media landscape in a similar fashion. The mismatch between the mainstream media and the public's sensibilities means there is a vast untapped market for news and views that are not now represented. To realize that potential, we only need three ingredients, and we already have them: first, free speech; second, capitalism and free markets; and the third ingredient is you, the consumers of news.

Free speech is under assault, most obviously on many college campuses, but also in the news media, which presents a conformist view to its audience and gets a politically segregated audience in return. Look at the letters section in *The New York Times*—virtually every reader who writes in agrees with the opinions of the paper. This isn't a miracle; it's a bubble. Liberals used to love to say, "I don't agree with your opinion, but I would fight to the death for your right to express it." You don't hear that anymore from the Left. Now they want to shut you up if you don't agree. And they are having some success.

But there is a countervailing force. Look at what happened this winter when the Left organized boycotts of department stores that carried Ivanka Trump's clothing and jewelry. Nordstrom folded like a cheap suit, but Trump's supporters rallied on social media and Ivanka's company had its best month ever. This is the model I have in mind for the media. It is similar to how FOX News got started. Rupert Murdoch thought there was an untapped market for a more fair and balanced news channel, and he recruited Roger Ailes to start it more than 20 years ago. Ailes found a niche market alright—half the country!

Incredible advances in technology are also on the side of free speech. The explosion of choices makes it almost impossible to silence all dissent and gain a monopoly, though certainly Facebook and Google are trying.

As for the necessity of preserving capitalism, look around the world. Nations without economic liberty usually have little or no dissent. That's not a coincidence. In this, I'm reminded of an enduring image from the Occupy Wall Street movement. That movement was a pestilence, egged on by President Obama and others who view other people's wealth as a crime against the common good. This attitude was on vivid display as the protesters held up their iPhones to demand the end of capitalism. As I wrote at the time, did they believe Steve Jobs made each and every Apple product one at a time in his garage? Did they not have a clue about how capital markets make life better, for more people than any other system known to man? They had no clue. And neither do many government officials, who think they can kill the golden goose and still get golden eggs.

Which brings me to the third necessary ingredient in determining where we go from here. It's you. I urge you to support the media you like. As the great writer and thinker Midge Decter once put it, "You have to join the side you're on." It's no secret that newspapers and magazines are losing readers and money and shedding staff. Some of them are good newspapers. Some of them are good magazines. There are also many wonderful, thoughtful, small publications and websites that exist on a shoestring. Don't let them die. Subscribe or contribute to those you enjoy. Give subscriptions to friends. Put your money where your heart and mind are. An expanded media landscape that better reflects the diversity of public preferences would, in time, help create a more level political and cultural arena. That would be a great thing. So again I urge you: join the side you're on.

The Roots of Our Partisan Divide

Christopher Caldwell

February 2020

American society today is divided by party and by ideology in a way it has perhaps not been since the Civil War. I have just published a book that, among other things, suggests why this is. It is called *The Age of Entitlement: America Since the Sixties*. It runs from the assassination of John F. Kennedy to the election of Donald J. Trump. You can get a good idea of the drift of the narrative from its chapter titles: 1963, Race, Sex, War, Debt, Diversity, Winners, and Losers.

I can end part of the suspense right now—Democrats are the winners. Their party *won* the 1960s—they gained money, power, and prestige. The GOP is the party of the people who lost those things.

One of the strands of this story involves the Vietnam War. The antiquated way the Army was mustered in the 1960s wound up creating a class system. What I'm referring to here is the so-called student deferment. In the old days, university-level education was rare. At the start of the First World War, only one in 30 American men was in a college or university, so student deferments were not culturally significant. By the time of Vietnam, almost half of American men were in a college or university, and student deferment remained in effect until well into the war. So if you were rich enough to study art history, you went to Woodstock and made love. If you worked in a garage, you went to Da Nang and made war. This produced a class division that many of the college-educated mistook for a moral division, particularly once we lost the war. The rich saw themselves as having avoided service in Vietnam not because they were more privileged or—heaven forbid—less brave, but because they were more decent.

Another strand of the story involves women. Today, there are two cultures of American womanhood—the culture of married women and the culture of single women. If you poll them on political issues, they tend to differ diametrically. It was feminism that produced this rupture. For women during the Kennedy administration, by contrast, there was one culture of femininity, and it united women from cradle to grave: Ninety percent of married women and 87 percent of unmarried women believed there was such a thing as "women's intuition." Only 16 percent of married women and only 15 percent of unmarried women thought it was excusable in some circumstances to have an extramarital affair. Ninety-nine percent of women, when asked the ideal age for marriage, said it was sometime before age 27. None answered "never."

But it is a third strand of the story, running all the way down to our day, that is most important for explaining our partisan polarization. It concerns how the civil rights laws of the 1960s, and particularly the Civil Rights Act of 1964, divided the country. They did so by giving birth to what was, in effect, a second constitution, which would eventually cause Americans to peel off into two different and incompatible constitutional cultures. This became obvious only over time. It happened so slowly that many people did not notice.

Because conventional wisdom today holds that the Civil Rights Act brought the country together, my book's suggestion that it pulled the country apart has been met with outrage. The outrage has been especially pronounced among those who have not read the book. So for their benefit I should make crystal clear that my book is *not* a defense of segregation or Jim Crow, and that when I criticize the long-term effects of the civil rights laws of the 1960s,

I do *not* criticize the principle of equality in general, or the movement for black equality in particular.

What I am talking about are the emergency mechanisms that, in the name of ending segregation, were established under the Civil Rights Act of 1964. These gave Washington the authority to override what Americans had traditionally thought of as their ordinary democratic institutions. It was widely assumed that the emergency mechanisms would be temporary and narrowly focused. But they soon escaped democratic control altogether, and they have now become the most powerful part of our governing system.

How Civil Rights Legislation Worked

There were two noteworthy things about the civil rights legislation of 1964 and 1965.

The first was its unprecedented concentration of power. It gave Washington tools it had never before had in peacetime. It created new crimes, outlawing discrimination in almost every walk of public and private life. It revoked—or repealed—the prevailing understanding of freedom of association as protected by the First Amendment. It established agencies to hunt down these new crimes—an expanded Civil Rights Commission, an Equal Employment Opportunity Commission (EEOC), and various offices of civil rights in the different cabinet agencies. It gave government new prerogatives, such as laying out hiring practices for all companies with more than 15 employees, filing lawsuits, conducting investigations, and ordering redress. Above all, it exposed every corner of American social, economic, and political life to direction from bureaucrats and judges.

To put it bluntly, the effect of these civil rights laws was to take a lot of decisions that had been made in the democratic parts of American government and relocate them to the bureaucracy or the judiciary. Only with that kind of arsenal, Lyndon Johnson and the drafters thought, would it be possible to root out insidious racism.

The second noteworthy thing about the civil rights legislation of the 1960s is that it was kind of a fudge. It sat uneasily not only with the First Amendment, but with the Constitution as a whole. The Voting Rights Act of 1965, passed largely to give teeth to the 14th Amendment's guarantee of equal rights for all citizens, did so by creating different levels of rights for citizens of southern states like Alabama and citizens of northern states like Michigan when it came to election laws.

The goal of the civil rights laws was to bring the sham democracies of the American South into conformity with the Constitution. But nobody's democracy is perfect, and it turned out to be much harder than anticipated to distinguish between democracy in the South and democracy elsewhere in the country. If the spirit of the law was to humiliate Southern bigots, the letter of the law put the entire country—all its institutions—under the threat of lawsuits and prosecutions for discrimination.

Still, no one was too worried about that. It is clear in retrospect that Americans outside the South understood segregation as a regional problem. As far as we can tell from polls, 70-90 percent of Americans outside the South thought that blacks in their part of the country were treated just fine, the same as anyone else. In practice, non-Southerners did not expect the new laws to be turned back on *themselves*.

The Broadening of Civil Rights

The problem is that when the work of the civil rights legislation was done—when *de jure* segregation was stopped—these new powers were not suspended or scaled back or reassessed. On the contrary, they intensified. The ability to set racial quotas for public schools was not in the original Civil Rights Act, but offices of civil rights started doing it, and there was no one strong enough to resist. Busing of schoolchildren had not been in the original plan, either, but once schools started to fall short of targets established by the bureaucracy, judges ordered it.

Affirmative action was a vague notion in the Civil Rights Act. But by the time of the Supreme Court's 1978 *Bakke* decision, it was an outright system of racial preference for non-whites. In that case, the plaintiff, Alan Bakke, who had been a U.S. Marine captain in Vietnam, saw his application for medical school rejected, even though his test scores were in the 96th, 94th, 97th, and 72nd percentiles. Minority applicants, meanwhile, were admitted with, on average, scores in the 34th, 30th, 37th, and 18th percentiles. And although the Court decided that Bakke himself deserved admission, it did not do away with the affirmative action programs that kept him out. In fact, it institutionalized them, mandating "diversity"—a new concept at the time—as the law of the land.

Meanwhile other groups, many of them not even envisioned in the original legislation, got the hang of using civil rights law. Immigrant advocates, for instance: Americans never voted for bilingual education, but when the Supreme Court upheld the idea in 1974, rule writers in the offices of civil rights simply established it, and it exists to this day. Women, too: the EEOC battled Sears, Roebuck & Co. from 1973 to 1986 with every weapon at its disposal, trying to prove it guilty of sexism—ultimately failing to prove even a single instance of it.

Finally, civil rights came to dominate—and even overrule—legislation that had nothing to do with it. The most traumatic example of this was the Immigration Reform and Control Act of 1986. This legislation was supposed to be the grand compromise on which our modern immigration policy would be built. On the one hand, about three million illegal immigrants who had mostly come north from Mexico would be given citizenship. On the other hand, draconian laws would ensure that the amnesty would not be an incentive to future migrants, and that illegal immigration would never get out of control again. So there were harsh "employer sanctions" for anyone who hired a non-citizen. But once the law passed, what happened? Illegal immigrants got their amnesty. But the penalties on illegal hiring turned out to be fake—because, to simplify just a bit, asking an employee who "looks Mexican" where he was born or about his citizenship status was held to be a violation of his civil rights. Civil rights law had made it impossible for Americans to get what they'd voted for through their representatives, leading to decades of political strife over immigration policy that continues to this day.

A more recent manifestation of the broadening of civil rights laws is the "Dear Colleague" letter sent by the Obama Education Department's Office for Civil Rights in 2011, which sought to dictate sexual harassment policy to every college and university in the country. Another is the overturning by judges of a temporary ban on entry from certain countries linked to terrorism in the first months of the Trump administration in 2017.

These policies, *qua* policies, have their defenders and their detractors. The important thing for our purposes is how they were established and enforced. More and more areas of American life have been withdrawn from voters' democratic control and delivered up to the bureaucratic and judicial emergency mechanisms of civil rights law. Civil rights law has become a second constitution, with powers that can be used to override the Constitution of 1787.

The New Constitution

In explaining the constitutional order that we see today, I'd like to focus on just two of its characteristics.

First, it has a *moral* element, almost a metaphysical element, that is usually more typical of theocracies than of secular republics. As we've discussed, civil rights law gave bureaucrats and judges emergency powers to override the normal constitutional order, bypassing democracy. But the key question is: Under what conditions is the government authorized to activate these emergency powers? It is a question that has been much studied by political thinkers in Europe. Usually when European governments of the past bypassed their constitutions by declaring emergencies, it was on the grounds of a military threat or a threat to public order. But in America, as our way of governing has evolved since 1964, emergencies are declared on a moral basis: people are suffering; their newly discovered rights are being denied. America can't wait anymore for the ordinary democratic process to take its course.

A moral ground for invoking emergencies sounds more humane than a military one. It is not. That is because, in order to justify its special powers, the government must create a class of officially designated malefactors. With the Civil Rights Act of 1964, the justification of this strong medicine was that there was a collection of Southern politicians who were so wily and devious, and a collection of Southern sheriffs so ruthless and depraved, that one could not, and was not morally obliged to, fight fair with them.

That pattern has perpetuated itself, even as the focus of civil rights has moved to American institutions less obviously objectionable than segregation. Every intervention in the name of rights requires the identification of a malefactor. So very early on in the gay marriage debate, those who believed in traditional marriage were likened to segregationists or to those who had opposed interracial marriage.

Joe Biden recently said: "Let's be clear: Transgender equality is the civil rights issue of our time. There is no room for compromise when it comes to basic human rights." Now, most Americans, probably including Joe Biden, know very little about transgenderism. But this is an assertion that Americans are not going to be permitted to advance their knowledge by discussing the issue in public or to work out their differences at the ballot box. As civil rights laws have been extended by analogy into other areas of American life, the imputation of moral non-personhood has been aimed at a growing number of people who have committed no sin more grievous than believing the same things they did two years ago, and therefore standing in the way of the progressive juggernaut.

The second characteristic of the new civil rights constitution is what we can call *intersectionality*. This is a sociological development. As long as civil rights law was limited to protecting the rights of Southern blacks, it was a stable system. It had the logic of history behind it, which both justified and focused its application. But if other groups could be given the privilege of advancing their causes by bureaucratic fiat and judicial decree, there was the possibility of a gradual building up of vast new coalitions, maybe even electoral majorities. This was made possible because almost anyone who was not a white heterosexual male could benefit from civil rights law in some way.

Seventy years ago, India produced the first modern minority-rights based constitution with a long, enumerated list of so-called "scheduled tribes and castes." Eventually, inter-group horse trading took up so much of the country's attention that there emerged a grumbling group of "everyone else," of "ordinary Indians." These account for many of the people behind the present prime minister, Narendra Modi. Indians who like Modi say he's the candidate of average citizens. Those who don't like him, as most of the international media do not, call him a "Hindu nationalist."

We have a version of the same thing happening in America. By the mid-1980s, the "intersectional" coalition of civil rights activists started using the term "people of color" to describe itself. Now, logically, if there really is such a thing as "people of color," and if they are demanding a larger share of society's rewards, they are *ipso facto* demanding that "*non*-people of color" get a smaller share. In the same way that the Indian constitution called forth the idea of a generic "Hindu," the new civil rights constitution created a group of "non-people of color." It made white people a political reality in the United States in a way they had never been.

Now we can apply this insight to parties. So overpowering is the hegemony of the civil rights constitution of 1964 over the Constitution of 1787, that the country naturally sorts itself into a party of those who have benefitted by it and a party of those who have been harmed by it.

A Party of Bigots and a Party of Totalitarians

Let's say you're a progressive. In fact, let's say you are a progressive gay man in a gay marriage, with two adopted children. The civil rights version of the country is everything to you. Your whole way of life depends on it. How can you back a party or a politician who even wavers on it? Quite likely, your whole moral idea of yourself depends on it, too. You may have marched in gay pride parades carrying signs reading "Stop the Hate," and you believe that people who opposed the campaign that made possible your way of life, your marriage, and your children, can only have done so for terrible reasons. *You* are on the side of the glorious marchers of Birmingham, and *they* are on the side of Bull Connor. To you, the other party is a party of bigots.

But say you're a conservative person who goes to church, and your seven-year-old son is being taught about "gender fluidity" in first grade. There is no avenue for you to complain about this. You'll be called a bigot at the very least. In fact, although you're not a lawyer, you have a vague sense that you might get fired from your job, or fined, or that something else bad will happen. You also feel that this business has something to do with gay rights. "Sorry," you ask, "when did I vote for this?" You begin to suspect that taking your voice away from you and taking your vote away from you is the main goal of these rights movements. To you, the other party is a party of totalitarians.

And that's our current party system: the bigots versus the totalitarians.

If either of these constitutions were totally devoid of merit, we wouldn't have a problem. We could be confident that the wiser of the two would win out in the end. But each of our two constitutions contains, for its adherents, a great deal worth defending to the bitter end. And unfortunately, each constitution must increasingly defend itself against the other.

When gay marriage was being advanced over the past 20 years, one of the common sayings of activists was: "The sky didn't fall." People would say: "Look, we've had gay marriage in Massachusetts for three weeks, and I've got news for you! The sky didn't fall!" They were right in the short term. But I think they forgot how delicate a system a democratic constitutional republic is, how difficult it is to get the formula right, and how hard it is to see when a government begins—slowly, very slowly—to veer off course in a way that can take decades to become evident.

Then one day we discover that, although we still deny the sky is falling, we do so with a lot less confidence.

Who Is in Control?
The Need to Rein in Big Tech

Allum Bokhari

January 2021

In January, when every major Silicon Valley tech company permanently banned the President of the United States from its platform, there was a backlash around the world. One after another, government and party leaders—many of them ideologically opposed to the policies of President Trump—raised their voices against the power and arrogance of the American tech giants. These included the President of Mexico, the Chancellor of Germany, the government of Poland, ministers in the French and Australian governments, the neoliberal center-right bloc in the European Parliament, the national populist bloc in the European Parliament, the leader of the Russian opposition (who recently survived an assassination attempt), and the Russian government (which may well have been behind that attempt).

Common threats create strange bedfellows. Socialists, conservatives, nationalists, neoliberals, autocrats, and anti-autocrats may not agree on much, but they all recognize that the tech giants have accumulated far too much power. None like the idea that a pack of American hipsters in Silicon Valley can, at any moment, cut off their digital lines of communication.

I published a book on this topic prior to the November election, and many who called me alarmist then are not so sure of that now. I built the book on interviews with Silicon Valley insiders and five years of reporting as a Breitbart News tech correspondent. Breitbart created a dedicated tech reporting team in 2015—a time when few recognized the danger that the rising tide of left-wing hostility to free speech would pose to the vision of the World Wide Web as a free and open platform for all viewpoints.

This inversion of that early libertarian ideal—the movement from the freedom of information to the control of information on the Web—has been the story of the past five years.

When the Web was created in the 1990s, the goal was that everyone who wanted a voice could have one. All a person had to do to access the global marketplace of ideas was to go online and set up a website. Once created, the website belonged to that person. Especially if the person owned his own server, no one could deplatform him. That was by design, because the Web, when it was invented, was competing with other types of online services that were not so free and open.

It is important to remember that the Web, as we know it today—a network of websites accessed through browsers—was not the first online service ever created. In the 1990s, Sir Timothy Berners-Lee invented the technology that underpins websites and web browsers, creating the Web as we know it today. But there were other online services, some of which predated Berners-Lee's invention. Corporations like CompuServe and Prodigy ran their own online networks in the 1990s—networks that were separate from the Web and had access points that were different from web browsers. These privately-owned networks were open to the public, but CompuServe and Prodigy owned every bit of information on them and could kick people off their networks for any reason.

In these ways the Web was different. No one owned it, owned the information on it, or could kick anyone off. That was the idea, at least, before the Web was captured by a handful of corporations.

We all know their names: Google, Facebook, Twitter, YouTube, Amazon. Like Prodigy and CompuServe back in the '90s, they own everything on their platforms, and they have the police power over what can be said and who can participate. But it matters a lot more today than it did in the '90s. Back then, very few people used online services. Today everyone uses them—it is practically impossible not to use them. Businesses depend on them. News publishers depend on them. Politicians and political activists depend on them. And crucially, citizens depend on them for information.

Today, Big Tech doesn't just mean control over online information. It means control over news. It means control over commerce. It means control over politics. And how are the corporate tech giants using their control? Judging by the three biggest moves they have made since I wrote my book—the censoring of the *New York Post* in October when it published its blockbuster stories on Biden family corruption, the censorship and eventual banning from the Web of President Trump, and the coordinated takedown of the upstart social media site Parler—it is obvious that Big Tech's priority today is to support the political Left and the Washington establishment.

Big Tech has become the most powerful election-influencing machine in American history. It is not an exaggeration to say that if the technologies of Silicon Valley are allowed to develop to their fullest extent, without any oversight or checks and balances, then we will never have another free and fair election. But the power of Big Tech goes beyond the manipulation of political behavior. As one of my Facebook sources told me in an interview for my book: "We have thousands of people on the platform who have gone from far right to center in the past year, so we can build a model from those people and try to make everyone else on the right follow the same path." Let that sink in. They don't just want to control information or even voting behavior—they want to manipulate people's worldview.

Is it too much to say that Big Tech has prioritized this kind of manipulation? Consider that Twitter is currently facing a lawsuit from a victim of child sexual abuse who says that the company repeatedly failed to take down a video depicting his assault, and that it eventually agreed to do so only after the intervention of an agent from the Department of Homeland Security. So

Twitter will take it upon itself to ban the President of the United States, but is alleged to have taken down child pornography *only after* being prodded by federal law enforcement.

———

How does Big Tech go about manipulating our thoughts and behavior? It begins with the fact that these tech companies strive to know everything about us—our likes and dislikes, the issues we're interested in, the websites we visit, the videos we watch, who we voted for, and our party affiliation. If you search for a Hannukah recipe, they'll know you're likely Jewish. If you're running down the Yankees, they'll figure out if you're a Red Sox fan. Even if your smart phone is turned off, they'll track your location. They know who you work for, who your friends are, when you're walking your dog, whether you go to church, when you're standing in line to vote, and on and on.

As I already mentioned, Big Tech also monitors how our beliefs and behaviors change over time. They identify the types of content that can change our beliefs and behavior, and they put that knowledge to use. They've done this openly for a long time to manipulate consumer behavior—to get us to click on certain ads or buy certain products. Anyone who has used these platforms for an extended period of time has no doubt encountered the creepy phenomenon where you're searching for information about a product or a service—say, a microwave—and then minutes later advertisements for microwaves start appearing on your screen. These same techniques can be used to manipulate political opinions.

I mentioned that Big Tech has recently demonstrated ideological bias. But it is equally true that these companies have huge economic interests at stake in politics. The party that holds power will determine whether they are going to get government contracts, whether they're going to get tax breaks, and whether and how their industry will be regulated. Clearly, they have a commercial interest in political control—and currently no one is preventing them from exerting it.

To understand how effective Big Tech's manipulation could become, consider the feedback loop.

As Big Tech constantly collects data about us, they run tests to see what information has an impact on us. Let's say they put a negative news story about someone or something in front of us, and we don't click on it or read it. They keep at it until they find content that has the desired effect. The feedback loop constantly improves, and it does so in a way that's undetectable.

What determines what appears at the top of a person's Facebook feed, Twitter feed, or Google search results? Does it appear there because it's popular or because it's gone viral? Is it there because it's what you're interested in? Or is there another reason Big Tech wants it to be there? Is it there because Big Tech has gathered data that suggests it's likely to nudge your thinking or your behavior in a certain direction? How can we know?

What we *do* know is that Big Tech openly manipulates the content people see. We know, for example, that Google reduced the visibility of Breitbart News links in search results by 99 percent in 2020 compared to the same period in 2016. We know that after Google introduced an update last summer, clicks on Breitbart News stories from Google searches for "Joe Biden" went to zero and stayed at zero through the election. This didn't happen gradually, but in one fell swoop—as if Google flipped a switch. And this was discoverable through the use of Google's own traffic analysis tools, so it isn't as if Google cared that we knew about it.

Speaking of flipping switches, I have noted that President Trump was collectively banned by Twitter, Facebook, Twitch, YouTube, TikTok, Snapchat, and every other social media platform you can think of. But even before that, there was manipulation going on. Twitter, for instance, reduced engagement on the President's tweets by over 80 percent. Facebook deleted posts by the President for spreading so-called disinformation.

But even more troubling, I think, are the invisible things these companies do. Consider "quality ratings." Every Big Tech platform has some version of this, though some of them use different names. The quality rating is what determines what appears at the top of your search results, or your Twitter or Facebook feed, etc. It's a numerical value based on what Big Tech's algorithms determine in terms of "quality." In the past, this score was determined by criteria that were somewhat objective: if a website or post contained viruses, malware, spam, or copyrighted material, that would negatively impact its quality score. If a video or post was gaining in popularity, the quality score would increase. Fair enough.

Over the past several years, however—and one can trace the beginning of the change to Donald Trump's victory in 2016—Big Tech has introduced all sorts of new criteria into the mix that determines quality scores. Today, the algorithms on Google and Facebook have been trained to detect "hate speech," "misinformation," and "authoritative" (as opposed to "non-authoritative") sources. Algorithms analyze a user's network, so that whatever users follow on social media—e.g., "non-authoritative" news outlets—affects the user's quality score. Algorithms also detect the use of language frowned on by Big Tech—e.g., "illegal immigrant" (bad) in place of "undocumented immigrant" (good)—and adjust quality scores accordingly. And so on.

This is not to say that you are informed of this or that you can look up your quality score. All of this happens invisibly. It is Silicon Valley's version of the social credit system overseen by the Chinese Communist Party. As in China, if you defy the values of the ruling elite or challenge narratives that the elite labels "authoritative," your score will be reduced and your voice suppressed. And it will happen silently, without your knowledge.

This technology is even scarier when combined with Big Tech's ability to detect and monitor entire networks of people. A field of computer science called "network analysis" is dedicated to identifying groups of people with shared interests, who read similar websites, who talk about similar things, who have similar habits, who follow similar people on social media, and who share similar political viewpoints. Big Tech companies are able to detect when particular information is flowing through a particular network—if there's a news story or a post or a video, for instance, that's going viral among conservatives or among voters as a whole. This gives them the ability to shut down a story they don't like before it gets out of hand. And these systems are growing more sophisticated all the time.

———

If Big Tech's capabilities are allowed to develop unchecked and unregulated, these companies will eventually have the power not only to suppress existing political movements, but to anticipate and prevent the emergence of new ones. This would mean the end of democracy as we know it, because it would place us forever under the thumb of an unaccountable oligarchy.

The good news is, there is a way to rein in the tyrannical tech giants. And the way is simple: take away their power to filter information and filter data on our behalf.

All of Big Tech's power comes from their content filters—the filters on "hate speech," the filters on "misinformation," the filters that distinguish "authoritative" from "non-authoritative" sources, etc. Right now these filters are switched on by default. We as individuals can't turn them off. But it doesn't have to be that way.

The most important demand we can make of lawmakers and regulators is that Big Tech be forbidden from activating these filters without our knowledge and consent. They should be prohibited from doing this—and even from nudging us to turn on a filter—under penalty of losing their Section 230 immunity as publishers of third party content. This policy should be strictly enforced, and it should extend even to seemingly non-political filters like relevance and popularity. Anything less opens the door to manipulation.

Our ultimate goal should be a marketplace in which third party companies would be free to design filters that could be plugged into services like Twitter, Facebook, Google, and YouTube. In other words, we would have two separate categories of companies: those that host content and those that create filters to sort through that content. In a marketplace like that, users would have the maximum level of choice in determining their online experiences. At the same time, Big Tech would lose its power to manipulate our thoughts and behavior and to ban legal content—which is just a more extreme form of filtering—from the Web.

This should be the standard we demand, and it should be industry-wide. The alternative is a kind of digital serfdom. We don't allow old-fashioned serfdom anymore—individuals and businesses have due process and can't be evicted because their landlord doesn't like their politics. Why shouldn't we also have these rights if our business or livelihood depends on a Facebook page or a Twitter or YouTube account?

This is an issue that goes beyond partisanship. What the tech giants are doing is so transparently unjust that all Americans should start caring about it—because under the current arrangement, we are all at their mercy. The World Wide Web was meant to liberate us. It is now doing the opposite. Big Tech is increasingly in control. The most pressing question today is: how are we going to take control back?

Critical Race Theory:
What It Is and How to Fight It

Christopher F. Rufo

March 2021

Critical race theory is fast becoming America's new institutional orthodoxy. Yet most Americans have never heard of it—and of those who have, many don't understand it. It's time for this to change. We need to know what it is so we can know how to fight it.

In explaining critical race theory, it helps to begin with a brief history of Marxism. Originally, the Marxist Left built its political program on the theory of class conflict. Marx believed that the primary characteristic of industrial societies was the imbalance of power between capitalists and workers. The solution to that imbalance, according to Marx, was revolution: the workers would eventually gain consciousness of their plight, seize the means of production, overthrow the capitalist class, and usher in a new socialist society.

During the 20th century, a number of regimes underwent Marxist-style revolutions, and each ended in disaster. Socialist governments in the Soviet Union, China, Cambodia, Cuba, and elsewhere racked up a body count of nearly 100 million of their own people. They are remembered for their gulags, show trials, executions, and mass starvations. In practice, Marx's ideas unleashed man's darkest brutalities.

By the mid-1960s, Marxist intellectuals in the West had begun to acknowl-edge these failures. They recoiled at revelations of Soviet atrocities and came to realize that workers' revolutions would never occur in Western Europe or the United States, where there were large middle classes and rapidly improving standards of living. Americans in particular had never developed a sense of class consciousness or class division. Most Americans believed in the American dream—the idea that they could transcend their origins through education, hard work, and good citizenship.

But rather than abandon their Leftist political project, Marxist scholars in the West simply adapted their revolutionary theory to the social and racial unrest of the 1960s. Abandoning Marx's economic dialectic of capitalists and workers, they substituted race for class and sought to create a revolutionary coalition of the dispossessed based on racial and ethnic categories.

Fortunately, the early proponents of this revolutionary coalition in the U.S. lost out in the 1960s to the civil rights movement, which sought instead the fulfillment of the American promise of freedom and equality under the law. Americans preferred the idea of improving their country to that of overthrowing it. The vision of Martin Luther King, Jr., President Johnson's pursuit of the Great Society, and the restoration of law and order promised by President Nixon in his 1968 campaign defined the post-1960s American political consensus.

But the radical Left has proved resilient and enduring—which is where critical race theory comes in.

What It Is

Critical race theory is an academic discipline, formulated in the 1990s, built on the intellectual framework of identity-based Marxism. Relegated for many years to universities and obscure academic journals, over the past decade it has increasingly become the default ideology in our public institutions. It has been injected into government agencies, public school systems, teacher training programs, and corporate human resources departments in the form of diversity training programs, human resources modules, public policy frameworks, and school curricula.

There are a series of euphemisms deployed by its supporters to describe critical race theory, including "equity," "social justice," "diversity and inclusion," and "culturally responsive teaching." Critical race theorists, masters of language construction, realize that "neo-Marxism" would be a hard sell. *Equity*, on the other hand, sounds non-threatening and is easily confused with the American principle of *equality*. But the distinction is vast and important. Indeed, equality—the principle proclaimed in the Declaration of Independence, defended in the Civil War, and codified into law with the 14th and 15th Amendments, the Civil Rights Act of 1964, and the Voting Rights Act of 1965—is explicitly rejected by critical race theorists. To them, equality represents "mere nondiscrimination" and provides "camouflage" for white supremacy, patriarchy, and oppression.

In contrast to equality, equity as defined and promoted by critical race theorists is little more than reformulated Marxism. In the name of equity, UCLA Law Professor and critical race theorist Cheryl Harris has proposed suspending private property rights, seizing land and wealth and redistributing them along racial lines. Critical race guru Ibram X. Kendi, who directs the Center for Antiracist Research at Boston University, has proposed the creation of a federal Department of Antiracism. This department would be independent of (i.e., unaccountable to) the elected branches of government, and would have the power to nullify, veto, or abolish any law at any level of government and curtail the speech of political leaders and others who are deemed insufficiently "antiracist."

One practical result of the creation of such a department would be the overthrow of capitalism, since according to Kendi, "In order to truly be antiracist, you also have to truly be anti-capitalist." In other words, identity is the means and Marxism is the end.

An equity-based form of government would mean the end not only of private property, but also of individual rights, equality under the law, federalism, and freedom of speech. These would be replaced by race-based redistribution of wealth, group-based rights, active discrimination, and omnipotent bureaucratic authority. Historically, the accusation of "anti-Americanism" has been overused. But in this case, it's not a matter of interpretation—critical race theory prescribes a revolutionary program that would overturn the principles of the Declaration and destroy the remaining structure of the Constitution.

How It Works

What does critical race theory look like in practice? Last year, I authored a series of reports focused on critical race theory in the federal government. The FBI was holding workshops on intersectionality theory. The Department of Homeland Security was telling white employees they were committing "microinequities" and had been "socialized into oppressor roles." The Treasury Department held a training session telling staff members that "virtually all white people contribute to racism" and that they must convert "everyone in the federal government" to the ideology of "antiracism." And the Sandia National Laboratories, which designs America's nuclear arsenal, sent white male executives to a three-day reeducation camp, where they were told that "white male culture" was analogous to the "KKK," "white supremacists," and "mass killings." The executives were then forced to renounce their "white male privilege" and write letters of apology to fictitious women and people of color.

This year, I produced another series of reports focused on critical race theory in education. In Cupertino, California, an elementary school forced first-graders to deconstruct their racial and sexual identities, and rank themselves according to their "power and privilege." In Springfield, Missouri, a middle school forced teachers to locate themselves on an "oppression matrix," based on the idea that straight, white, English-speaking, Christian males are members of the oppressor class and must atone for their privilege and "covert white supremacy." In Philadelphia, an elementary school forced fifth-graders to celebrate "Black communism" and simulate a Black Power rally to free 1960s radical Angela Davis from prison, where she had once been held on charges of murder. And in Seattle, the school district told white teachers that they are guilty of "spirit murder" against black children and must "bankrupt [their] privilege in acknowledgement of [their] thieved inheritance."

I'm just one investigative journalist, but I've developed a database of more than 1,000 of these stories. When I say that critical race theory is becoming the operating ideology of our public institutions, it is not an exaggeration—from the universities to bureaucracies to K-12 school systems, critical race theory has permeated the collective intelligence and decision-making process of American government, with no sign of slowing down.

This is a revolutionary change. When originally established, these government institutions were presented as neutral, technocratic, and oriented towards broadly-held perceptions of the public good. Today, under the increasing sway of critical race theory and related ideologies, they are being turned against the American people. This isn't limited to the permanent bureaucracy in Washington, D.C., but is true as well of institutions in the states, even in red states, and it is spreading to county public health departments, small Midwestern school districts, and more. This ideology will not stop until it has devoured all of our institutions.

Futile Resistance

Thus far, attempts to halt the encroachment of critical race theory have been ineffective. There are a number of reasons for this.

First, too many Americans have developed an acute fear of speaking up about social and political issues, especially those involving race. According to a recent Gallup poll, 77 percent of conservatives are afraid to share their political beliefs publicly. Worried about getting mobbed on social media, fired from their jobs, or worse, they remain quiet, largely ceding the public debate to those pushing these anti-American ideologies. Consequently, the institutions themselves become monocultures: dogmatic, suspicious, and hostile to a diversity of opinion. Conservatives in both the federal government and public school systems have told me that their "equity and inclusion" departments serve as political offices, searching for and stamping out any dissent from the official orthodoxy.

Second, critical race theorists have constructed their argument like a mousetrap. Disagreement with their program becomes irrefutable evidence of a dissenter's "white fragility," "unconscious bias," or "internalized white supremacy." I've seen this projection of false consciousness on their opponents play out dozens of times in my reporting. Diversity trainers will make an outrageous claim—such as "all whites are intrinsically oppressors" or "white teachers are guilty of spirit murdering black children"—and then when confronted with disagreement, they adopt a patronizing tone and explain that participants who feel "defensiveness" or "anger" are reacting out of guilt and shame. Dissenters are instructed to remain silent, "lean into the discomfort," and accept their "complicity in white supremacy."

Third, Americans across the political spectrum have failed to separate the premise of critical race theory from its conclusion. Its premise—that American history includes slavery and other injustices, and that we should examine and learn from that history—is undeniable. But its revolutionary conclusion—that America was founded on and defined by racism and that our founding principles, our Constitution, and our way of life should be overthrown—does not rightly, much less necessarily, follow.

Fourth and finally, the writers and activists who have had the courage to speak out against critical race theory have tended to address it on the theoretical level, pointing out the theory's logical contradictions and dishonest account of history. These criticisms are worthy and good, but they move the debate into the academic realm, which is friendly terrain for proponents of critical race theory. They fail to force defenders of this revolutionary ideology to defend the practical consequences of their ideas in the realm of politics.

Political Engagement

No longer simply an academic matter, critical race theory has become a tool of political power. To borrow a phrase from the Marxist theoretician Antonio Gramsci, it is fast achieving "cultural hegemony" in America's public institutions. More and more, it is driving the vast machinery of the state and society. If we want to succeed in opposing it, we must address it politically at every level.

Critical race theorists must be confronted with and forced to speak to the facts. Do they support public schools separating first-graders into groups of "oppressors" and "oppressed"? Do they support mandatory curricula teaching that "all white people play a part in perpetuating systemic racism"? Do they support public schools instructing white parents to become "white traitors" and advocate for "white abolition"? Do they want those who work in government to be required to undergo this kind of reeducation? How about managers and workers in corporate America? How about the men and women in our military? How about every one of us?

There are three parts to a successful strategy to defeat the forces of critical race theory: governmental action, grassroots mobilization, and an appeal to principle.

We already see examples of governmental action. Last year, one of my reports led President Trump to issue an executive order banning critical race theory-based training programs in the federal government. President Biden rescinded this order on his first day in office, but it provides a model for governors and municipal leaders to follow. This year, several state legislatures have introduced bills to achieve the same goal: preventing public institutions from conducting programs that stereotype, scapegoat, or demean people on the basis of race. And I have organized a coalition of attorneys to file lawsuits against schools and government agencies that impose critical race theory-based programs on grounds of the First Amendment (which protects citizens from compelled speech), the Fourteenth Amendment (which provides equal protection under the law), and the Civil Rights Act of 1964 (which prohibits public institutions from discriminating on the basis of race).

On the grassroots level, a multiracial and bipartisan coalition is emerging to do battle against critical race theory. Parents are mobilizing against racially divisive curricula in public schools and employees are increasingly speaking out against Orwellian reeducation in the workplace. When they see what is happening, Americans are naturally outraged that critical race theory promotes three ideas—race essentialism, collective guilt, and neo-segregation—which violate the basic principles of equality and justice. Anecdotally, many Chinese-Americans have told me that having survived the Cultural Revolution in their former country, they refuse to let the same thing happen here.

In terms of principles, we need to employ our own moral language rather than allow ourselves to be confined by the categories of critical race theory. For example, we often find ourselves debating "diversity." Diversity as most of us understand it is generally good, all things being equal, but it is of secondary value. We should be talking about and aiming at *excellence*, a common standard that challenges people of all backgrounds to achieve their potential. On the scale of desirable ends, excellence beats diversity every time.

Similarly, in addition to pointing out the dishonesty of the historical narrative on which critical race theory is predicated, we must promote the true story of America—a story that is honest about injustices in American history, but that places them in the context of our nation's high ideals and the progress we have made towards realizing them. Genuine American history is rich with stories of achievements and sacrifices that will move the hearts of Americans—in stark contrast to the grim and pessimistic narrative pressed by critical race theorists.

Above all, we must have courage—the fundamental virtue required in our time. Courage to stand and speak the truth. Courage to withstand epithets. Courage to face the mob. Courage to shrug off the scorn of the elites. When enough of us overcome the fear that currently prevents so many from speaking out, the hold of critical race theory will begin to slip. And courage begets courage. It's easy to stop a lone dissenter; it's much harder to stop 10, 20, 100, 1,000, 1,000,000, or more who stand up together for the principles of America.

Truth and justice are on our side. If we can muster the courage, we will win.

Our Increasingly Unrecognizable Civilization

Mark Steyn

April/May 2021

I live about 20 minutes south of the Canadian border, which used to be called the longest undefended frontier in the world. People moved freely back and forth across it all day every day. But now it's been closed for over a year. At one point my daughter asked me to drive her up there, because there was a 30-minute opportunity for people on one side to talk to their friends on the other. "Sad!" as President Trump would say. It was like Checkpoint Charlie in Berlin during the Cold War, except that *both* sides are now like East Berlin.

I don't know how this happened, but it is just one indication that America, and the West in general, have become almost unrecognizable from what they were not that long ago.

Look at just three things we have lost.

One is equality before the law, something absolutely essential to a free society. In its place, we now have politicized law. If a policeman fatally shoots someone, whether his name is released to the public depends on whether the shooting is consistent with the preferred narrative of the ruling class. A policeman recently took down a young woman who was threatening the life of another young woman with a knife, and that policeman was immediately identified—indeed, his photo was posted and he was threatened by NBA superstar LeBron James on Twitter. On the other hand, we know nothing of the policeman who shot dead an unarmed woman in the U.S. Capitol on January 6. His name will apparently never be released to the public.

Second, border control. Functioning societies, at least since the Peace of Westphalia three centuries ago, have borders. America has no southern border and no plans to get one. The official position of our government seems to be that any of the seven billion persons on this planet has a right to come and stay in the U.S. for three years, until his or her assigned court date comes up. As the number of people with pending cases continues to grow, that three years will extend out to five or seven or 15 years. If we get all seven billion people to come here, the court system will break down entirely and maybe we can go back to having a functioning border.

And third, dare I bring up the fact that it is a real question whether we can go back to agreeing to have open and honest elections? And if we don't have open and honest elections, control of our borders, and equality before the law, then we don't have the conditions for politics or free government.

And here's the thing. It is not at all clear to me that many of America's conservative politicians understand the seriousness of all this. You can see it in the fact that they go around trying to scare people with the specter of a "radical socialist agenda." For well over a year now, we have been living in a world in which it's accepted as normal that the state has essentially unlimited power—and in which our freedom to decide for ourselves has been diminished almost to invisibility. Why do these conservative politicians think the words "radical socialist agenda" still scare anyone in a time when the state can tell us whether we can have Aunt Mabel over for Christmas? They are completely out of touch.

Over the same period as the pandemic lockdowns, we have seen an escalation of so-called wokeness. And if you look at one of the most startling manifestations of this, transgender fanaticism—which involves, after all, the abolition of biological sex and, I'm sorry to have to say it, the physical mutilation of children—one notices that America is farther down this road than any other country in the Western world. In other words, at this moment of crisis for Western Civilization, or for what we used to call Christendom, the leading country of the free world is pulling the wrong way.

Think of it. Your daughter has been training since she was a little girl to run in school sports. Now at 17, she's in the state high school track championships, and you are forbidden even to notice that she's competing against a woman who is 6'2" with thighs like tugboats, a great touch of five o'clock shadow on her face, and the most muscular bosom you've ever seen. You're not supposed to notice the craziness of this, and the craziness is at its craziest right here in America.

We traditionally think of France as being a bit screwy, but today there are French intellectuals who regard themselves as hardcore leftists and yet who think America has gone bonkers on this transgender issue. President Macron himself has said that American wokeness is an existential threat to the French Republic, and he even found bureaucrats in France's education bureaucracy who agreed. There is not a single bureaucrat in the Department of Education in Washington, D.C., who would agree, but there are apparently a few in Paris.

If you look further east in Europe to the lands that were once behind the Iron Curtain—to Hungary, Poland, and the Czech Republic, which still function as conventional nation-states calculating their best interests—you find tremendous fear of the threat of wokeness that is being exported, sometimes aggressively, from America. So it is here in the U.S. where we have to put the stake through these ideas.

But again, even most of our conservative leaders and institutions seem oblivious. School districts in America are talking about revising their curricula to cover transgender issues from grade school on. Now, I went to an English boys' school, and we were expected to pick up sexuality on our own time. In those days people would have looked puzzled if you had said, "We're going to have to cancel geography or Latin, because we need to put gay studies in there." These days, instead of going off behind the bike shed during recess to learn about sex, kids need to sneak behind the bike shed to do a little bit of closeted geography or closeted Latin. It's completely backwards. And yet what do we hear from most conservative politicians? That it would be nice to offer people a tax cut!

We are way beyond tax cuts. We're broke. We're just a smidgen away from $30 trillion in federal debt—something with no historical precedent. Talking about tax cuts today is like talking about VAT tax refunds on the Titanic. It's not actually what's necessary at the moment.

Another big issue that should take our minds off tax cuts is China. I can't get over the way we in the U.S. have been ordered by our governors and the CDC to punish ourselves by living small, shrunken lives, while the people in China who loosed this pandemic on the world have paid no price for it.

Dr. Fauci has been a federal government bureaucrat since 1968. He's the J. Edgar Hoover of public health. He talks about the COVID virus as if we're at war. But he seems to think a country wins a war by taking it out on its own population rather than the enemy, which is what we've done.

Which do you think was the only major economy to grow in 2020? It's not a hard question. America's economy shrank 3.5 percent last year. The economies of Germany and Japan shrank almost five percent. France's, Italy's, and India's economies all shrank over eight percent, and the economy of the United Kingdom was down ten percent. China's economy, on the other hand, grew 2.3 percent in 2020, and first quarter growth for 2021 in China set a new world record—it was up over 18.3 percent. The COVID pandemic has been hugely profitable for China.

U.S. policy towards China since the 1990s represents perhaps the biggest strategic miscalculation by any great power in human history. Just as communism was wobbling and beginning to fall everywhere else, we helped Beijing come up with the first economically viable form of communism.

At first we were told it was only our manufacturing that we would ship to China. After all, we were told, it wasn't economically viable for Americans to make widgets. Remember the talk in the '90s? We were going to be the "knowledge economy." All the clever people told us this. We weren't going to have mills and factories, but we were going to be the knowledge economy. Well, in case you haven't noticed, China's got the entire knowledge economy for itself now. It makes our laptops and our smartphones and it's out front with Huawei and 5G. It also makes the batteries that power our gizmos and the chips that run our cars. When COVID struck, we found out fast that the Chinese not only make our viruses, they also make the personal protective equipment that protects us against the viruses—and all of our medicines to boot! Those wily Chinese get you both coming and going.

China is now the number one global power. You can define this militarily, where it now has the largest surface fleet on the planet. You can define it economically. But the way I define it is to look at who gets its way in the world. New Zealand has just effectively pulled out of the Five Eyes intelligence-sharing arrangement—an arrangement between the U.S., the U.K., Canada, Australia, and New Zealand, the oldest such arrangement on the planet. New Zealand has pulled out with respect to China because it doesn't want to offend China. I would think Canada might be the next to go. Or look at the World Health Organization. America pays for it, but Chairman Xi in Beijing calls the shots. China gets its way now, and the U.S. doesn't.

We need politicians with a sense of urgency about these problems, but all they seem to have is urgency about things that aren't urgent. Look at climate change. People say we need to take action over climate change or else rising sea levels are going to overwhelm the Maldives in the Indian Ocean in the 22nd century. That's the century after this one, which is still quite young. These same people say about the immediate crisis on the southern border that it's "a natural phenomenon beyond the control of politicians." But changing the weather in order to lower the sea levels that will threaten the Maldives in the Indian Ocean in the next century is within the power of politicians? In general, our leaders are urgent about nothing that matters and not in the least bit urgent about things that matter very much.

The things our news media talks about incessantly, whether it's transgender bathrooms or Confederate statues being toppled or the totally dishonest national conversation on race—nothing like this is heard in China as it goes along steadily strengthening its position as the world's leading power. The Chinese don't find themselves stuck in these sterile, drain-circling, dishonest public conversations about identity politics. These conversations are a waste of time. And one thing we should demand of our politicians is that they talk about things that *aren't* a waste of time.

At the root of our problems is that we have seen the emergence of a true ruling class, like Grand Dukes in medieval Europe. Its members intermarry. They send their kids to the same schools. They circulate back and forth between government and the private sector. And over time it has become increasingly easy to identify members of this class.

John Kerry gave a commencement address a couple of years ago in which he told the students, "You are going to be the first generation to live in a borderless world." And for the elite, the idea of a borderless world rings true. A typical member of the ruling class will get a job with a firm like Goldman Sachs, work for a couple of years in Hong Kong, then move on for a couple of years in Geneva, and then maybe come back to America. What are borders to such a person? Meanwhile, for the common American, COVID has literally ended, to a large degree, any freedom of movement. They live in the farthest thing from a borderless world. Oftentimes they're trapped in a town that is dying because of the open-border, cheap-labor policies advocated by people like John Kerry.

Our political division in America today is a class division, and we need to expose it as such whenever we see it. The ruling class tries to keep racial and other forms of division stirred up in our politics so that we don't notice the class protection racket they are running. Look at that guy from Twitter, Jack Dorsey, who wears a beard like he's playing the hobo in a Charlie Chaplin silent film. I wouldn't mind betting that when he's called to testify in Congress, he has his valet hook on the beard and lower him into the clothes that make him look like he's been sleeping in a dumpster. Then at night after the cameras are off he's like Lord Grantham in *Downton Abbey*, spending an hour being dressed for dinner. Our elites have become incredibly good at theater.

Getting back to the southern border, it perfectly symbolizes the bifurcation of our society. We're told there's a health emergency. We're told we can't open our businesses or attend weddings or funerals. Yet at the same time, every day, thousands of people pour across the southern border, test positive for COVID, and are then driven to a nice hotel and put up there at taxpayers' expense.

It's also interesting to compare the southern border with the northern. Prior to the pandemic, when the border with Canada was open, my kids had their Kinder Eggs confiscated by the Department of Homeland Security when we would cross the border going south into Vermont. Kinder Eggs are chocolate eggs with a kid's toy inside. They are sold in Canada, but they are banned in the U.S. because the Food and Drug Administration calls the toy a "non-nutritive embed"—and that's good enough to send Homeland Security agents swinging into action! There is always a big crackdown before Easter on Kinder Eggs. So at the northern border there are lots of things, down to Kinder Eggs, that are illegal. But at the southern border you can come in with pretty much anything you want, including COVID. Why is that? It is because some groups serve the needs of the ruling class and others don't. License is extended to the former and not the latter.

People ask me, "Why are you going on about Kinder Eggs? They're not important. It's more important that so-and-so is up two points in Iowa and three points in New Hampshire. That could be a real game changer." To which I answer no, that's not how it works. If they take the small freedoms away from you, whether it's the freedom to eat Kinder Eggs or to enjoy a high pressure shower, you will lose all the larger freedoms, which is the world we're in now.

I used to get occasional pushback when I'd talk about rights. "Rights are abstract things," people would say—"they don't have anything to do with our real lives." Well, after the last year, we know they have everything to do with our real lives. When you're told you can't open your hair salon, when you're told you can't have family or friends over for dinner, when you're told you must wear a mask in your own garden, there's nothing abstract about it. This is where all the stupid Kinder Egg laws have been trending for years. And it's why we need to push back.

I made a little joke earlier about studying transgenderism in grade school, but it's not a laughing matter. Education is the biggest structural defect in our society. We have an almost entirely corrupt and abusive education establishment. And in one corner of Governor Whitmer's Michigan, of all places, Hillsdale College stands against this. Hillsdale's literature, I've noted through the years, talks a lot about the College's 177 years of being rooted in the soil of Michigan. And this reminds me of the fact that if you do not have roots, you are not a functioning society. You can't just be flotsam and jetsam, bobbing around on the currents of the age, wheresoever they tend. If you do that, you're cut off from your roots.

This is what's so frightening about the trends in education today. Cromwell told his portrait painter, "Paint me, warts and all." That's not what is happening in America, where the trend in education is to paint only America's warts. So even the great Kate Smith, who sang "God Bless America" for years, is having her statue taken down because she made a racially insensitive record in 1931. Well you know who really had a racially insensitive record in 1931? The Democratic Party. But unlike Kate Smith's statue, it's still around.

President Macron of France is not my favorite chap—he's a sinister globalist for one thing. But he made an admirable stand when he announced that not one French statue would be taken down and not a single French street name would be changed, because they are all part of French history. And "Bingo!" as Peter Navarro likes to say, the statue toppling and street-name changing in France went away. Why can't American conservatives show that kind of strength? The Senate Minority Leader says he personally would not be bothered if the historical names of U.S. military bases are changed. The editor of *National Review* says that he wouldn't be bothered about taking down Confederate statues. But of course it doesn't stop there—now they're going for all the statues. Washington, Jefferson, Lincoln, McKinley, and on and on. The point conservatives need to grasp is, unless you're prepared to surrender everything, don't surrender anything.

I'll end by pointing out that the Left wins because it seizes language. Take the policy of letting people vote who are not U.S. citizens and shouldn't be voting. The Left calls this policy "counting every vote." Therefore someone who wants to make sure voters are citizens is *opposed* to "counting every vote." If we don't take back the language, we will lose the truth. Even on FOX News, I have noticed, news anchors now talk about "gender assigned at birth," as if that's something different from one's biological sex. There may be 57 genders, but there are only two biological sexes.

Don't surrender the language. Reclaim the language. It's the first step to recovering our civilization.

ECONOMICS

Whatever Happened to Free Enterprise?

Ronald Reagan

January 1978

G overnment, by going outside its proper province, has caused many, if not most, of the problems that vex us.

How much are we to blame for what has happened? Beginning with the traumatic experience of the Great Depression, we the people have turned more and more to government for answers that government has neither the right nor the capacity to provide. Unfortunately, government as an institution always tends to increase in size and power, and so government attempted to provide the answers.

The result is a fourth branch of government added to the traditional three of executive, legislative, and judicial: a vast federal bureaucracy that is now being imitated in too many states and too many cities, a bureaucracy of enormous power that determines policy to a greater extent than any of us realize, very possibly to a greater extent than our own elected representatives. And it can't be removed from office by our votes.

More than anything else, a new political economic mythology, widely believed by too many people, has increased government's ability to interfere as it does in the marketplace. Profit is a dirty word, blamed for most of our social ills. In the interest of something called "consumerism," free enterprise is becoming far less free. Property rights are being reduced, and even eliminated, in the name of environmental protection. It is time that a voice be raised on behalf of the 73 million independent wage earners in this country, pointing out that profit, property rights, and freedom are inseparable, and you cannot have the third unless you continue to be entitled to the first two.

Even many of us who believe in free enterprise have fallen into the habit of saying when something goes wrong: "There ought to be a law." Sometimes I think there ought to be a law against saying that there ought to be a law.

In spite of all the evidence that points to the free market as the most efficient system, we continue down a road that is bearing out the prophecy of Tocqueville, a Frenchman who came here 130 years ago. He was attracted by the miracle that was America. Think of it: Our country was only 70 years old and already we had achieved such a miraculous living standard, such productivity and prosperity, that the rest of the world was amazed. So he came here and he looked at everything he could see in our country, trying to find the secret of our success, and then went back and wrote a book about it. Even then, 130 years ago, he saw signs prompting him to warn us that if we weren't constantly on the guard, we would find ourselves covered by a network of regulations controlling every activity. He said if that came to pass we would one day find ourselves a nation of timid animals with government the shepherd.

It all comes down to this basic premise: If you lose your economic freedom, you lose your political freedom and, in fact, all freedom. Freedom is something that cannot be passed on genetically. It is never more than one generation away from extinction. Every generation has to learn how to protect and defend it. Once freedom is gone, it is gone for a long, long time. Already, too many of us, particularly those in business and industry, have chosen to switch rather than fight.

We should take inventory and see how many things we can do ourselves that we have come to believe only a government can do.

The most dangerous myth is that business can be made to pay a larger share of taxes, thus relieving the individual. Politicians preaching this are either deliberately dishonest or economically illiterate, and either one should scare us. Business doesn't pay taxes, and who better than business could make this message known? Only people pay taxes, and people pay as consumers every tax that is assessed against a business. Passing along their tax costs is the only way businesses can make a profit and stay in operation.

The federal government has used its taxing power to redistribute earnings to achieve a variety of social reforms. Politicians love those indirect business taxes, because it hides the cost of government. During the New Deal days, an undersecretary of the Treasury wrote a book in which he said that taxes can serve a higher purpose than just raising revenue. He said they could be an instrument of social and economic control to redistribute wealth and income and to penalize industries and economic groups. We need to put an end to that kind of thinking.

To win this battle against Big Government, we must communicate with each other. We must support the doctor in his fight against socialized medicine, the oil industry in its fight against crippling controls and repressive taxes, and the farmer, who hurts more than most because of government harassment and rule-changing in the middle of the game. All of these issues concern each one of us, regardless of what our trade or profession may be. Corporate America must begin to realize that it has allies in the independent businessmen and women, the shopkeepers, the craftsmen, the farmers, and the professions. All these men and women are organized in a great variety of ways, but right now we only talk in our own organizations about our own problems. What we need is a liaison between these organizations to realize how much strength we as a people still have if we will use that strength.

We have had enough of sideline kibitzers telling us the system they themselves have disrupted with their social tinkering can be improved or saved if we will only have more of that tinkering or even government planning and management. They play fast and loose with a system that for 200 years made us the light of the world and the refuge for people all over the world who yearn to breathe free. It is time we recognized that the system, no matter what our problems are, has never failed us once. Every time we have failed the system, usually by lacking faith in it, usually by saying that we have to change and do something else. A Supreme Court Justice has said the time has come, is indeed long overdue, for the wisdom, ingenuity, and resources of American business to be marshaled against those who would destroy it.

What specifically should be done? The first essential for the businessman is to confront the problem as a primary responsibility of corporate management. It has been said that history is the patter of silken slippers descending the stairs and the thunder of hobnail boots coming up. Back through the years we have seen people fleeing the thunder of those boots to seek refuge in this land. Now too many of them have seen the signs, signs that were ignored in their homeland before the end came, appearing here. They wonder if they will have to flee again. But they know there is no place to run to. Will we, before it is too late, use the vitality and the magic of the marketplace to save this way of life, or will we one day face our children, and our children's children, when they ask us where we were and what we were doing on the day that freedom was lost?

Coping with Ignorance

F. A. Hayek

July 1978

It is to me not only a great honor but also the discharge of an intellectual duty and a real pleasure to be allowed to deliver a Ludwig von Mises memorial lecture. There is no single man to whom I owe more intellectually, even though he was never my teacher in the institutional sense of the word.

I came originally from the other of the two original branches of the Austrian school. While Mises had been an inspired pupil of Eugen Boehm von Bawerk, who died comparatively early and whom I knew only as a friend of my grandfather before I knew what the word "economics" meant, I was personally a pupil of his contemporary, friend, and brother-in-law, Friedrich von Wieser. I was attracted by him, I admit, because unlike most of the other members of the Austrian school, he had a good deal of sympathy with a mild Fabian socialism to which I was inclined as a young man. He in fact prided himself that his theory of marginal utility had provided the basis of progressive taxation, which then seemed to me one of the ideals of social justice.

It was he who, just retiring as I graduated, sent me with a letter of introduction to Ludwig von Mises, who as one of the directors of a new temporary government office concerned with settling certain problems arising out of the treaty of St. Germain, was looking for young lawyers with some understanding of economics and knowledge of foreign languages. I remember vividly how, almost exactly 56 years ago, after presenting to Mises my letter of introduction by Wieser, in which I was described as a promising young economist, Mises said, "Well, I've never seen you at my lectures."

That was almost completely true. I had looked in at one of his lectures and found that a man so conspicuously antipathetic to the kind of Fabian views which I then held was not the sort of person to whom I wanted to go. But of course things changed.

The meeting was the beginning. After a short conversation, Mises asked, "When can you start work?" This led to a long, close collaboration. First, for five years, he was my official chief in that government office and then vice president of an institute of business cycle research which we had created together. During these ten years he certainly had more influence on my outlook of economics than any other man.

It was essentially his second great work, *Die Gemein Wirtscaft* of 1922, which appeared in English translation only 15 years later as *Socialism*, that completely won me over to his views. And then in his *Privatseminar*, as we called the little discussion group which met at his office, I became gradually intimately familiar with his thinking.

I do not wish however to claim to be an authoritative interpreter of Mises' views. Although I do owe him a decisive stimulus at a crucial point of my intellectual development, and continuous inspiration through a decade, I have perhaps most profited from his teaching because I was not initially his student at the university, an innocent young man who took his word for gospel, but came to him as a trained economist, trained in a parallel branch of Austrian economics from which he gradually, but never completely, won me over. Though I learned that he usually was right in his conclusions, I wasn't always satisfied by his arguments, and retained to the end a certain critical attitude which sometimes forced me to build different constructions, which however, to my great pleasure, usually led to the same conclusions. I am to the present moment pursuing the questions which he made me see, and that, I believe is the greatest benefit one scientist can confer on one of the next generation.

I do not know whether my making our incurable ignorance of most of the particular circumstances which determine the course of this great society the central point of the scientific approach would have Mises' approval. It is probably a development that goes somewhat beyond his views, because Mises himself was still much more a child of the rationalist age of enlightenment and of continental rather than of English liberalism, in the European sense of the word, than I am myself.

But I do flatter myself that he sympathized with my departure in this direction, which I like to describe briefly as a movement back from Voltaire to Montesquieu. It is the outcome of this development about which I am now going to speak.

I've come to believe that both the aim of the market order, and therefore the object of explanation of the theory of it, is to cope with the inevitable ignorance of everybody of most of the particular facts which determine this order. By a process which men did not understand, their activities have produced an order much more extensive and comprehensive than anything they could have comprehended, but on the functioning of which we have become utterly dependent.

Even 200 years after Adam Smith's *Wealth of Nations*, it is not yet fully understood that it is the great achievement of the market to have made a far-ranging division of labor possible, that it brings about a continuous adaptation of economic effect to millions of particular facts or events which in their totality are not known and cannot be known to anybody. A real understanding of the process which brings this about was long blocked by post-Smithian classical economics which adopted a labor or cost theory of value.

The misconception that costs determined prices prevented economists for a long time from recognizing that it was prices which operated as the indispensable signals telling producers what costs it was worth expending on the production of the various commodities and services, and not the other way around. It was the costs which they had expended which determined the prices of things produced.

It was this crucial insight which finally broke through and established itself about a hundred years ago through the so-called marginal revolution in economics.

The chief insight gained by modern economists is that the market is essentially an ordering mechanism, growing up without anybody wholly understanding it, that enables us to utilize widely dispersed information about the significance of circumstances of which we are mostly ignorant. However, the various planners (and not only the planners in the socialist camp) and dirigists have still not yet grasped this.

I do not believe that it is merely present ignorance, which we expect future advance of knowledge will remove, which makes a rational effort at central planning wholly impossible. I believe such a central utilization of necessarily widely dispersed knowledge of particular and temporary circumstances must forever remain impossible. We can have a far-ranging division of labor only by relying on the impersonal signals of prices.

That here and now we economists do not know enough to be justified to undertake such a task as the planning of the whole economic system seems to me so obvious that I find it increasingly difficult to treat the contrary belief with any respect.

It is a basic fact that we as scientists have to explain the results of the actions of men, which produces a sort of order by following signals inducing them to adapt to facts which they do not know. It creates a comparable or similar problem of coping with ignorance such as the people in the economics world encounter even more than the people who undertake to explain this process.

It is a difficulty which all attempts at a theoretical explanation of the market process face, though it appears that not many economists have been clearly aware of the source of the difficulties which they encounter.

If the chief problem of economic decisions is one of coping with the inevitable ignorance, the task of a science of economics trying to explain the joint effects of hundreds of thousands of such decisions on men in many different positions has to deal with an ignorance as it were, of a second order of magnitude because the explaining economist does not even know what all the acting people know; he has to provide an explanation without knowing the determining facts, not even knowing what the individual members in the economic system know about these facts.

We are in this respect not in the happy position in which the theorists of a relatively simple phenomena find themselves. When they have formed a hypothesis about how two or three variables are interrelated, they can test such a hypothesis by inserting into their abstract formula, observing values replacing the blanks, and then see whether the conclusions are correct.

Our problem is that even if we have thought out a beautiful and possibly correct theory of the complex phenomena with which we have to deal, we can never ascertain all the concrete specific data of a particular position, simply because we do not know all that which the acting people know. But it is the joint results of those actions which we want to predict.

If the market really achieves a utilization of more information than any participant in this market process possesses, the outcome must depend on more particular facts than the scientific observer can insert into his tentative hypothesis which is intended to explain the whole process.

There are two possible ways in which economists have endeavored at least partly to overcome this difficulty.

The first, represented by what today we call micro-economics, resignedly accepts the fact that because of this difficulty we can never achieve a full explanation, or an exact prediction of the particular outcome of a given situation, but must instead be content with what I have occasionally called a "pattern prediction" or, earlier a "prediction of the principle." All we can achieve is to say what kinds of things will not happen and what sort of pattern the resulting situation will show, without being able to predict a particular outcome.

This kind of micro-economics attempts, by the construction of simplified models in which all the kinds of attitudes and circumstances we meet in the real life are represented, to simulate the kind of movements and changes which we observe in the real world.

Such a theory can tell us what sort of changes we can expect in the real world, the general character of which our model indicates, which reduces (not so much in scale as in the number of distinct elements), the facts with which we have to deal, to make its workings still comprehensible or surveyable.

I still believe that this is the only approach which is entitled to regard itself as scientific. Being scientific involves in this connection a frank admission of how limited our powers of prediction really are. It still does lead to some falsifiable predictions, namely what sorts of events are possible in a given situation and which are not.

It is, in this sense, an empirical theory even though it consists largely, but not entirely, of propositions which are self-evident once they are stated. Indeed, I doubt whether micro-economic theory has ever discovered any new facts. Decreasing returns, decreasing marginal productivity or marginal utility, decreasing marginal rates of substitution were of course all phenomena familiar to ordinary people even if these did not call them by that name. In fact, it is only because ordinary people knew these facts, long before economists discovered their importance, that they have always been among the determinants of how the market actually functions. What the economic theorists found out was merely the relevance of these particular facts for the decision of individuals in their interactions with other persons.

It is the obscuring of the empirical fact of people learning what others do by a process of communication of knowledge which has always made me reluctant to accept von Mises' claim of an a priori character of the whole of economic theory, although I agree with him that much of it consists merely in working out the logical implications of certain initial facts.

I recognize with him micro-economic theory as the only legitimate economic theory because, and insofar as, it recognizes the inevitable limitation of our possible knowledge of the objective facts which determine any given situation; and we need claim no more that we are entitled to claim.

I will not deny that we find also in the micro-economic literature a good deal of indefensible pretense of a great deal more.

There is, of course, in the first instance, the frequent abuse of the convenient conception of "equilibrium" toward which the market process is said to tend. I will not say that there are not forces at work which can usefully be described as equilibrating tendencies.

But equilibrating forces are of course at work in any stream of a liquid and must be taken into account in any attempt to analyze the flow of such a stream. Such a stream in the physical sense of the word of course will never reach a state of equilibrium. And the same is true of the economic efforts of the production and use of goods and services where every part may all the time tend toward a partial or local equilibrium, but long before that is reached the circumstances to which the local efforts adapt themselves will have changed themselves as a result of similar processes. All we can claim for the achievement of micro-economic theory is that the signals which the prices constitute will always make the individuals change their plans in the direction made necessary by factual charges of which they have no direct knowledge—not that this process will ever lead to what some economists call an equilibrium.

Not content with this limited insight, which economics can in fact supply, economists ambitious to make it more precise have often spoiled micro-economics by a tendency, which we shall encounter in a more systematic form when I pass on to the second type of approach, macro-economics. They tried to deal with our inescapable ignorance of the data required for a full explanation, the macro-economic one, by trying measurements I shall discuss later.

I will at this stage make only two further comments on this. The first is that it is an erroneous belief, characteristic of bad mathematicians, that mathematics is essentially quantitative and that, therefore, to build on the great achievements of the founders of mathematical economics, men like Jevons, Walras, and Pareto, one has to introduce quantitative data obtained by measurements. That was certainly not the intention of the founders of mathematical economics. They understood much better than their successors that algebraic mathematical formulae are the pre-eminent method for describing abstract patterns without assuming or possessing particular information about the specific magnitudes involved. One great mathematician has indeed described a mathematician as a maker of patterns. In this sense mathematics can be very helpful to us.

The second point which I want to make is that a particular reason which in the physical sciences make measurements of concrete magnitudes the hallmark of scientific procedure for a very definite reason do not apply to the explanation of human action. The true reason why the physical sciences must rely on measurements is that it has been recognized that things which appear alike to our senses frequently do not behave in the same manner, and that sometimes things which appear alike to us behave very differently if examined.

The physicist, to arrive at valid theories, was often compelled to substitute for the classification of different objects which our senses provide to us a different classification which was based solely on the relations of objective things toward each other.

Now this is really what measurement amounts to: a classification of objects according to the manner in which they act on other objects. But to explain human action all that is relevant is how the things appear to human beings, to acting men. This depends on whether men regard two things as the same or different kinds of things, not what they really are, unknown to them. For our purposes the results of measurements (at least so far as these are not performed by the people whose actions we want to explain) are wholly uninteresting.

The belief derived from physics that measurement is an essential foundation of all sciences is very old. There was more than 300 years ago a German philosopher named Erhard Weigel who strove to construct a universal science which he proposed to call Pantometria, based as the name says on measuring everything. Much of economics, and if I may add in parenthesis much of contemporary psychology, has indeed become Pantometria in a sense in the principle that if you don't know what measurements mean, measure anyhow because that is what science does. The social sciences building at the University of Chicago indeed still bears since it was built 40 years ago on its outside an inscription taken from the famous physicist Lord Kelvin: "When you cannot measure, your knowledge is meager and unsatisfactory." I will admit that that may be true, but it is certainly not scientific to insist on measurement where you don't know what your measurements mean. There are cases where measurements are not relevant. What has done much damage to micro-economics is striving for a pseudo-exactness by imitating methods of the physical sciences which have to deal with what are fundamentally much more simple phenomena. And the assumption that it is possible to ascertain all the relevant particular facts still completely dominates the alternative methods of dealing with our constitutional ignorance, which economists have tried to overcome. This of course, is what has come to be called macro-economics as distinct from micro-economics.

The basic idea on which this approach proceeds is fairly simple and obvious. If we cannot know all the individual facts which determine individual action and thereby the economic process, we must start from the most comprehensive information which we can obtain about them, and that is the statistical figures about aggregates and averages.

Again, the model which is followed is provided by the physical sciences which, where they have to deal with true mass phenomena such as the movement of millions of molecules with which thermodynamics has to deal, where we admittedly know nothing about the movement of any individual molecule, the law of large numbers enables us to discover statistical regularities or probabilities which indeed, in this way, provide an adequate foundation for reliable predictions.

The trouble is, unfortunately, that in the disciplines which endeavor to explain the structure of society, we do not have to deal with true mass phenomena.

The events which we must take into account in any attempt to predict the outcome of particular social processes are never so numerous as to enable us to substitute ascertained probabilities for information about the individual events. As a distinguished thinker, the late Warren Weaver of the Rockefeller Foundation has pointed out, both in the biological and in the social sciences frequently we cannot rely on probabilities, or the law of large numbers, because unlike the positions which exist in the physical sciences, where statistical evidence of probabilities can be substituted for information on particular facts, we have to deal with what he calls organized complexity, where we cannot expect to find permanent constant relations between aggregates or averages.

Indeed, this intermediate field between the simple phenomena of the physical sciences, where everything can be explained by theoretical formulae which contain no more than two or three unknowns, and the instances where a large enough number of events to be able to deal with true mass phenomena to rely on probability is our subject. In the social sciences we have to deal with something which Warren Weaver called "organized complexity," phenomena which are not made up of sufficiently large numbers of similar events to enable us to ascertain the probabilities for their occurrence.

In order to provide a full explanation we would have to have information about every single event which you can never possibly obtain. But while micro-theorists have resigned themselves to the consequent limitations of our powers and admit that we must be content with what I've called "mere pattern predictions," many of the more ambitious and impatient students of these problems refuse to recognize these limitations to out possible knowledge, and possible power of prediction, and therefore also of our possible power of control.

What drives people to the pursuit of statistical research is usually the hope of discovering in this way new facts of general and not merely historical importance. But this hope is inevitably disappointed. I certainly do not wish to underrate the importance of historical information about the particular situation. I doubt, however, whether the observation and measurement of true mass phenomena has significantly improved our understanding of the market process. What we can find by this procedure, as by all observation of particular circumstances, may possibly be special relations, determined by the particular circumstances of the moment and the place, which indeed, perhaps for some time may enable us to make correct predictions. But with general laws which help to explain how at different places the course of economic affairs is determined, these quantitative relations between measurable magnitudes have precious little to do. Indeed, even the very moderate hopes which I myself had at one time concerning the usefulness of such economic forecasts based on observed statistical regularities has mostly been disappointed. The concrete course of the process of adaptation to unknown circumstances cannot be predicted. All we can predict is certain abstract features of the process, not its concrete manifestations.

It is now frequently assumed that at least the theory of money, in the nature of that subject, must be macro-theory. I can see no reason whatever for this. The cause for this belief is apparently the fact that the value of money is usually conceived as corresponding to an average of prices. But that is no more true than it is of the value of any other commodity. I do not see for instance, that our habitual use of index numbers of prices, although undoubtedly very convenient for many purposes, has in any way assisted our understanding of the effect of monetary changes, or to draw relevant conclusions, except, perhaps about the behavior of index numbers.

The interesting problems are those of the effect of monetary changes on particular prices, and about these index numbers or changes of general price levels, tell us nothing.

It seems to me more and more that the immense efforts which during the great popularity of macro-economics over the last 30 or 40 years have been devoted to it, were largely misspent, and that if we want to be useful in the future we shall have to be content to improve and spread the admittedly limited insights which micro-economics conveys.

I believe it is only micro-economics which enables us to understand the crucial functions of the market process: that it enables us to make effective use of information about thousands of facts of which nobody can have full knowledge.

The Real Cost of Regulation

John Stossel

May 2001

When I started 30 years ago as a consumer reporter, I took the approach that most young reporters take today. My attitude was that capitalism is essentially cruel and unfair, and that the job of government, with the help of lawyers and the press, is to protect people from it. For years I did stories along those lines—stories about Coffee Association ads claiming that coffee "picks you up while it calms you down," or Libbey-Owens-Ford Glass Company ads touting the clarity of its product by showing cars with their windows rolled down. I and other consumer activists said, "We've got to have regulation. We've got to police these ads. We've got to have a Federal Trade Commission." And I'm embarrassed at how long it took me to realize that these regulations make things worse, not better, for ordinary people.

The damage done by regulation is so vast, it's often hard to see. The money wasted consists not only of the taxes taken directly from us to pay for bureaucrats, but also of the indirect cost of all the lost energy that goes into filling out the forms. Then there's the distraction of creative power. Listen to Jack Faris, president of the National Federation of Independent Business: "If you're a small businessman, you have to get involved in government or government will wreck your business." And that's what happens. You have all this energy going into lobbying the politicians, forming the trade associations and PACs, and trying to manipulate the leviathan that's grown up in Washington, D.C., and the state capitals. You have many of the smartest people in the country today going into law, rather than into engineering or science. This doesn't create a richer, freer society. Nor do regulations only depress the economy. They depress the spirit. Visitors to Moscow before the fall of communism noticed a dead-eyed look in the people. What was that about? I don't think it was about fear of the KGB. Most Muscovites didn't have intervention by the secret police in their daily lives. I think it was the look that people get when they live in an all-bureaucratic state. If you go to Washington, to the Environmental Protection Agency, I think you'll see the same thing.

One thing I noticed that started me toward seeing the folly of regulation was that it didn't even punish the obvious crooks. The people selling the breast-enlargers and the burn-fat-while-you-sleep pills got away with it. The Attorney General would come at them after five years, they would hire lawyers to gain another five, and then they would change the name of their product or move to a different state. But regulation did punish legitimate businesses.

When I started reporting, all the aspirin companies were saying they were the best, when in fact aspirin is simply aspirin. So the FTC sued and demanded corrective advertising. Corrective ads would have been something like, "Contrary to our prior ads, Excedrin does not relieve twice as much pain." Of course these ads never ran. Instead, nine years of costly litigation finally led to a consent order. The aspirin companies said, "We don't admit doing anything wrong, but we won't do it again." So who won?

Unquestionably the lawyers did. But did the public? Aspirin ads are more honest now. They say things like, "Nothing works better than Bayer"—which, if you think about it, simply means, "We're all the same." But I came to see that the same thing would have happened without nearly a decade of litigation, because markets police themselves. I can't say for certain how it would have happened. I think it's a fatal conceit to predict how markets will work. Maybe Better Business Bureaus would have gotten involved. Maybe the aspirin companies would have sued each other. Maybe the press would have embarrassed them. But the truth would have gotten out. The more I watched the market, the more impressed I was by how flexible and reasonable it is compared to government-imposed solutions.

Market forces protect us even where we tend most to think we need government. Consider the greedy, profit-driven companies that have employed me. CBS, NBC, and ABC make their money from advertisers, and they've paid me for 20 years to bite the hand that feeds them. Bristol-Myers sued CBS and me for $23 million when I did the story on aspirin. You'd think CBS would have said, "Stossel ain't worth that." But they didn't. Sometimes advertisers would pull their accounts, but still I wasn't fired. Ralph Nader once said that this would never happen except on public television. In fact the opposite is true: Unlike PBS, almost every local TV station has a consumer reporter. The reason is capitalism: More people watch stations that give honest information about their sponsors' products. So although a station might lose some advertisers, it can charge the others more. Markets protect us in unexpected ways.

Alternatives to the Nanny State

People often say to me, "That's okay for advertising. But when it comes to health and safety, we've got to have OSHA, the FDA, the CPSC" and the whole alphabet soup of regulatory agencies that have been created over the past several decades. At first glance this might seem to make sense. But by interfering with free markets, regulations almost invariably have nasty side effects. Take the FDA, which saved us from thalidomide—the drug to prevent morning sickness in pregnant women that was discovered to cause birth defects. To be accurate, it wasn't so much that the FDA saved us, as that it was so slow in studying thalidomide that by the end of the approval process, the drug's awful effects were being seen in Europe. I'm glad for this. But since the thalidomide scare, the FDA has grown ten-fold in size, and I believe it now does more harm than good. If you want to get a new drug approved today, it costs about $500 million and takes about ten years. This means that there are drugs currently in existence that would improve or even save lives, but that are being withheld from us because of a tiny chance they contain carcinogens. Some years ago, the FDA held a press conference to announce its long-awaited approval of a new beta-blocker, and predicted it would save 14,000 American lives per year. Why didn't anybody stand up at the time and say, "Excuse me, doesn't that mean you killed 14,000 people last year by not approving it?" The answer is, reporters don't think that way.

Why, in a free society, do we allow government to perform this kind of nanny-state function? A reasonable alternative would be for government to serve as an information agency. Drug companies wanting to submit their products to a ten-year process could do so. Those of us who choose to be cautious could take only FDA-approved drugs. But others, including people with terminal illnesses, could try non-approved drugs without sneaking off to Mexico or breaking the law. As an added benefit, all of us would learn something valuable by their doing so. I'd argue further that we don't need the FDA to perform this research. As a rule, government agencies are inefficient. If we abolished the FDA, private groups like the publisher of Consumer Reports would step in and do the job better, cheaper, and faster. In any case, wouldn't that be more compatible with what America is about? Patrick Henry never said, "Give me absolute safety or give me death!"

Lawyers and Liability

If we embrace the idea of free markets, we have to accept the fact that trial lawyers have a place. Private lawsuits could be seen as a supplement to Adam Smith's invisible hand: the invisible fist. In theory they should deter bad behavior. But because of how our laws have evolved, this process has gone horribly wrong. It takes years for victims to get their money, and most of the money goes to lawyers. Additionally, the wrong people get sued. A Harvard study of medical malpractice suits found that most of those getting money don't deserve it, and that most people injured by negligence don't sue. The system is a mess. Even the cases the trial lawyers are most proud of don't really make us safer. They brag about their lawsuit over football helmets, which were thin enough that some kids were getting head injuries. But now the helmets are so thick that kids are butting each other and getting other kinds of injuries. Worst of all, they cost over $100 each. School districts on the margin can't afford them, and as a result some are dropping their football programs. Are the kids from these schools safer playing on the streets? No.

An even clearer example concerns vaccines. Trial lawyers sued over the Diphtheria-Pertussis-Tetanus Vaccine, claiming that it wasn't as safe as it might have been. Although I suspect this case rested on junk science, I don't know what the truth is. But assuming these lawyers were right, and that they've made the DPT vaccine a little safer, are we safer? When they sued, there were 20 companies in America researching and making vaccines. Now there are four. Many got out of the business because they said, "We don't make that much on vaccines. Who needs this huge liability?" Is America better off with four vaccine makers instead of 20? No way.

These lawsuits also disrupt the flow of information that helps free people protect themselves. For example, we ought to read labels. We should read the label on tetracycline, which says that it won't work if taken with milk. But who reads labels anymore? I sure don't. There are 21 warning labels on stepladders—"Don't dance on stepladders wearing wet shoes," etc.—because of the threat of liability. Drug labels are even crazier. If anyone were actually to read the two pages of fine print that come with birth control pills, they wouldn't need to take the drug. My point is that government and lawyers don't make us safer. Freedom makes us safer. It allows us to protect ourselves. Some say, "That's fine for us. We're educated. But the poor and the ignorant need government regulations to protect them." Not so. I sure don't know what makes one car run better or safer than another. Few of us are automotive engineers. But it's hard to get totally ripped off buying a car in America. The worst car you can find here is safer than the best cars produced in planned economies. In a free society, not everyone has to be an expert in order for markets to protect us. In the case of cars, we just need a few car buffs who read car magazines. Information gets around through word-of-mouth. Good companies thrive and bad ones atrophy. Freedom protects the ignorant, too.

Admittedly there are exceptions to this argument. I think we need some environmental regulation, because now and then we lack a market incentive to behave well in that area. Where is the incentive for me to keep my waste-treatment plant from contaminating your drinking water? So we need some rules, and some have done a lot of good. Our air and water are cleaner thanks to catalytic converters. But how much regulation is enough? President Clinton set a record as he left office, adding 500,000 new pages to the Federal Register—a whole new spiderweb of little rules for us to obey. How big should government be? For most of America's history, when we grew the fastest, government accounted for five percent or less of GDP. The figure is now 40 percent. This is still less than Europe. But shouldn't we at least have an intelligent debate about how much government should do? The problem is that to have such a debate, we need an informed public. And here I'm embarrassed, because people in my business are not helping that cause.

Fear-Mongering: A Risky Business

A turning point came in my career when a producer came into my office excited because he had been given a story by a trial lawyer—the lazy reporter's best friend—about Bic lighters spontaneously catching fire in people's pockets. These lighters, he told me, had killed four Americans in four years. By this time I'd done some homework, so I said, "Fine. I'll do the exploding lighter story after I do stories on plastic bags, which kill 40 Americans every four years, and five-gallon buckets, which kill 200 Americans (mostly children) every four years." This is a big country, with 280 million people. Bad things happen to some of them. But if we frighten all the rest about ant-sized dangers, they won't be prepared when an elephant comes along. The producer stalked off angrily and got Bob Brown to do the story. But several years later, when ABC gave me three hour-long specials a year in order to keep me, I insisted the first one be called, "Are We Scaring Ourselves to Death?" In it, I ranked some of these risks and made fun of the press for its silliness in reporting them.

Risk specialists compare risks not according to how many people they kill, but according to how many days they reduce the average life. The press goes nuts over airplane crashes, but airplane crashes have caused fewer than 200 deaths per year over the past 20 years. That's less than one day off the average life. There is no proof that toxic-waste sites like Love Canal or Times Beach have hurt anybody at all, despite widely reported claims that they cause 1,000 cases of cancer a year. (Even assuming they do, and assuming further that all these cancer victims die, that would still be less than four days off the average life.) House fires account for about 4,500 American deaths per year—18 days off the average life. And murder, which leads the news in most towns, takes about 100 days off the average life. But to bring these risks into proper perspective, we need to compare them to far greater risks like driving, which knocks 182 days off the average life. I am often asked to do scare stories about flying—"The Ten Most Dangerous Airports" or "The Three Most Dangerous Airlines"—and I refuse because it's morally irresponsible. When we scare people about flying, more people drive to Grandma's house, and more are killed as a result. This is statistical murder, perpetuated by regulators and the media.

Even more dramatic is the fact that Americans below the poverty line live seven to ten fewer years than the rest of us. Some of this difference is self-induced: poor people smoke and drink more. But most of it results from the fact that they can't afford some of the good things that keep the rest of us alive. They drive older cars with older tires; they can't afford the same medical care; and so on. This means that when bureaucrats get obsessed about flying or toxic-waste sites, and create new regulations and drive up the cost of living in order to reduce these risks, they shorten people's lives by making them poorer. Bangladesh has floods that kill 100,000 people. America has comparable floods and no one dies. The difference is wealth. Here we have TVs and radios to hear about floods, and cars to drive off in. Wealthier is healthier, and regulations make the country poorer. Maybe the motto of OSHA should be: "To save four, kill ten."

Largely due to the prevalence of misleading scare stories in the press, we see in society an increasing fear of innovation. Natural gas in the home kills 200 Americans a year, but we accept it because it's old. It happened before we got crazy. We accept coal, which is awful stuff, but we're terrified of nuclear power, which is probably cleaner and safer. Swimming pools kill over 1,000 Americans every year, and I think it's safe to say that the government wouldn't allow them today if they didn't already exist. What about vehicles that weigh a ton and are driven within inches of pedestrians by 16-year-olds, all while spewing noxious exhaust? Cars, I fear, would never make it off the drawing board in 2001.

What's happened to America? Why do we allow government to make decisions for us as if we were children? In a free society we should be allowed to take risks, and to learn from them. The press carps and whines about our exposure to dangerous new things—invisible chemicals, food additives, radiation, etc. But what's the result? We're living longer than ever. A century ago, most people my age were already dead. If we were better informed, we'd realize that what's behind this longevity is the spirit of enterprise, and that what gives us this spirit—what makes America thrive—isn't regulation. It's freedom.

The Entrepreneur
As American Hero

Walter E. Williams

March 2005

Let's start off talking about the entrepreneur with a brief discussion of the sources of income. Some of the rhetoric one hears gives the impression that income is somehow distributed—that there's a dealer of dollars. Thus, one might think that the reason some Americans have more income than others is that the dollar dealer is a racist, a sexist, or a multi-nationalist who deals out dollars unfairly. Alternatively, some suggest that the reason that some Americans are richer than others is because they got to the pile of money first and took an unfair share. In either case, justice requires that government take the ill-gotten gains of the few and restore them to their rightful owners—in other words, redistribute income. While no one actually describes the sources of income this way, the logic of some arguments about the need to redistribute implies such a vision.

In truth, in a free society, income is earned through pleasing and serving one's fellow man. I mow your lawn, repair your roof or teach your kid economics. In turn you give me dollars. We can think of dollars as certificates of performance. With these certificates of performance in hand, I go to my grocer and ask him to give me a pound of steak and a six-pack of beer that my fellow man produced. In effect the grocer says, "You're making a claim on something your fellow man produced. You're asking him to serve you—but did you serve him?" I say, "Yes I did." The grocer responds, "Prove it!" That's when I show him my certificates of performance—namely, the money my fellow man paid me to mow his lawn.

Contrast the morality of having to serve one's fellow man as a condition of being served by him with the alternative. Government can say to me, "Williams, you don't have to serve your fellow man in order to have a claim on what he produces. As long as you're loyal to us, we will take what your fellow man produces and give it to you."

Obviously, some people are more effective at serving and pleasing their fellow man than others. They earn a greater number of certificates of performance (i.e., higher income) and hence have greater claims on what their fellow man produces. Take Luciano Pavarotti. Why is his income much higher than mine? It's because of discriminating people like you. You will plunk down $75 to hear him sing an aria from *La Bohème*; but how much would you be willing to pay to hear me do the same? Those who would call Pavarotti's income unfair and would have government take part of it to give to others are essentially saying, "We disagree with the decisions of millions upon millions of people acting voluntarily that resulted in Pavarotti's higher income. We are going to use the coercive powers of government to cancel out the full effect of those decisions through income redistribution." I might add that income redistribution is simply a legal version of what a thief does—namely, take the rightful property of one person for the benefit of another. The primary distinction between his behavior and that of Congress is legality.

For the most part, in a free society, people who are wealthy have become so through effectively serving their fellow man. Cyrus McCormick and his reaping machine, Thomas Watson, the founder of IBM, and Lloyd Conoverk, who created the antibiotic tetracycline in the employ of Pfizer are just a few of the exceptional contributors. And while these people and their companies became extremely wealthy, society benefitted far more than they did in terms of the value of healthier lives and the millions and possibly billions of lives saved.

Capitalism Raises All Boats

Propaganda and stubborn ignorance has it that the advances of capitalism benefit only the rich. But the evidence, as I've already pointed out, refutes that. Let's look at more: The rich have always been able to afford entertainment, but it was the development and marketing of radio and television that made entertainment accessible to the common man. The rich have never had the drudgery of washing and ironing clothing, beating out carpets or waxing floors.

It was the development and mass production of washing machines, wash and wear clothing, vacuum cleaners, and no-wax floors that spared the common man of this drudgery. At one time, only the rich could afford automobiles, telephones, and computers. Now all but a tiny percentage of Americans enjoy these goods.

Today, as it has always been, the direct impetus for technological innovation and progress has been the entrepreneurial search for profits and the competitive economy. As Stephen Moore and Julian L. Simon point out in their book, *25 Wonderful Trends of the 20th Century*, over the course of the last 100 years life expectancy rose from 47 to 77 years of age; deaths from infectious disease fell from 700 to 50 per 100,000 of the population; agricultural workers fell from 35 to 2.5 percent of the workforce; auto ownership rose from one to 91 percent of the population; patents granted rose from 25,000 to 150,000 a year; and controlling for inflation, household assets rose from $6 trillion to $41 trillion just between 1945 and 1998.

Let's consider another factor that is nearly completely ignored. The output and wealth generated through free enterprise contributes to a more civilized society and civilized relationships. For most of mankind's existence, he has had to spend most of his time simply eking out a living. In pre-industrial society and in many places in the world still today, the most optimistic scenario for the ordinary citizen was to be able to eke out enough to meet his physical needs for another day. But with the rise of capitalism and the concomitant rise in human productivity that yielded seemingly ceaseless economic progress, it was no longer necessary for mankind to spend his entire day simply providing for minimum physical needs. People were able to satisfy their physical needs with less and less time. This made it possible for people to have the time and resources to develop spiritually and culturally. In other words, the rise of capitalism enabled the gradual extension of civilization to greater and greater numbers of people. More of them have time available to read and become educated in the liberal arts and gain more knowledge about the world around them. Greater wealth permits them to attend the arts, afford recreation, contemplate more fulfilling and interesting life activities and do other culturally enriching activities that were formerly within the purview of only the rich. How was all this achieved? In a market system, enterprise profits are performance-related; they come about through a process of finding out what human wants are not being met and finding ways to meet them.

In reference to the motivations of the entrepreneur Adam Smith says this: "By directing that industry in such a manner as its produce may be of the greatest value, he intends only his own gain, and he is in this, as in many other cases, led by an invisible hand to promote an end which was no part of his intention." That might very well describe an entrepreneur like Thomas Watson, Sr., founder of IBM. Such previously unimaginable human progress as we have seen in recent decades is the direct result of having methods of handling large amounts of data accurately and rapidly. From the 1930s onward, IBM was at the forefront in the development of the machinery to do this. The huge benefits we enjoy as a result of IBM's pioneering work was no part of the intention of Thomas Watson or his successors. They were in it for their gain—profits.

In Defense of Profit

Profit has almost become a dirty word, so let me spend a few minutes talking about the magnitude of profits and the role that profits play in a free market economy. As to this magnitude, only roughly six cents of each dollar companies take in represent after-tax profits. By far, wages are the largest part of that dollar, representing about 60 cents. As percentages of 2002 national income, after-tax profits represented about five percent and wages about 71 percent.

I'll discuss first what might be called normal profit and later turn to the more emotional topic of "windfall profits"—what some have labeled "obscene profits." Normal profit is the opportunity cost of using entrepreneurial abilities in the production of a good. It's what the entrepreneur could have earned in his next best alternative—say, another business venture. Just as wages, rent, and interest must be paid in order to employ the services of labor, land, and capital, normal profits must be paid to employ entrepreneurial services—the decisions, innovations, and risks that drive economic progress.

Whether an entrepreneur makes a profit depends essentially on two things. The first is whether he is producing a good that consumers value and are willing to pay for; the second is whether he's using the scarce resources of society in the most efficient manner to produce the good.

Let's look at an example of the role of profits in providing incentives to produce what the consumer wants. Remember 1985, when Coca Cola introduced the "new" Coke? Pepsi Cola president Roger Enrico called it "the Edsel of the '80s," representing one of the greatest marketing debacles that decade. Who made the Coca Cola Company bring back the old Coke? Was it Congress, the courts, the president, or other government officials who were acting in the interests of soda-drinking Americans? No, it was the specter of negative profits (i.e., losses) that convinced Coca Cola to bring back the old Coke. Thus, one role of profits is to discover what consumers want and, if producers make mistakes, correct them.

Profits also force producers to employ resources wisely. If producers waste inputs, their production costs will be higher. In order to cover their cost, they must charge prices higher than what consumers are willing to pay. After a while the company will incur unsustainable losses and go out of business. As a result, the company's resources will become available to someone else who'll put them to wiser use. This process is short-circuited if government offers bailouts in the forms of guaranteed loans, subsidies, or restrictions on competitive products from abroad such as tariffs and import quotas. Government "help" enables failing companies to continue squandering resources. In this context it is important to remember that a business going bankrupt doesn't meant that its productive resources will vanish into thin air. It means someone else will own them.

So-called windfall profits are profits above and beyond those needed to keep an entrepreneur producing a good or service. But they serve a vital social function. They serve as a signal that there are unmet human wants. One of the best examples of the role of windfall profits are those that arise in the wake of a disaster and are often condemned as price gouging. In the wake of a disaster, such as a hurricane, there is an immediate change in scarcity conditions and that's reflected in higher prices for goods and services. Say a family of four sees their home damaged or destroyed. At before-disaster prices, they might decide to rent two adjoining hotel rooms. However, when they arrive at the hotel and see that room prices have doubled, they might easily decide to tough it out in a single room. Doing so makes a room available for someone else whose home was damaged and needs a place to spend the night. Thus, higher prices give people incentive to economize on scarce resources.

In the wake of Florida's Hurricane Andrew, windfall profits played a vital, though unappreciated role. Plywood destined to be shipped to the Midwest, West, and Northeast suddenly was rerouted to South Florida. Lumber mills increased production. Truckers and other workers worked overtime in order to increase the availability of plywood and other construction materials to Floridians. Rising plywood prices meant something else as well. All that plywood heading south meant plywood prices rose in other locations, discouraging "lower valued" uses of plywood such as home improvement projects. After all, rebuilding and repairing destroyed homes is a "higher valued" use of plywood.

What caused these market participants to do what was in the social interest, namely, sacrifice or postpone alternative uses for plywood? The answer reveals perhaps the most wonderful feature of this process. Rising prices and opportunities for higher profits encouraged people to do voluntarily what was in the social interest: help their fellow man recover from a disaster.

Williams' Law

At this juncture let me say a few words about the modern push for corporate social responsibility. Do corporations have a social responsibility? Yes, and Nobel Laureate Professor Milton Friedman put it best in 1970 when he said that in a free society "there is one and only one social responsibility of business—to use its resources and engage in activities designed to increase its profits so long as it stays within the rules of the game, which is to say, engages in open and free competition without deception or fraud."

It is only people, not businesses, who have responsibilities. A CEO is an employee, an employee of shareholders and customers. The failure of the corporate executive community to recognize this, and engage in activities unrelated to the pursuit of profits, means national wealth will be lower, product prices will be higher and the return on investment lower.

If we care about people's wants, rather than beating up on profit-making enterprises, we should pay more attention to government-owned non-profit organizations. A good example are government schools. Many squander resources and produce a shoddy product while administrators, teachers, and staff earn higher pay and perks, and customers (taxpayers) are increasingly burdened. Unlike other producers, educationists don't face the rigors of the profit discipline, and hence they're not as accountable. Ditto the U.S. Postal Service. They often provide shoddy and surly services, but the management and workers receive increasingly higher wages while customers pay higher and higher prices. Again, wishes of customers can be safely ignored because there's no bottom line discipline of profits.

Here's Williams' law: Whenever the profit incentive is missing, the probability that people's wants can be safely ignored is the greatest. It's not just the post office and schools but delivery of other government services, such as garbage collection, as well. If a poll were taken asking people which services they are most satisfied with and which they are most dissatisfied with, for-profit organizations (supermarkets, computer companies, and video stores) would dominate the first list, while non-profit organizations (schools, post offices, and offices of motor vehicle registration) would dominate the latter. In a free economy, the pursuit of profits and serving people are one and the same. No one argues that the free enterprise system is perfect, but it's the closest we'll come here on Earth.

Free to Choose: A Conversation with Milton Friedman

July 2006

Larry Arnn: In *Free to Choose*, in the chapter on "The Tyranny of Controls," you argue that protectionism and government intervention in general breed conflict and that free markets breed cooperation. How do you reconcile this statement with the fact that we think of free markets as being competitive?

Milton Friedman: They are competitive, but they are competitive over a broad range. The question is, how do you make money in a free market? You only make money if you can provide someone with something he or she is willing to pay for. You can't make money any other way. Therefore, in order to make money, you have to promote cooperation. You have to do something that your customer wants you to do. You don't do it because he orders you to. You don't do it because he threatens to hit you over the head if you don't. You do it because you offer him a better deal than he can get anywhere else. Now that's promoting cooperation. But there are other people who are trying to sell to him, too. They're your competitors. So there is competition among sellers, but cooperation between sellers and buyers.

LA: In the chapter on "The Tyranny of Controls," you seem gloomy about the prospects for India. Why?

MF: I was in India in 1955 on behalf of the American government to serve as an economic adviser to the minister of finance. I concluded then that India had tremendous potential, but none of it was being achieved. That fact underlies the passage you are referring to in *Free to Choose*. Remember, *Free to Choose* aired in January 1980, and as of that time there had been no progress in India. The population had grown, but the standard of living was as low as it had been in 1955. Now, in the past ten or 15 years, there has been movement in India, and maybe those hidden potentials I saw in 1955 will finally be achieved. But, there is still great uncertainty there.

LA: In that same chapter, you wrote the following about China: "Letting the genie of…initiative out of the bottle even to this limited extent will give rise to political problems that, sooner or later, are likely to produce a reaction toward greater authoritarianism. The opposite outcome, the collapse of communism and its replacement by a market system, seems far less likely." What do you think about that statement today?

MF: I'm much more optimistic about China today than I was then. China has made great progress since that time. It certainly has not achieved complete political freedom, but it has come closer. It certainly has a great deal more economic freedom. I visited China for the first time in 1980 right after the publication of *Free to Choose*. I had been invited by the government to lecture on how to stop inflation, among other things. China at that time was in a pretty poor state. The hotel we stayed in showed every sign of being run by a communist regime. We returned to China twice, and each time, the changes were tremendous. In 1980, everybody was wearing the dull and drab Mao costume; there were bicycles all over the place and very few cars. Eight years later, we started to see some color in the clothes, there were things available for sale that hadn't been available before, and free markets were breaking out all over the place. China has continued to grow at a dramatic rate. But in the section of *Free to Choose* you refer to, I talked about the political conflict that was coming—and that broke out in Tiananmen Square. The final outcome in China will not be decided until there is a showdown between the political tyranny on the one hand and economic freedom on the other—they cannot coexist.

LA: Let me ask you about demographic trends. Columnist Mark Steyn writes that in ten years, 40 percent of young men in the world are going to be living in oppressed Muslim countries. What do you think the effect of that is going to be?

MF: What happens will depend on whether we succeed in bringing some element of greater economic freedom to those Muslim countries. Just as India in 1955 had great but unrealized potential, I think the Middle East is in a similar situation today. In part this is because of the curse of oil. Oil has been a blessing from one point of view, but a curse from another. Almost every country in the Middle East that is rich in oil is a despotism.

LA: Why do you think that is so?

MF: One reason, and one reason only—the oil is owned by the governments in question. If that oil were privately owned and thus someone's private property, the political outcome would be freedom rather than tyranny. This is why I believe the first step following the 2003 invasion of Iraq should have been the privatization of the oil fields. If the government had given every individual over 21 years of age equal shares in a corporation that had the right and responsibility to make appropriate arrangements with foreign oil companies for the purpose of discovering and developing Iraq's oil reserves, the oil income would have flowed in the form of dividends to the people—the shareholders—rather than into government coffers. This would have provided an income to the whole people of Iraq and thereby prevented the current disputes over oil between the Sunnis, Shiites, and Kurds, because oil income would have been distributed on an individual rather than a group basis.

LA: Many Middle Eastern societies have a kind of tribal or theocratic basis and long-held habits of despotic rule that make it difficult to establish a system of contract between strangers. Is it your view that the introduction of free markets in such places could overcome those obstacles?

MF: Eventually, yes. I think that nothing is so important for freedom as recognizing in the law each individual's natural right to property, and giving individuals a sense that they own something that they're responsible for, that they have control over, and that they can dispose of.

LA: Is there an area here in the United States in which we have not been as aggressive as we should in promoting property rights and free markets?

MF: Yes, in the field of medical care. We have a socialist-communist system of distributing medical care. Instead of letting people hire their own physicians and pay them, no one pays his or her own medical bills. Instead, there's a third party payment system. It is a communist system and it has a communist result. Despite this, we've had numerous miracles in medical science. From the discovery of penicillin, to new surgical techniques, to MRIs and CAT scans, the last 30 or 40 years have been a period of miraculous change in medical science. On the other hand, we've seen costs skyrocket. Nobody is happy: physicians don't like it, patients don't like it. Why? Because none of them are responsible for themselves. You no longer have a situation in which a patient chooses a physician, receives a service, gets charged, and pays for it. There is no direct relation between the patient and the physician. The physician is an employee of an insurance company or an employee of the government. Today, a third party pays the bills. As a result, no one who visits the doctor asks what the charge is going to be—somebody else is going to take care of that. The end result is third party payment and, worst of all, third party treatment.

LA: Following the recent expansion in prescription drug benefits and Medicare, what hope is there for a return to the free market in medical care?

MF: It does seem that markets are on the defensive, but there is hope. The expansion of drug benefits was accompanied by the introduction of health savings accounts—HSAs. That's the one hopeful sign in the medical area, because it's a step in the direction of making people responsible for themselves and for their own care. No one spends somebody else's money as carefully as he spends his own.

LA: On the subject of Social Security, let me read to you a passage from *Free to Choose*: "As we have gone through the literature on Social Security, we have been shocked at the arguments that have been used to defend the program. Individuals who would not lie to their children, their friends, their colleagues, whom all of us would trust implicitly in the most important personal dealings, have propagated a false view of Social Security. Their intelligence and exposure to contrary views make it hard to believe that they have done so unintentionally and innocently. Apparently they have regarded themselves as an elite group within society that knows what is good for other people better than those people do for themselves." What do you think of these words today?

MF: I stick by every word there. But there has been progress since then. Let me explain: *Free to Choose* was produced and shown on television for the first time in January 1980. President Reagan was elected in November 1980. To get a clear picture of what has happened since the publication of *Free to Choose*, we really need to look at what happened before and after the election of Ronald Reagan. Before Reagan, non-defense government spending—on the federal, state, and local levels—as a percentage of national income was rising rapidly. Between the early 1950s and 1980, we were in a period of what I would call galloping socialism that showed no signs of slowing. Following the election of Ronald Reagan, there was an abrupt and immediate halt to this expansion of government. But even under Reagan, government spending as a percentage of national income didn't come down: It has held constant from that time to now. Although the early years of the current Bush presidency did see spending increases, national income has risen, too. We have achieved some success at our first task: stopping the growth of government. The second task is to shrink government spending and make government smaller. We haven't done that yet, but we are making some progress. I should also mention as a cautionary tale that, prior to Reagan, the number of pages in the Federal Register was on the rise, but Reagan succeeded in reducing this number substantially. However, once Reagan was out of office, the number of pages in the Register began to rise even more quickly. We have not really succeeded in that area.

There have been real changes in our society since *Free to Choose* was published. I'm not attributing them to *Free to Choose*—I'm not saying that's the reason—but in general, there has been a complete change in public opinion. This change is probably due as much to the collapse of the Soviet Union as it is to what Friedrich Hayek or Milton Friedman or somebody else wrote. Socialism used to mean the ownership and operation of the means of production, but nobody gives it that meaning today. There is no country in the world attempting to be socialist in that sense except North Korea. And perhaps Russia is moving in that direction. Conversely, opinion has not shifted far enough in terms of the dangers of big government and the deleterious effects it can have, and that's where we're facing future problems. This clarifies the task facing institutions such as Hillsdale College: We must make clear that the only reason we have our freedom is because government is so *inefficient*. If the government were efficient in spending the approximately 40 percent of our income that it currently manages, we would enjoy less freedom than we do today.

LA: In *Free to Choose* you discuss Abraham Lincoln's "House Divided" speech, which you relate to the great task that the American people face. Like Lincoln, you argue that a house divided against itself cannot stand: America is going to be a government intervention country or it's going to be a free market country, but it cannot continue indefinitely as a mixture of both. Do you still believe that?

MF: Yes, I very much believe that, and I believe that we've been making some headway since *Free to Choose* appeared. However, even though it is real headway compared to what was happening before, we are mostly holding ground.

LA: What do you think are the major factors behind the economic growth we have experienced since the publication of *Free to Choose*?

MF: Economic growth since that time has been phenomenal, which has very little to do with most of what we've been talking about in terms of the conflict between government and private enterprise. It has much more to do with the technical problem of establishing sound monetary policy. The economic situation during the past 20 years has been unprecedented in the history of the world. You will find no other 20-year period in which prices have been as stable—relatively speaking—in which there has been as little variability in price levels, in which inflation has been so well-controlled, and in which output has gone up as regularly. You hear all this talk about economic difficulties, when the fact is we are at the absolute peak of prosperity in the history of the world. Never before have so many people had as much as they do today. I believe a large part of that is to be attributed to better monetary policy. The improved policy is a result of the acceptance of the view that inflation is a monetary phenomenon, not a real phenomenon. We have accepted the view that central banks are primarily responsible for maintaining stable prices and nothing else.

LA: Do you think the Great Depression was triggered by bad monetary policy at a crucial moment?

MF: Absolutely. Unfortunately, it is still the case that if you ask people what caused the Great Depression, nine out of ten will probably tell you it was a failure of business. But it's absolutely clear that the Depression was a failure of government and not a failure of business.

LA: You don't think the Smoot-Hawley tariff caused the Depression?

MF: No. I think the Smoot-Hawley tariff was a bad law. I think it did harm. But the Smoot-Hawley tariff by itself would not have made one quarter of the labor force unemployed. However, reducing the quantity of money by one third *did* make a quarter of the labor force unemployed. When I graduated from undergraduate college in 1932, I was baffled by the fact that there were idle machines and idle men and you couldn't get them together. Those men wanted to cooperate; they wanted to work; they wanted to produce what they wore; and they wanted to produce the food they ate. Yet something had gone wrong: The government was mismanaging the money supply.

LA: Do you think our government has learned its lesson about how to manage the money supply?

MF: I think that the lesson has been learned, but I don't think it will last forever. Sooner or later, government will want to raise funds without imposing taxes. It will want to spend money it does not have. So I hesitate to join those who are predicting two percent inflation for the next 20 years. The temptation for government to lay its hands on that money is going to be very hard to resist. The fundamental problem is that you shouldn't have an institution such as the Federal Reserve, which depends for its success on the abilities of its chairman. My first preference would be to abolish the Federal Reserve, but that's not going to happen.

LA: I want to talk now about education and especially about vouchers, because I know they are dear to your heart. Why do you think teachers unions oppose vouchers?

MF: The president of the National Education Association was once asked when his union was going to do something about students. He replied that when the students became members of the union, the union would take care of them. And that was a correct answer. Why? His responsibility as president of the NEA was to serve the members of his union, not to serve public purposes. I give him credit: The trade union has been very effective in serving its members. However, in the process, they've destroyed American education. But you see, education isn't the union's function. It's our fault for allowing the union to pursue its agenda. Consider this fact: There are two areas in the United States that suffer from the same disease—education is one and health care is the other. They both suffer from the disease that takes a system that should be bottom-up and converts it into a system that is top-down. Education is a simple case. It isn't the public purpose to build brick schools and have students taught there. The public purpose is to provide education.

Think of it this way: If you want to subsidize the production of a product, there are two ways you can do it. You can subsidize the producer or you can subsidize the consumer. In education, we subsidize the producer—the school. If you subsidize the student instead—the consumer—you will have competition. The student could choose the school he attends and that would force schools to improve and to meet the demands of their students.

LA: Although you discuss many policy issues in *Free to Choose*, you have turned much of your attention to education, and to vouchers as a method of education reform. Why is that your focus?

MF: I don't see how we can maintain a decent society if we have a world split into haves and have-nots, with the haves subsidizing the have-nots. In our current educational system, close to 30 percent of the youngsters who start high school never finish. They are condemned to low-income jobs. They are condemned to a situation in which they are going to be at the bottom. That leads in turn to a divisive society; it leads to a stratified society rather than one of general cooperation and general understanding. The effective literacy rate in the United States today is almost surely less than it was 100 years ago. Before government had any involvement in education, the majority of youngsters were schooled, literate, and able to learn. It is a disgrace that in a country like the United States, 30 percent of youngsters never graduates from high school. And I haven't even mentioned those who drop out in elementary school. It's a disgrace that there are so many people who can't read and write. It's hard for me to see how we can continue to maintain a decent and free society if a large subsection of that society is condemned to poverty and to handouts.

LA: Do you think the voucher campaign is going well?

MF: No. I think it's going much too slowly. What success we have had is almost entirely in the area of income-limited vouchers. There are two kinds of vouchers: One is a charity voucher that is limited to people below a certain income level. The other is an education voucher, which, if you think of vouchers as a way of transforming the educational industry, is available to everybody. How can we make vouchers available to everybody? First, education ought to be a state and local matter, not a federal matter. The 1994 Contract with America called for the elimination of the Department of Education. Since then, the budget for the Department of Education has tripled. This trend must be reversed. Next, education ought to be a parental matter. The responsibility for educating children is with parents. But in order to make it a parental matter, we must have a situation in which parents are free to choose the schools their children attend. They aren't free to do that now. Today the schools pick the children. Children are assigned to schools by geography—by where they live. By contrast, I would argue that if the government is going to spend money on education, the money ought to travel with the children. The objective of such an expenditure ought to be educated children, not beautiful buildings. The way to accomplish this is to have a universal voucher. As I said in 1955, we should take the amount of money that we're now spending on education, divide it by the number of children, and give that amount of money to each parent. After all, that's what we're spending now, so we might as well let parents spend it in the form of vouchers.

LA: I have one more question for you. You describe a society in which people look after themselves because they know the most about themselves, and they will flourish if you let them. You, however, are a crusader for the rights of others. For example, you say in *Free to Choose*—and it's a very powerful statement—a tiny minority is what matters. So is it one of the weaknesses of the free market that it requires certain extremely talented and *disinterested* people who can defend it?

MF: No, that's not right. The self-interest of the kind of people you just described is promoting public policy. That's what they're interested in doing. For example, what was my self-interest in economics? My self-interest to begin with was to understand the real mystery and puzzle that was the Great Depression. My self-interest was to try to understand why that happened, and that's what I enjoyed doing—that was my self-interest. Out of that I grew to learn some things—to have some knowledge. Following that, my self-interest was to see that other people understood the same things and took appropriate action.

LA: Do you define self-interest as what the individual wants?

MF: Yes, self-interest is what the individual wants. Mother Teresa, to take one example, operated on a completely self-interested basis. Self-interest does not mean narrow self-interest. Self-interest does not mean monetary self-interest. Self-interest means pursuing those things that are valuable to you but which you can also persuade others to value. Such things very often go beyond immediate material interest.

LA: Does that mean self-interest is a synonym for self-sacrifice?

MF: If you want to see how pervasive this sort of self-interest is that I'm describing, look at the enormous amount of money contributed after Hurricane Katrina. That was a tremendous display of self-interest: The self-interest of people in that case was to help others. Self-interest, rightly understood, works for the benefit of society as a whole.

Entrepreneurship in American History

John Steele Gordon

February 2014

The word "entrepreneur"—one who undertakes, manages, and assumes the risk of a new enterprise—comes from the French, where it literally means "undertaker." The word was borrowed into English in the mid-19th century—perhaps the golden age of the entrepreneur—when the number of new economic niches was exploding and the hand of government was at its lightest in history. The activity of entrepreneurship, of course, is much older, going back to ancient times. As for America, our nation was founded, quite literally, by entrepreneurs.

In 1607 the Virginia Company sent three ships across the Atlantic and unloaded 109 passengers at what became Jamestown, Virginia. They were embarked on a new business enterprise that they hoped would be profitable— American plantations. The Virginia Company was a joint-stock company, a relatively new invention that allowed people to invest in enterprises without running the risk of losing everything if the business did not succeed. By limiting liability, corporations greatly increased the number of people who could dare to become entrepreneurs by pooling their resources while avoiding the possibility of ruin. Thus the corporation was one of the great inventions of the Renaissance, along with printing, double-entry bookkeeping, and the full-rigged ship.

Allowing incorporation as a matter of law, rather than requiring an act of the executive or of the legislature, began in the United States as early as 1811, when New York State passed a general incorporation law for certain businesses, including anchor makers—I suspect an anchor manufacturer had a friend in Albany. Soon enlarged in scope, the ability to incorporate simply by filling out the right forms freed the process from politics, and the number of corporations exploded. There had been only seven companies incorporated in British North America, but the state of Pennsylvania alone incorporated more than 2,000 between 1800 and 1860.

Unfortunately for the stockholders of the Virginia Company, the business of American plantations was a very new one and had a steep learning curve—a curve that would be encountered again and again as the American economy developed and new industries were born. It is a curve all would-be entrepreneurs must climb to be successful. The Virginia Company did not climb that curve quickly enough, and made just about every mistake that it could make: It tried to run Jamestown as a company town; it searched for gold, of which Virginia has none, instead of planting crops; and it failed at establishing a glass-making industry. Eventually Jamestown was nearly abandoned. Only when John Rolfe introduced West Indian tobacco in 1612 did Virginia find an export that had a market in Europe—indeed a market that grew explosively and made Virginia rich. But by that time it was far too late for the Virginia Company, which went broke.

In fact, of course, most entrepreneurs do fail.

———

It has not been nearly well enough noted that the American colonies, while many ended up in royal hands, were not founded by the English state. Several, such as Massachusetts Bay, Plymouth, and Virginia, were founded by profit-seeking corporations. Others, such as Pennsylvania and Maryland, were founded by proprietors. To be sure, many of these enterprises had non-entrepreneurial motives, such as providing a refuge for religious dissenters. John Winthrop wanted the Puritans to establish a "shining city on a hill"; William Penn thought of Pennsylvania as a "Holy Experiment" where Quakers could live in peace. But Plymouth, Massachusetts Bay, and Pennsylvania were also expected to show a profit. "Though I desire to extend religious freedom," said Penn, "yet I want some recompense for my troubles."

New York, of course, was founded by the Dutch, not the English, and profit was the sole reason for settling on Manhattan. Indeed, so bent on money making were the Dutch that they did not get around to building a church for 17 years, worshiping instead in the fort. When they did finally build a church, they named it for St. Nicholas, and Santa Claus has been the patron saint of New York ever since.

Even after the British took the colony in 1664, the Dutch devotion to commerce remained. Harking back to the early source of its economic success, the fur trade, the city's seal remains a beaver surrounded by wampum. Even today, that little hustly-bustly Dutch village lies at the heart of the world's most important and powerful city, and making money is still New York's chief business.

Even in the theocracy that was early New England, the entrepreneurial spirit burned bright. Unlike the colonies on the Chesapeake, there was no cash crop that could be grown in New England's stony soil and short growing season. Perhaps the closest thing to a cash crop was that singular beast, the Atlantic cod. Pulled from the great fishing waters off New England in prodigious numbers, it was salted, dried, and shipped to Europe to provide cheap protein for the masses. Even today, there is a carving of a codfish hanging in the Massachusetts State House. Perhaps because New England lacked a true cash crop, its economy became much more diverse than those of the Southern colonies. Shipping and shipbuilding, lumber, fishing, slaving, and rum distilling became mainstays of the New England economy and produced its earliest fortunes.

Also very important to the evolving New England economy was iron, a commodity that had by then been indispensable for 3,000 years. At first this iron had to be imported at vast expense from foundries in England. John Winthrop the younger—son of the man who coined the phrase "shining city on a hill"—saw opportunity and, a born entrepreneur, he seized it. There was plenty of iron ore available, but to make iron he needed something

America did not then have—capital. So he sailed to England in 1641 to get it. Why, one might well wonder, would English capitalists invest in a major industrial enterprise located in a wilderness 3,000 miles away? The answer lay in something America *did* have in indescribable abundance—wood. Charcoal was as indispensable as ore to iron smelting, and whereas England's forests were being rapidly cut down, America had well over a million square miles of forest. So Winthrop was able to argue that combining America's cheap raw materials with England's capital would produce a product that could be sold at a profit, not only in Massachusetts but in England as well.

Winthrop called the new company the Company of Undertakers—note the word, the literal translation of "entrepreneur"—to which the government of Massachusetts granted a 21-year monopoly on iron production, an exemption from taxation, and the right to export iron once local demand was met. (Obviously, cozy relations between government and industry is not wholly a recent phenomenon.) The Saugus Iron Works, as it is known, was a financial failure, as so many first attempts are. But it is now a national historic site—and well it should be, for it was the start of a great American industry.

By the end of the colonial era, the colonies were producing one-seventh of the world's pig iron. A little over 100 years later, the U.S. was producing more iron and steel than Britain and Germany combined, and producing them so efficiently that we were an exporter to those countries. Much of that iron and steel was manufactured by Andrew Carnegie, who had arrived in America a penniless immigrant from Scotland in the 1840s. When he sold out to J. P. Morgan in 1901, Morgan congratulated him on becoming "the richest man in the world."

The Saugus Iron Works was contemporaneous with the beginning of one of the handmaidens of American entrepreneurship, American invention. The first patent awarded to an American resident was given to Joseph Jenks in 1646 for a device that improved the manufacture of edged tools, such as sickles. It was the beginning of the "Yankee ingenuity" that has characterized America's economy ever since, from that first machine tool to bifocal glasses, the cotton gin, automated flour mills, the high-pressure steam engine, interchangeable parts, the McCormick reaper, the oil industry, the airplane, Coca-Cola, the affordable automobile, the digital computer, and Twitter. For an example of how great a synergistic effect entrepreneurship and invention have had on each other, consider that when Twitter went public last year, the stock offering produced no fewer than 1,600 newly-minted millionaires.

By the time the 13 colonies declared independence, they were, after only 169 years, the richest place on earth per capita. No wonder the British fought so hard to suppress the rebellion. While statistics from the late 18th century can be scarce—the very word "statistics" wouldn't be coined until the early 19th century—there is one powerful statistic indicating just how much better off Americans were than their British cousins: Soldiers in the Continental Army were, on average, a full two inches taller than their British counterparts.

Adam Smith's The Wealth of Nations was published the same year as independence was declared. Being very young, America did not have the burden of hundreds of years of economic cronyism. There were no aristocrats, no guilds, no ancient monopolies or hereditary tariffs as there were in continental Europe. And therefore Karl Marx was wrong, at least about America, when he wrote, "Men make their own history, but they do not make it as they please; they do not make it under circumstances chosen by themselves, but under circumstances directly encountered and transmitted from the past." We had less past than any other country, and therefore we could make our own history, creating the most Smithian economy in the western world. To be sure, it was not purely Smithian. People in government will always try to help those who are powerful at the expense of those who might become so. But the U.S. has consistently come closer to the Smithian ideal, over a longer period of time, than any other major nation.

Nothing encourages entrepreneurial activity more than the freedom to take risk. Consider one of my favorite early American entrepreneurs, Frederic Tudor. In 1806, he decided to sell ice. He wanted to get it where it was cheap, New England, and sell it where it was dear, the Southern states and the West Indies. Everyone laughed. But his secret was a waste product that a great New England industry was more than happy to supply him with for free—sawdust, an excellent insulator. So Tudor combined two cheap things and made them valuable simply by moving their location. By 1820 he was shipping 2,000 tons of ice a year to as far away as Calcutta, getting as much as 25 cents a pound. By 1850, ice was one of New England's largest exports. By 1900, of course, the trade was dead, thanks to the invention of refrigeration. We call that creative destruction.

A second great spur to entrepreneurship is the freedom to fail. And no country in the world has been as consistently tolerant of economic failure as the United States. While bankruptcy in Europe has always been regarded as a moral as well as a financial failure, this has not been the case here— possibly because we are descendants of people who sought a second chance by immigrating. There were, to be sure, debtors prisons in colonial and early America, and some very distinguished people spent time in them—including James Wilson, one of the first justices of the Supreme Court. But debtors prison, a remarkably counter-productive institution—after all, how do you pay off your debts while you're cooling your heels in jail?—was abandoned in the U.S. earlier than elsewhere. It ended under federal law in 1833, and most states had followed suit by 1850. Great Britain wouldn't abolish debtors prison until 1869.

As a result of this freedom to fail without suffering social opprobrium, many entrepreneurs were able on their second or third try to strike it rich. Consider Henry Flagler, who began his business career in the wholesale commodity business and prospered so well that he was making a then vast income of about $50,000 a year by the time of the Civil War. When the war drove the price of salt through the roof, Flagler invested heavily in a salt company in Michigan. When the war ended, however, the price of salt collapsed, as did the business. Flagler, who had risen from the son of an itinerant preacher to the "one percent," was broke. He had to borrow money from his father-in-law—at ten percent interest, no less—in order to feed and house his family. But only five years later, Flagler was a founding partner of Standard Oil, with one-sixth of the company. Later, after running Standard Oil became a matter of management rather than entrepreneurship, Flagler used his Standard Oil millions to create the modern state of Florida, turning it from a semi-tropical wilderness to a tourist mecca and agricultural powerhouse. No American had as much influence on the shaping of a state as Henry Flagler had on Florida, except perhaps Brigham Young in Utah.

Or consider Isaac Merritt Singer. He was on his own by the time he was twelve, and only basically literate—a character straight out of Dickens. At 19 he obtained an apprenticeship in a machine shop and soon demonstrated a marked talent for mechanics. Unfortunately for Singer, he wanted to be an actor—a profession for which he had little talent. Singer tinkered on the side and invented a rock drill, but he was so desperate for money that he sold the patent for a mere $2,000. Only when he gave up acting in middle age did he turn his attention full time to mechanics, and soon after that he invented a new kind of sewing machine that had a great advantage over previous kinds: It actually worked. Once the patent situation was settled—it was the first use of what is now a standard model for dealing with complex inventions to which many people contribute pieces, the patent pool—he made a vast fortune, as the sewing machine revolutionized, and industrialized, the clothing industry.

It's not hard to see why: A shirt that took a seamstress 14 hours to sew by hand could now be produced in an hour-and-a-quarter. Many clothing workers feared for their livelihoods. But of course the effect of the sewing machine was to enlarge their business, not destroy it. As the price of ready-made clothes dropped, the increasing market for them made up for the lower price many times over. This is one of the fundamental means by which capitalism has made the world a richer place for everyone.

———

By the time of Isaac Singer's death in 1875, the American economy was being transformed by the emergence of giant corporations, with tens of thousands of employees and thousands of stockholders. Lagging far behind were the rules needed for such an economy to operate for the benefit of all. Many thought a plutocracy threatened, and plutocracy threatens a country's entrepreneurial spirit quite as much as an overbearing government—especially if the plutocrats and politicians get together, as they are wont to do in their mutual, if short-term, self-interest. This, of course, is the very essence of crony capitalism that has kept so many countries poor and could threaten this country's prosperity.

Standard Oil was able to muscle many small operators into selling out by threatening ruin if they did not. Standard's relationship with the railroads allowed them to ship much more cheaply than the smaller refiners, and it often received an under-the-table kickback on the oil the small operators did ship. Standard would always offer what it regarded as a fair price, but it was "take it or leave it"—and leaving it was usually not an option.

The lack of rules sometimes led to theft of the stockholders' investments in all but name. In earlier times, an organization's managers were almost always owners as well, and thus had an identity of interest with the owners. But as capital requirements rose, managers often came to be, at best, small shareholders. So the self-interest of management and that of shareholders diverged.

The Union Pacific Railroad, for instance, was chartered by the federal government to build part of the transcontinental railroad. The newly installed management organized a construction company owned by themselves, gave it a fancy French name, Crédit Mobilier, and hired themselves to build the railroad. And guess what? They overcharged. To make sure Congress didn't make trouble, they cut key members in on the deal, allowing them to pay for Crédit Mobilier stock using the enormous quarterly dividends—often 100 percent of par value—that they were paid. The result was a bankrupt railroad that had been shoddily constructed.

Managers also did not have to make regular reports to their stockholders in most cases and, even when they did, could keep the books as they pleased. Wall Street, with a powerful interest in knowing the truth about the corporations whose securities were traded and underwritten there, began imposing regular accounting rules and quarterly, audited reports. The result was a far more honest capital market, where entrepreneurs could come in search of financing with the certainty that they would be treated fairly and have their risk-taking properly rewarded if the idea was a success. That was a huge spur to entrepreneurship

Government also sought to police the marketplace, but with far less success than Wall Street. Railroads were brought under a federal regulatory regime that quickly evolved into a cartel called the Interstate Commerce Commission. Trucking came under its control in the 1930s and airlines were regulated by their own cartel, the Civil Aeronautics Board. Cartels and monopolies, of course, prevent competition and thus entrepreneurship. That, in turn, prevents the creative destruction that is so vital to capitalism.

After the ICC and CAB lost their rate setting and route allocating powers in the late 1970s, transportation costs—a transaction cost—dropped from 15 percent of GDP to only ten percent, allowing lower prices for almost all goods. At the same, time innovation flourished. Old legacy airlines, unable to compete in the new environment, disappeared. New airlines with new strategies, such as Southwest and Jet Blue, emerged. Entrepreneurship returned to transportation from where it had long been absent.

With the birth of the digital age, there has been a new golden age of entrepreneurship. Thousands of new niches have become available to exploit, many of which can be exploited very cheaply. The result has been the greatest inflorescence of fortune-making—and fortune-making usually implies entrepreneurship—in human history. In 1982 it took $82 million to have a place on the *Forbes* list. Today it takes over $1 billion.

———

The opportunities for people with ideas and a willingness to take risks are plentiful in America, and there is plenty of capital available to bring those ideas to life. On top of that, mechanisms to bring ideas and capital together are more robust than they have been in the past. So the future of entrepreneurship in this most entrepreneurial of countries remains bright. The only fear is that an overbearing government, bent on managing the American economy— supposedly for the good of all, but actually for the benefit of bureaucrats and politicians—will strangle the goose that has laid so many golden eggs. That is always a danger, for government is just as subject to the law of self-interest as the marketplace. Unfortunately, the process of creative destruction is far less vigorous in government, which is a monopoly by its nature.

On the other hand, government regularly displays an incompetence so extraordinary that reform becomes possible. We are witnessing such a display now with the launch of Obamacare. Obamacare, of course, seeks to rid one-sixth of the American economy of even a vestige of entrepreneurship and turn it over to the public sector.

I'm always an optimist, so I think good things will come out of this. Let us hope so.

CULTURE

Frank Capra's America and Ours

John Marini

March 2015

Filmmaker Frank Capra was not an American by birth or blood. Consequently he did not understand America, as many Americans do today, in terms of personal categories of identity such as race, ethnicity, gender, or sexuality. He understood America in terms of its political principles—the moral principles of America that can be shared by all who understand them and are willing to live up to them. This was Abraham Lincoln's understanding as well. In a speech in Chicago in 1858, Lincoln noted that many citizens of that time did not share the blood of the "old men" of America's Founding generation. But, he continued,

> when they look through the old Declaration of Independence they find that those old men say that "We hold these truths to be self-evident, that all men are created equal," and then they feel that that moral sentiment taught in that day evidences their relation to those men, that it is the father of all moral principles in them, and that they have a right to claim it as though they were blood of the blood, and flesh of the flesh of the men who wrote that Declaration, and so they

are. That is the electric cord in that Declaration that links the hearts of patriotic and liberty-loving men together, that will link those patriotic hearts as long as the love of freedom exists in the minds of men throughout the world.

Frank Capra was born in Sicily in 1897 and came to America in 1903. Yet by the 1930s, his movies—movies like *Mr. Deeds Goes to Town, Mr. Smith Goes to Washington,* and *Meet John Doe*—were said to embody the best in America. Capra's films were nominated for 35 Academy Awards and won eight, including two for best picture and three for best director. But Capra's star faded after the Second World War, and by the end of the revolutionary decade of the 1960s, the actor and director John Cassavetes could say: "Maybe there never was an America in the thirties. Maybe it was all Frank Capra." By that time, Capra's films were widely viewed as feel-good fantasies about a country that never was. But is that view correct?

Capra, like Lincoln, believed that our inherited political edifice of liberty and equal rights is a fundamental good. He believed that if our treasure is in the ideas of our fathers, it is the duty of each generation to make those ideas live through the proper kind of education—including through literature and art, including his own art of filmmaking. Accordingly, he believed it is important to celebrate the deeds of those ordinary individuals who continue to exercise the virtues necessary to maintain those ideas.

In celebrating these deeds in his movies, Capra rejected social or economic theories based on progressivism or historicism—theories in which the idea of natural right is replaced with struggles for power based on categories such as race and class. Such theories had taken root not only in Soviet Russia and Nazi Germany, but elsewhere in the West—especially in the universities. As political theorist Hannah Arendt observed during World War II:

Among ideologies few have won enough prominence to survive the hard competitive struggle of persuasion, and only two have come out on top and essentially defeated all others: the ideology which interprets history as an economic struggle of classes, and the other that interprets history as a natural fight of races. The appeal of both to large masses was so strong that they were able to obtain state support and establish themselves as official national doctrines. But far beyond the boundaries in which race-thinking and class-thinking have developed into obligatory patterns of thought, free public opinion has adopted them to such an extent that not only intellectuals but great masses of people will no longer accept any presentation of past or present facts that is not in agreement with these views.

It is not surprising, then, that Capra's films came to be viewed by critics, especially after the 1960s, through the lens of those economic or social theories.

—————

Capra was often thought to be a populist. But Capra did not assume that a virtuous opinion existed in the people, or that the people simply needed mobilizing. He was aware that the modern public is created by modern mass media whose techniques spawn mass society, posing a danger to individual freedom. Capra wrote that his films "embodied the rebellious cry of the individual against being trampled into an ort by massiveness—mass production, mass thought, mass education, mass politics, mass wealth, mass conformity." He did not believe in the use of mass power to improve society or to right historical wrongs. Reform, he thought, must take place through moral regeneration—thus through moral education.

Consider Capra's 1939 film, *Mr. Smith Goes to Washington*, in which an idealistic man goes to Congress, runs into rampant corruption, becomes despondent, is later inspired at the Lincoln Memorial, decides against hope to stand on principle, and prevails. Capra had doubts about making *Mr. Smith*. While in Washington preparing for the film, he attended a press conference in which President Roosevelt outlined the great problems facing the nation. Capra wondered whether it was a good time to make a dramatic comedy about Washington politics. In his troubled state he visited the Lincoln Memorial, where he saw a boy reading Lincoln's words to an elderly man. He decided, he later wrote, that he "must make the film, if only to hear a boy read Lincoln to his grandpa." He left the Lincoln Memorial that day, he recalled, with this growing conviction about our film: The more uncertain are the people of the world... the more they need a ringing statement of America's democratic ideals. The soul of our film would be anchored in Lincoln. Our Jefferson Smith [the film's lead character, played by Jimmy Stewart] would be a young Abe Lincoln, tailored to the rail-splitter's simplicity, compassion, ideals, humor.... It is *never* untimely to yank the rope of freedom's bell.

When watching *Mr. Smith*, it is important to notice where Capra locates the corruption. FDR customarily attacked "economic royalists," or the private corruption of corporations and monopolies. For FDR, the solution to corruption was to be found through the government and through the unions, which would combat the economic forces of the private sphere. But in *Mr. Smith*, Capra located the corruption not in the private but in the political sphere—it was the politicians who had usurped the institutions of government on behalf of their own interests and the special interests. When Smith goes to Washington he reveres a Senator from his state who had been a friend of his father. Smith's father, a newspaperman, had been killed while defending an independent prospector against a mining syndicate that was likely in cahoots with the union. Capra, like Smith and his father, understood America in terms of a *common* good—a good established by the principles of equality and liberty as the foundation of *individual* rights.

The setting of *Mr. Smith* is deliberately timeless. There is no mention of the Depression or of impending war. There is no indication of partisanship. What Capra hopes to bring to life are the words that have been carved in stone on Washington, D.C.'s monuments, but which are now forgotten. That is Jefferson Smith's purpose as well. In a central scene in the movie, gazing at the lighted dome of the Capitol, Smith says:

Boys forget what their country means by just reading "the land of the free" in history books. Then they get to be men, they forget even more. Liberty is too precious a thing to be buried in books.... Men should hold it up in front of them every single day... and say, "I'm free to think and to speak. My ancestors couldn't. I can. And my children will."

What Smith is advocating in the film is the establishment of a boys camp that will teach them about the principles of their country. Moreover, it is not to be paid for by the taxpayers, but with a loan from the government to be paid for by the boys themselves. At the climax of Smith's battle in the Senate, he says this:

> Get up there with that lady that's up on top of this Capitol dome— that lady that stands for liberty. Take a look at this country through her eyes.... You won't just see scenery. You'll see...what man's carved out for himself after centuries of fighting...for something better than just jungle law—fighting so he can stand on his own two feet, free and decent—like he was created, no matter what his race, color, or creed. That's what you'd see. There's no place out there for graft or greed or lies—or compromise with human liberties. And if that's what the grown-ups have done with this world that was given to them, then we better get those boys camps started fast and see what the kids can do. It's not too late.... *Great principles don't get lost once they come to light. They're right here. You just have to see them again.*

For Capra, like Lincoln, the problem is how to make people see the principles again.

The politicians in Washington in 1939 did not like their portrayal in *Mr. Smith*. Many tried to keep the movie from being shown. Capra thought it to be a ringing defense of democracy—and the people agreed. It was a tremendous success, not only in America, but throughout the world. In 1942, a month before the Nazi occupation of France was to begin, the Vichy government asked the French people what films they wanted to see before American and British films were banned by the Germans. The great majority wanted to see *Mr. Smith*. One theater in Paris played the movie for 30 straight nights.

———

By the time America entered World War II, Capra had become America's most popular director and was president of the Screen Directors Guild. Yet four days after Pearl Harbor he left Hollywood to join the Armed Forces. He was sent to Washington and was given an office next to the Army Chief of Staff, General George Marshall. Marshall was worried that millions of men would be conscripted, many right off of the farm, having little idea of the reason for the war. He assigned Capra to make "a series of documented, factual-information films—the first in our history—that will explain to our boys in the Army *why* we are fighting, and the *principles* for which we are fighting." Capra was nearly cowed by the assignment. He had never made a documentary. But after giving it some thought, he brilliantly dramatized the difference between the countries at war by using their own films and documentaries, in this way illustrating the character and danger of tyranny.

After the war, with the danger gone, it became increasingly clear that American intellectuals, who had rejected the political principles of the American Founding, had not understood the phenomenon of tyranny. For them, it was simply historical conditions that had established the distinction between right and wrong—or between friend and enemy—during the war. For them, in fighting the Nazis, America had simply been fighting a social movement. Subsequently, they looked on those who still revered America's Founding principles as representing a reactionary economic and social movement to be opposed here at home. For the same reason, Capra's wartime documentaries— known collectively as *Why We Fight*—came to be seen merely as propaganda.

Capra never thought of his documentaries as propaganda. He saw them as recognizing the permanent human problems—those problems that reveal the distinction between right and wrong, good and evil, justice and injustice. The fundamental distinction in politics is between freedom and slavery or democracy and tyranny. Winston Churchill said of Capra's wartime documentaries, "I have never seen or read any more powerful statement of our cause or of our rightful case against the Nazi tyranny." In his view, they were not propaganda at all. Churchill insisted that they be shown to every British soldier and in every theater in England. At the end of the war in 1945, General Marshall awarded Capra the Distinguished Service Medal. And on Churchill's recommendation, Capra was awarded the Order of the British Empire Medal in 1962.

———

Capra's last great movie, *It's a Wonderful Life,* was made in 1946. Shortly before making it, he said, "There are just two things that are important.

One is to strengthen the individual's belief in himself, and the other, even more important right now, is to combat a modern trend toward atheism." This movie, he wrote, summed up his philosophy of filmmaking: "First, to exalt the worth of the individual; to champion man—plead his causes, protest any degradation of his dignity, spirit or divinity." Capra understood that Hollywood would be changing, because the culture and society had begun to change. The historical and personal categories of class and race had become political, and self-expression and self-indulgence had replaced those civic virtues that require self-restraint. In his 1971 autobiography—imagine what he would think today—he wrote that "practically all the Hollywood filmmaking of today is stooping to cheap salacious pornography in a crazy bastardization of a great art to compete for the 'patronage' of deviates."

In 1982, when he was in his 85th year, Capra was awarded the American Film Institute's Life Achievement Award. In his acceptance speech, he touched on the things that had been most important in his life. He spoke of celebrating his sixth birthday in steerage on a 13-day voyage across the Atlantic. He recalled the lack of privacy and ventilation, and the terrible smell. But he also remembered the ship's arrival in New York Harbor, when his father brought him on deck and showed him the Statue of Liberty: "Cicco look!" his illiterate peasant father had said. "Look at that! That's the greatest light since the star of Bethlehem! That's the light of freedom! Remember that. Freedom." Capra remembered. In his speech to the Hollywood elite so many years later, he revealed his formula for moviemaking. He said: "The art of Frank Capra is very, very simple. It's the love of people. Add two simple ideals to this love of people—the freedom of each individual and the equal importance of each individual—and you have the principle upon which I based all my films."

It is hard to think of a better way to describe Frank Capra's view of the world, and America's place in fulfilling its purpose, than to turn to another great American who made his living in the world of motion pictures. Ronald Reagan was a friend and admirer of Frank Capra. They were very much alike. The inscription that Reagan had carved on his tombstone could have been written by Capra: "I know in my heart that man is good. That what is right will always eventually triumph. And there is purpose and worth to each and every life." Both Capra and Reagan looked to a benevolent and enduring Providence, and the best in man's nature, as the ultimate grounds of political right. For them, as for Lincoln, America was more than a geographical location or a place where citizens shared a common blood or religion, or belonged to a common culture or tradition. America was a place where an enlightened understanding of "the Laws of Nature and of Nature's God" had made it possible to establish those principles of civil and religious liberty that gave "purpose and worth to each and every life."

Capra was aware that the moral foundations established by those principles, as well as belief in God, had become endangered by the transformations in American life following World War II. He saw the necessity of reviving the moral education necessary to preserve the conditions of freedom, because he understood that in a democracy, the people must not only participate in the rule of others, they must also learn to govern themselves.

In his last and most personal tribute to his adopted country, Capra recalled his family's arrival at Union Station in Los Angeles after their long journey across America in 1903. When they got off the train, his mother and father got on their knees and kissed the ground. Capra's last words to his assembled audience were these: "For America, for just allowing me to live here, I kiss the ground." Capra did not believe that he had a right to be a citizen of America. Rather he was grateful for the privilege of living in America. He understood that freedom not only offers economic opportunity, but establishes a duty for all citizens—a duty to preserve the conditions of freedom not only for themselves, but for their posterity. Only those willing to bear the burdens of freedom have a right to its rewards.

For Capra, the real America was to be understood in terms of its virtues, which are derived from its principles. In his view, his art was dedicated to keeping those virtues alive—by making those principles live again in the speeches and deeds of that most uncommon phenomenon of human history, the American common man. It was the simple, unsophisticated, small-town common American that Capra celebrated in his films. But for Capra, as for his friend John Ford, no one epitomized this phenomenon better than Abraham Lincoln.

For American elites today, and for too many of the American people as well, the past has come to seem no longer meaningful to the present, and the celebration of the heroes of the past, like Lincoln, has come to seem naïve. Looking ahead, I'm afraid, the moral regeneration of America that Capra had hoped to bring about will require more than a Capra. It will require a Lincoln.

The Negative Impact of the #MeToo Movement

Heather Mac Donald

April 2018

O ur nation is about to be transformed, thanks to the #MeToo movement. I am not speaking about a cessation of sexual predation in the workplace. If that were the only consequence of #MeToo, the movement would clearly be a force for good. Unfortunately, its effects are going to be more sweeping and destructive. #MeToo is going to unleash a new torrent of gender and race quotas throughout the economy and culture, on the theory that all disparities in employment and institutional representation are due to harassment and bias. The resulting distortions of decision-making will be largely invisible; we will usually not know of the superior candidates for a job who were passed over in the drive for gender parity. But the net consequence will be a loss of American competitiveness and scientific achievement.

Pressures for so-called diversity, defined reductively by gonads and melanin, are of course nothing new. Since the 1990s, every mainstream institution has lived in terror of three lethal words: "all white male," an epithet capable of producing paroxysms of self-abasement. Silicon Valley start-ups and science labs quake before the charge of being all or mostly male; their varied ethnic demographics earn them no protection from the diversity racket.

The New York Times recently criticized the board of fashion giant H&M for being "entirely white." We can therefore infer that there are females on the H&M board, or else the *Times* would have let loose with the bigger gun: "all white male." When both categories of alleged privilege—white and male—overlap, an activist is in the diversity sweet spot, his power over an institution at its zenith.

But however pervasive the diversity imperative was before, the #MeToo movement is going to make the previous three decades look like a golden age of meritocracy. No mainstream institution will hire, promote, or compensate without an exquisite calculation of gender and race ratios. Males in general, and white males in particular, will have to clear a very high bar in order to justify further deferring that halcyon moment of gender equity.

Hollywood and the media are already showing the #MeToo effect. At this year's Oscar awards lunch, the president of the Academy of Motion Picture Arts and Sciences, John Bailey, prefaced his remarks by noting that he was a "75-year-old white man." Bailey was trying to get out ahead of the curve, since if he hadn't pointed out this shameful status, feminist crusaders in the press and the industry would have done so for him. Witness actress Natalie Portman's sneer in presenting the best director prize at the 2018 Golden Globe awards: "And here are the all-male nominees." Such shallow bean counting is now going to become the automatic response to any perceived lack of "diversity" in entertainment.

Naturally, Bailey announced reparations for the Academy's predominantly white male profile: henceforth it would "balance gender, race, ethnicity, and religion" in all its activities and would double its female and minority members by 2020. Needless to say, this was not enough. Outside the lunch, the National Hispanic Media Coalition protested the lack of proportional ethnic representation in Oscar nominations and acting roles.

CBS is considering only females to fill the anchor slot at *Face the Nation*, to catch up with *The Today Show*, which now has two female anchors. The Recording Academy, which oversees the Grammys, has promised to overcome the "unconscious biases that impede female advancement" in the music industry, after bean-counting complaints from *The Wall Street Journal's* pop music critic and female music executives.

The prospect of left-wing entertainment moguls having to sacrifice their box office judgment to identity politics is an unalloyed pleasure, and of little consequence to society at large. But quota-izing will hardly be limited to Hollywood.

Major publishing houses are analyzing their author lists by gender and race and making publishing decisions accordingly. What books get reviewed and who reviews them will increasingly be determined according to gender and race. There are likely no major newspapers that are not tallying reporter and op-ed bylines, as well as the topics they cover, by gender and race. In 2005, professional feminist Susan Estrich preposterously accused Michael Kinsley, then running the *Los Angeles Times* editorial pages, of excluding female writers. Naturally, Estrich ignored the fact that males are disproportionately interested in public affairs, as demonstrated by lopsided sex ratios among op-ed submissions and letters to the editor. Eighty-seven percent of contributors to Wikipedia are male. There are no allegedly sexist gatekeepers at Wikipedia screening out females; contributions are anonymous and open to all. But males are more oriented towards highly fact-based realms.

Now, however, sterile bean-counting exercises such as Estrich's have gone in-house. In response to the #MeToo movement, *The New York Times* created a "gender editor" who presides over a "gender initiative" to infuse questions of gender throughout all the *Times'* coverage. A recent front-page product of this #MeToo initiative covered the earth-shattering problem facing NFL cheerleaders: to wit, they have a dress code and are forbidden from fraternizing with the players. Despite these allegedly patriarchal conditions, females are still lining up to be hired, to the puzzlement of the *Times*.

Publisher Meredith Corp. has come in for the usual criticism after buying the floundering Time, Inc. late last year. "They're basically all middle-aged white males from the Midwest," grumbled a *Time* staffer, who, you would think, would be in no position to complain. Dow Jones, the publisher of *The Wall Street Journal*, is offering leadership training exclusively to females to try to meet its short-term goal of 40 percent female executives.

Corporate boardrooms, executive suites, and management structures are going to be scoured for gender and race imbalances. Diversity trainers are already sensing a windfall from #MeToo. Gender, diversity, and inclusion were the dominant themes at this January's World Economic Forum in Davos,

Switzerland. The conference was chaired exclusively by women. Windows were emblazoned with slogans like "Diversity is good for business" and "Gender equality is a social and economic issue." CEOs shared their techniques for achieving gender equity. It's actually quite simple: pay managers based on their record of hiring and promoting females and minorities, as Hilton CEO Christopher Nassetta explained. Never mind the fact that by introducing irrelevant criteria such as race and gender into an evaluation process, you will inevitably end up with less qualified employees.

U.S. banks and financial institutions are facing pressure from shareholder groups to release data on the number and compensation of females and minorities in their upper ranks. Immediate punishment befalls anyone in business who has the courage to criticize this war on merit. The chief creative officer of the advertising firm M&C Saatchi wrote last year that he was "bored of diversity being prioritized over talent." Saatchi atoned for this heresy with a frenzy of female hirings and promotions.

Amazingly, John Williams—a white man—squeaked into the presidency of the Federal Reserve Bank of New York this April, to the outrage of the diversocrats. Don't be surprised if he is the last to do so. "The New York Fed has never been led by a woman or a person of color, and that needs to change," announced New York Senator Kirsten Gillibrand. Williams' "progress," as *The New York Times* called it, in "diversifying" senior leadership when he was president of the San Francisco Fed undoubtedly made his unfortunate race and sex more palatable to the search committee.

#MeToo enforcers are even going after classical music. *New Yorker* music critic Alex Ross triggered outrage against the Chicago Symphony Orchestra and the Philadelphia Orchestra in February when he tweeted that they had programmed no female composers in their 2018-2019 seasons. Never mind that the CSO was even then performing Jennifer Higdon's Low Brass Concerto—a piece commissioned by the Chicago, Philadelphia, and Baltimore orchestras—at Carnegie Hall. It is ludicrous to suggest that these institutions are discriminating against female composers, but Ross and his followers demand affirmative programming quotas.

The public radio show, *Performance Today*, ran a series of shows in March about gender and racial inequities in classical music. At a time of diminishing classical music audiences, it is profoundly irresponsible to direct the poison of identity politics at our most precious musical institutions. Doing so only encourages potential young listeners and culturally ignorant philanthropists (I'm thinking of you, Bill Gates) to stay away. Facts are facts, and throughout most of music history, the greatest composers have been male. No amount of digging through score archives, however useful that enterprise may be for discovering unfamiliar works, is going to unearth a female counterpart to Bach, Mozart, Beethoven, Schubert, Chopin, or Brahms. So what? We should simply be grateful—profoundly grateful—for the music these men created.

Orchestra boards will pay penance for their own inadequate diversity by a mad rush on female conductors, whose numbers are minuscule. It was already difficult two years ago to land a U.S. conducting position for a universally esteemed white male conductor, reports his agent. Now it would be nearly impossible, the agent believes, adding: "If I had a trans conductor, I would be rich."

Academia, the source of identity politics, will double down on its diversity quota-izing in the wake of #MeToo. A panel at the annual American Economic Association meeting in January charged that gender discrimination was pervasive in economics—an argument that fit into the "larger national examination of bias and abuse toward women in the work force," *The New York Times* reminded readers. In March, the *Chronicle of Higher Education* and Priya Satia, former diversity chair of Stanford University's Department of History, went into diversity meltdown over a history conference that Hoover Institution Fellow Niall Ferguson had organized. Though Ferguson had invited females to speak, none had accepted. Not good enough, according to Professor Satia. Ferguson should have suspended the conference entirely unless he could persuade females and minorities to participate. Although Satia did not identify any scholarly gaps that resulted from the actual lineup, Stanford University was so shaken by the controversy that it issued a statement on behalf of the president and provost assuring the public that it had made its concerns about the lack of diversity known to the conference organizers.

STEM departments—departments of science, technology, engineering, and math—have been under enormous pressure from the federal government to hire by gender and race. Now they are creating their own internal diversity enforcers, notwithstanding the massive diversity bureaucracies already in place. UCLA's Engineering Department now has its own diversity dean. Audrey Pool O'Neal, the director of UCLA's Women in Engineering program justified this sinecure with the usual role model argument for gender- and race-conscious decision-making. "Female students let me know how much they appreciate seeing a woman of color in front of their classroom," she told the UCLA student newspaper.

Why not appreciate seeing the most qualified scholar in front of your classroom? Any female student who thinks she needs a female professor in order to envision a scientific career has declared herself a follower rather than a pioneer—and a follower based on a characteristic that is irrelevant to intellectual achievement. Marie Curie did not need female role models to investigate radioactivity. She was motivated by a passion to understand the world. That should be reason enough for anyone to plunge headlong into the search for knowledge.

Silicon Valley is a #MeToo diversity bonanza waiting to happen. It's not for nothing that the Mountain View headquarters of Google is referred to as the "Google campus"; the culture of the Silicon Valley behemoth is an echo chamber of shrill academic victimology. Managers and employees reflexively label dissenters from left-wing orthodoxy as misogynists and racists. It is assumed that the lack of proportional representation of female, black, and Hispanic engineers at the company is due to bias on the part of every other type of engineer.

In August 2017, Google fired computer engineer James Damore for writing a memo suggesting that the lack of 50-50 gender proportionality at Google and other tech firms may not be due to bias, but rather to different career predilections on the part of males and females. He cited psychological research establishing that on average, males and females are attracted to different types of work: males to more abstract, idea-centered work, females to more human-centered, relational activities. Damore was not disparaging the scientific skills of the female engineers working at Google; he was trying to explain why there were not more of them. Nevertheless, Google accused Damore of using harmful gender stereotypes that put Google's female employees at risk of some unspecified trauma.

Google's adoption of the bathetic rhetoric of academic victimology to justify firing Damore was bad enough. But in January 2018, the National Labor Relations Board released a memo upholding Google's action on the same grounds: Damore had engaged in discrimination and sexual harassment by employing "harmful gender stereotypes." The reasoning behind the NLRB memo puts at risk the job of every academic scientist researching the biological and psychological differences between the sexes. The ideological imperatives of feminism are trumping the search for scientific truth. This is a dangerous position for a society to embrace.

The following month, a Google recruiter challenged Silicon Valley's quota mentality by refusing to obey an edict to purge white males from consideration for entry-level engineering interviews. The recruiter alleges in a lawsuit that he was promptly fired. Google, it seems, would rather not even know about potentially groundbreaking tech talent if it comes in the wrong color and shape.

Such distortions of meritocracy will become even more intense following #MeToo. The mad rush of investor funding into the biotech fraudster firm Theranos was undoubtedly due in large part to the sex of its founder. Elizabeth Holmes claimed to have invented an advanced blood-testing device. Even as her claims about the largely fictitious device unraveled, investors continued to give her unqualified support. Her blue chip board boasted two former secretaries of state and James Mattis, then head of the U.S. Central Command and now Secretary of Defense. Hilariously, the #MeToo-obsessed *New York Times* opined that it was "surprising" how long Holmes was allowed to operate "before regulators stepped in." Actually, what is surprising is that they stepped in at all, given the dominant narrative that the dearth of female start-ups is due to sexism on the part of venture capitalists and regulators.

Despite the billions of dollars that governments, companies, and foundations have poured into increasing the number of females in STEM, the gender proportions of the hard sciences have not changed much over the years. This is not surprising, given mounting evidence of the differences in interests and aptitudes between the sexes. Study after study has shown that females gravitate towards different types of jobs than men, as James Damore fatally observed. Females on average tend to choose fields that are perceived to make the world a better place, according to the common understanding of that phrase. A preschool teacher in the Bronx, profiled by *Bloomberg News*, exemplifies such a choice. She has a B.A. in neuroscience, but opted not to go to medical school so as to have an impact on poor and minority children. Her salary is a pittance compared to what she could earn as a clinical or research neurologist, but she said that pay is not her top motivation when it comes to choosing a job.

Even under the broad STEM umbrella, females seek jobs that are seen as directly helping others by a two-to-one ratio over males. Females make up 75 percent of workers in health-related jobs, but only 25 percent of workers in computer jobs and 14 percent of engineering workers, according to a Pew Research Center poll. In 2016, nearly 82 percent of obstetrics and gynecology residents were female—yet no one is complaining about gender bias against males. And in a resounding blow to the feminist narrative about bias in STEM, it turns out that the more gender equality in a country, the lower the percentage of females in STEM majors and fields. The more careers open to females, the less likely they are to choose math or science.

Finally, there is the most taboo subject of all: the non-identical distribution of high-end math skills. Males outnumber females on both the bottom rung of math cluelessness and the top rung of math insight. In the U.S., there are 2.5 males in the top .01 percent of math ability for every female in that category. This is not a matter of gender bias and cultural conditioning; gender differences in math precocity show up as early as kindergarten.

Given these different distributions of interests and skills, the only way to engineer gender proportionality in the hard sciences is to put a ceiling on male hires, no matter how gifted, until enough females can be induced to enter the field to balance out the males. And indeed, the National Science Foundation, which has announced that progress in science requires a "diverse STEM workforce," seems to be moving in that direction. This is undoubtedly good news for China, as it furiously pushes ahead with its unapologetically meritocratic system of science training and research. Not such good news for the rest of us, however.

The #MeToo movement has uncovered real abuses of power. But the solution to those abuses is not to replace valid measures of achievement with irrelevancies like gender and race. Ironically, the best solution to sexual predation is not more feminism, but less. By denying the differences between men and women, and by ridiculing the manly virtues of gentlemanliness and chivalry and the female virtues of modesty and prudence, feminism dissolved the civilizational restraints on the male libido. The boorish behavior that pervades society today would have been unthinkable in the past, when a traditional understanding of sexual propriety prevailed. Now, however, with the idea of "ladies and gentlemen" discredited and out of favor, boorishness is increasingly the rule.

Contrary to the feminist narrative, Western culture is in fact the least patriarchal culture in human history; rather than being forced to veil, females in our society can parade themselves in as scantily clad a manner as they choose; pop culture stars flaunt their promiscuity. As we have seen, every mainstream institution is trying to hire and promote as many females as possible.

As the #MeToo movement swells the demand for ever more draconian diversity mandates, a finding in a Pew Research Center poll on workplace equity is worth noting: the perception of bias is directly proportional to the number of years the perceiver has spent in an American university. The persistent claim of gender bias, in other words, is ideological, not empirical. But after #MeToo, it will have an even more disruptive effect.

Shall We Defend Our Common History?

Roger Kimball

February 2019

The recent news that the University of Notre Dame, responding to complaints by some students, would "shroud" its twelve 134-year-old murals depicting Christopher Columbus was disappointing. It was not surprising, however, to anyone who has been paying attention to the widespread attack on America's past wherever social justice warriors congregate.

Notre Dame, a Congregation of the Holy Cross institution, may not be particularly friendly to its Catholic heritage. But its president, the Rev. John Jenkins, demonstrated how jesuitical (if not, quite, Jesuit) he could be. Queried about the censorship, he said, apparently without irony, that his decision to cover the murals was not intended to conceal anything, but rather to tell "the full story" of Columbus's activities.

Welcome to the new Orwellian world where censorship is free speech and we respect the past by attempting to elide it.

Over the past several years, we have seen a rising tide of assaults on statues and other works of art representing our nation's history by those who are eager to squeeze that complex story into a box defined by the evolving rules of political correctness. We might call this the "monument controversy," and what happened at Notre Dame is a case in point: a vocal minority, claiming victim status, demands the destruction, removal, or concealment of some object of which they disapprove. Usually, the official response is instant capitulation.

As the French writer Charles Péguy once observed, "It will never be known what acts of cowardice have been motivated by the fear of not looking sufficiently progressive." Consider the frequent demands to remove statues of Confederate war heroes from public spaces because their presence is said to be racist. New York Governor Andrew Cuomo, for example, has recently had statues of Robert E. Lee and Stonewall Jackson removed from a public gallery. In New York City, Mayor Bill de Blasio has set up a committee to review "all symbols of hate on city property."

But it is worth noting that the monument controversy signifies something much larger than the attacks on the Old South or Italian explorers.

In the first place, the monument controversy involves not just art works or commemorative objects. Rather, it encompasses the resources of the past writ large. It is an attack on the past for failing to live up to our contemporary notions of virtue.

In the background is the conviction that we, blessed members of the most enlightened cohort ever to grace the earth with its presence, occupy a moral plane superior to all who came before us. Consequently, the defacement of murals of Christopher Columbus—and statues of later historical figures like Teddy Roosevelt—is perfectly virtuous and above criticism since human beings in the past were by definition so much less enlightened than we.

The English department at the University of Pennsylvania contributed to the monument controversy when it cheered on students who were upset that a portrait of a dead white male named William Shakespeare was hanging in the department's hallway. The department removed the picture and replaced it with a photograph of Audre Lorde, a black feminist writer. "Students removed the Shakespeare portrait," crowed department chairman Jed Esty, "and delivered it to my office as a way of affirming their commitment to a more inclusive mission for the English department." Right.

High schools across the country contribute to the monument controversy when they remove masterpieces like *Huckleberry Finn* from their libraries because they contain ideas or even just words of which they disapprove.

The psychopathology behind these occurrences is a subject unto itself. What has happened in our culture and educational institutions that so many students jump from their feelings of being offended—and how delicate they are, how quick to take offense!—to self-righteous demands to repudiate the thing that offends them? The more expensive education becomes the more it seems to lead, not to broader understanding, but to narrower horizons.

———

Although there is something thuggish and intolerant about the monument controversy, it is not quite the same as the thuggishness of the Roman emperor Caracalla, who murdered his brother and co-emperor Geta and had statues of Geta toppled and his image chiseled off coins. Nor is it quite the same as what happened when Soviet dictator Joseph Stalin exiled Leon Trotsky, had him airbrushed out of the *Great Soviet Encyclopedia*, and sent assassins to Mexico to finish the job.

Iconoclasm takes different forms. The disgusting attacks on the past and other religious cultures carried out by the Taliban, for example, are quite different from the toppling of statues of Saddam Hussein by liberated Iraqis after the Iraq War. Different again was the action of America's own Sons of Liberty in 1776, who toppled a statue of the hated George III and melted down its lead to make 40,000 musket balls. It is easy to sympathize with that pragmatic response to what the Declaration of Independence called "a long train of abuses and usurpations." It is worth noting, however, that George Washington censured even this action for "having much the appearance of a riot and a want of discipline."

While the monument controversy does depend upon a reservoir of iconoclastic feeling, it represents not the blunt expression of power or destructiveness but rather the rancorous, self-despising triumph of political correctness. The exhibition of wounded virtue, of what we now call "virtue-signaling," is key.

Consider some recent events at Yale University, an institution where preening self-infatuation is always on parade. Yale recently formed a Committee to Establish Principles on Renaming and a Committee on Art in Public Spaces. Members of the former prowl the campus looking for buildings, colleges, faculty chairs, lecture programs, and awards that have politically incorrect names. The latter police works of art and other images on campus, making sure that anything offensive to favored groups is covered or removed.

At the residential college formerly known as Calhoun College, for example—it's now called Grace Hopper College—the Committee ordered the removal of stained glass windows depicting slaves and other historical scenes of Southern life. Statues and other representations of John C. Calhoun have likewise been slotted for removal. Calhoun, an 1804 Yale graduate, was a leading statesman and political thinker of his day. But he was also an apologist for slavery, so he has to be erased from the record.

Of course, impermissible attitudes and images are never in short supply once the itch to stamp out history gets going. Two years ago it was Calhoun and representations of the Antebellum South. More recently it was a carving at an entrance to Yale's Sterling Memorial Library depicting an Indian and a Puritan. The Puritan, if you can believe it, was holding a musket—a gun! Who knows, perhaps he was a member of the NRA or at least could give inspiration to other members of that very un-Yale-like organization. According to Susan Gibbons, one of Yale's librarian-censors, the presence of an armed Puritan "at a major entrance to Sterling was not appropriate." Solution? Cover over the musket with a cowpat of stone—but leave the Indian's bow and arrow alone!

Actually, it turns out that the removable cowpat of stone was only a stopgap. The outcry against the decision struck a chord with Peter Salovey, Yale's president. "Such alteration," he noted, "represents an erasure of history, which is entirely inappropriate at a university." He's right about that. But if anyone has mastered the art of saying one thing while doing the opposite it is President Salovey. He spoke against "the erasure of history." But then, instead of merely altering the image, he announced that Yale would go full Taliban, removing the offending stonework altogether.

In the bad old days, librarians and college presidents were people who sought to protect the past, that vast storehouse of offensive attitudes and behavior that also just so happens to define our common inheritance. In our own more enlightened times, many librarians and college presidents collude in its effacement.

Someone might ask, "Who cares what violence a super-rich bastion of privilege and unaccountability like Yale perpetrates on its patrimony?" Well, we should all care. Institutions like Yale, Harvard, and Stanford are among the chief drivers of the "progressive" hostility to free expression and other politically correct attitudes that have insinuated themselves like a fever-causing virus into the bloodstream of public life. Instead of helping to preserve our common inheritance, they work to subvert it.

Spiriting away stonework in the Ivy League may seem mostly comical. But there is a straight line from those acts of morally righteous intolerance to far less comical examples of puritanical censure.

Consider the case of James Damore, the now former Google engineer who wrote an internal memo describing the company's cult-like "echo chamber" of political correctness and ham-handed efforts to nurture "diversity" in hiring and promotion. When the memo was publicized, it first precipitated controversy—then it provided Google CEO Sundar Pichai a high horse upon which to perch, declare Damore's memo "offensive and not OK," and then fire him. For what? For expressing his opinion in a company discussion forum designed to encourage free expression!

In one way, there was nothing new about Google's actions. Large companies have always tended to be bastions of conformity. Decades ago, everyone at IBM had to wear a white shirt and was strongly encouraged to espouse conservative social values. Today, everyone in Silicon Valley has to subscribe to the 95 theses of the social justice warrior's creed, beginning with certain dogmas about race, fossil fuels, sexuality, and the essential lovableness of jihadist Muslims. If you are at Google and dissent from this orthodoxy, you will soon find yourself not at Google.

The violence in Charlottesville, Virginia, in 2017 was a godsend to the self-appointed hate police. In its immediate aftermath, companies around the country took pains to declare their rejection of "hate," and ProPublica, the Southern Poverty Law Center, and other leftish thugs expanded their witch hunts beyond such targets as the "Daily Stormer"—a vile anti-Semitic website. After Charlottesville, for example, "Jihad Watch"—hardly a hate group website—was dropped by PayPal until a public outcry induced PayPal to reverse its decision. There have been other such casualties, and there will be many more.

Let's step back and ask ourselves what motivates the left-wing virtuecrats attempting to enforce their new regime of political correctness. Christian theologians tell us that the *visio beatifica*—the beatific vision of God—is the highest pleasure known to man. Alas, that communion is granted to very few in this life. For the common run of mankind, I suspect, the highest earthly pleasure is self-righteous moral infatuation.

Like a heartbeat, moral infatuation has a systolic and diastolic phase. In the systolic phase, there is an abrupt contraction of sputtering indignation: fury, outrage, high horses everywhere. Then there is the gratifying period of recovery: the warm bath of self-satisfaction, set like a jelly in a communal ecstasy of unanchored virtue signaling.

The communal element is key. While individuals may experience and enjoy moral infatuation, the overall effect is greatly magnified when shared. Consider the mass ecstasy that at first accompanied Maximilien Robespierre's effort to establish a Republic of Virtue during the French Revolution's Reign of Terror in 1793.

The response to Donald Trump's comments about the murderous violence that erupted in Charlottesville provides another vivid example. Trump's chief crime was to have suggested that there was "blame on both sides" as well as "good people" on both sides of the protest. I am not sure there was an abundance of "good people" on either side of the divide that day, although Trump's main point was to distinguish between lawful protest and hate-fueled violence. But forget about distinctions. The paroxysms of rage that greeted Trump were a marvel to behold, as infectious as they were unbounded. One prominent commentator spoke for the multitude when he described Trump's response as a "moral disgrace."

I didn't think so, but then I thought that the President was correct when he suggested that the alt-Left is just as much a problem as the alt-Right. Indeed, if we needed to compare the degree of iniquity of the neo-Nazis and Ku Klux Klanners, on the one hand, and Antifa and its fellow travelers on the other, I am not at all sure which would come out the worse. Real Nazis—the kind that popped up like mushrooms in Germany in the 1920s and 1930s—are scary. But American neo-Nazis? They are a tiny bunch of pathetic losers. The Ku Klux Klan was a terrorist group with millions of members in its earlier incarnations. Now it too is a tiny bunch—5,000 or 6,000 by most estimates—of impotent malcontents.

Antifa, on the other hand, has brought its racialist brand of violent protest to campuses and demonstrations around the country: smashing heads as well as property. I suspect that paid-up, full-time members of the group are few, but the ideology of identity politics that they feed upon is a gruesome specialty of the higher education establishment today.

I also thought that the President was right to ask where the erasure of history would end. At Charlottesville it was a statue of Robert E. Lee. But why stop there? Why not erase the entire history of the Confederacy? There are apparently some 1,500 monuments and memorials to the Confederacy in public spaces across the United States. According to one study, most of them were commissioned by Southern women, "in the hope of preserving a positive vision of antebellum life." A noble aspiration, inasmuch as the country had recently fought a civil war that devastated the South and left more than 700,000 Americans dead. These memorials were part of an effort to knit the broken country back together. Obliterating them would also be an attack on the effort of reconciliation.

And what about Thomas Jefferson and George Washington? They both owned slaves, as did 41 of the 56 signers of the Declaration of Independence. What about them? To listen to many race peddlers these days, you would think they regarded George Orwell's warning in *1984* as a how-to manual: "Every record has been destroyed or falsified," Orwell wrote,

> every book has been rewritten, every picture has been repainted, every statue and street and building has been renamed, every date has been altered. And that process is continuing day by day and minute by minute. History has stopped.

Plato was right when he said that politicians are essentially rhetoricians. Rhetoric succeeds or fails not because of its logic or intellectual substance, but on the question of its emotional appeal. By that standard, I'd say that Donald Trump, though often rhetorically effective, missed an important rhetorical opportunity at Charlottesville. He didn't understand that the politically correct dispensation that rules academia, the media, the Democratic Party, and large swathes of the corporate world requires a certain ritual homage to be paid to its reigning pieties about "racism" in America.

Doubtless there are things to criticize about Donald Trump. But being racist isn't among them. What infuriates his critics—but at the same time affords them so many opportunities to bathe in the gratifying fluid of their putative moral superiority—is that Trump refuses to collude in the destructive, politically correct charade according to which "racism" is the nearly ubiquitous cardinal sin of white America. He is having none of that, and his refusal to go along with the attempted moral blackmail is driving his critics to a fever pitch. They scream "racism" but, unlike other politicians, Trump refuses to cower in the corner whimpering. That he goes against their script infuriates them.

Back in 1965, the Frankfurt School Marxist Herbert Marcuse wrote an essay called "Repressive Tolerance." It is a totalitarian classic. Marcuse distinguished between two kinds of tolerance. First, there is what he called "bad" or "false" tolerance. This is the sort of tolerance that most of us would call "true" tolerance, the sort of thing your parents taught you and that undergirds liberal democracy. Second, there is what Marcuse calls "liberating tolerance," which he defined as "intolerance against movements from the Right, and toleration of movements from the Left."

So here we are. The old idea of tolerance was summed up in such chestnuts as, "I disapprove of what you say, but I will defend to the death your right to say it." The new dispensation is: "I disapprove of what you say, therefore you may not say it."

The Marxist-tinged ideology of the 1960s has had a few decades to marinate the beneficiaries of our free-market society, steeping them in the toxic nostrums that masquerade as moral imperatives in our colleges and universities. Today we find the graduates of those institutions manipulating the fundamental levers of political and corporate power.

The monument controversy shows the susceptibility of "liberating tolerance" to fanaticism. And it reminds us that in the great battle between the partisans of freedom and the inebriates of virtue, freedom is ultimately negotiable—until it rouses itself to fight back. At stake is nothing less than the survival of our common history.

"Faith and reason are mutually reinforcing"

Clarence Thomas

November 2019

This is a very special occasion—the 175th anniversary of Hillsdale and the dedication of Christ Chapel. This beautiful Chapel is a culmination of years of generosity, planning, and hard work. And the end result is at once stunning and glorious.

The Chapel's enduring beauty highlights the transcendence, the sovereignty, and the grace of God. It truly illustrates how architectural design can reflect the character of God and evoke a sense of reverence for His majesty.

Everyone involved in the financing, planning, and construction of this Chapel should rightly be proud. It is a magnificent accomplishment. But we've gathered here today not just to admire this beautiful Chapel—we have gathered here to dedicate it.

The word *dedicate* in this context means "to set apart and consecrate to a deity or to a sacred purpose." To dedicate this Chapel appropriately, then, it is worthwhile to reflect on the purposes for which we are setting apart this sacred place on a college campus.

The primary purpose of a chapel is to provide a place where man can enter the presence of God. It provides a sanctuary in which man can withdraw from the chaos of our world and seek a sacred stillness. For as Elijah learned on Mount Horeb, God so often comes to us not in the storms, not in the earthquakes or fires of life, but in stillness—in a "gentle whisper."

Accordingly, men and women have long sought respite from the noise and commotion of daily life, where they can "be still, and know that [He is] God," where they can seek an inner calm and a transcendent peace. Beautiful chapels, such as this one, provide that sacred space for stillness, a place for an encounter with the Divine. As the architect of this Chapel has written, "When you enter a church, it is as if you are entering through a gateway from the profane toward the sacred."

It is difficult to overstate the significance of the role that this Chapel will play in the life of Hillsdale College.

———

Although a chapel is a place for many activities, it also serves as a statement about the importance of those activities. The construction of a *college* chapel, in particular, is a public declaration that faith and reason are mutually reinforcing. And in 2019, the construction of a chapel is a bold act of leadership at a crucial time in our nation's history. So I would like to underscore briefly the broader significance of the decision that Hillsdale College has made in building Christ Chapel.

Beginning in the early 1900s, many elite private colleges and universities began to face questions about the continuing relevance of religious instruction on campus. These questions would have surprised the founders of those schools, many of which were created in part for the express purpose of providing religious instruction. But as time went on and as schools moved away from their religious roots, the relevance of religion to higher education was increasingly questioned, and campus chapels, in particular, came to be viewed as relics of a bygone era.

With the completion of Christ Chapel, Hillsdale College has staked out its position in this debate, and its decision serves as an example for all of us. The construction of so grand a chapel in 2019 does not happen by accident or as an afterthought. Christ Chapel reflects the College's conviction that a vibrant intellectual environment and a strong democratic society are fostered, not hindered, by a recognition of the Divine. Hillsdale College affirms, with the writer of Proverbs, that, "The fear of the Lord is the beginning of wisdom, and the knowledge of the Holy One is insight."

By constructing this Chapel, the College upholds the continued importance of its Christian roots, even as it respects the rights of each person to worship God according to the dictates of his own conscience. Our country was founded on the view that a correct understanding of the nature of God and the human person is critical to preserving the liberty that we so enjoy.

John Adams wrote, "Our Constitution was made only for a moral and religious People. It is wholly inadequate to the government of any other." He recognized that the preservation of liberty is not guaranteed. Without the guardrails supplied by religious conviction, popular sovereignty can devolve into mob rule, unmoored from any conception of objective truth.

As I think about our political culture today, I am reminded of Ronald Reagan's warning that, "Freedom is never more than one generation away from extinction. We didn't pass it to our children in the bloodstream. The only way they can inherit the freedom we have known is if we fight for it, protect it, defend it, and then hand it on to them . . . [to] do the same."

Each generation is responsible both to itself and to succeeding generations for preserving and promoting the blessings of liberty. Faith in God, more than anything else, fuels the strength of character and self-discipline needed to discharge ably that responsibility. That is why I am so encouraged by the construction of Christ Chapel.

Hillsdale College's Articles of Association affirm that "inestimable blessings" flow from "the prevalence of civil and religious liberty and intelligent piety in the land." The College was founded on the belief that "the diffusion of sound learning is essential to the perpetuity of these blessings." Thus Hillsdale College was founded on the understanding that the battle to preserve and promote freedom in our country will be waged in the hearts and minds of the people.

Rather than shrinking from the battle, Hillsdale is rising to the occasion by investing in the intellectual and spiritual development of its students, so they can provide God-honoring leadership in our country. Let it be said of them what was said of David, that he "served the counsel of God in his own generation."

Students, faculty, administrators, and friends of Hillsdale, let this Chapel be more than just an impressive building. Let it be a place where people enter the presence of a majestic God. Let it be a house of worship, of prayer, of meditation, and of celebration before God. Let it be a haven of rest for the weary, a place of healing for the wounded, a place of comfort for the grieving, and a source of hope for the despairing and forgotten.

Let it point to a day when "the dwelling of God" will be "with men," when God himself will "wipe away every tear" and mend every wound. Let it be a place where tomorrow's leaders discern their callings and grow firm in their convictions. Let it stand as a bold declaration to a watching world that faith and learning are rightly understood as complements, and that both are essential to the preservation of the blessings of liberty.

Let this Chapel equip and inspire us to honor God in whatever He calls us to do. For as Saint Paul wrote in his Letter to the Romans, "From Him and through Him and to Him are all things. To Him be the glory forever. Amen."

May God bless each of you. May God bless Hillsdale. And may God bless this wonderful country.

American Sports Are Letting Down America

Jason Whitlock

July/August 2020

Nearly 30 years ago, in a 1993 Nike commercial, professional basketball legend Charles Barkley fired the first shot at the "role model" concept popularized by Columbia University sociologist Robert K. Merton in the aftermath of the 1960s counterculture movement. "I am not a role model," Barkley proclaimed in the half-minute spot. "I'm not paid to be a role model. I'm paid to wreak havoc on the basketball court. Parents should be role models. Just because I dunk a basketball doesn't mean I should raise your kids."

Barkley's words landed with a force every bit the equal of former NFL quarterback Colin Kaepernick's National Anthem knee 23 years later. Former Vice President Dan Quayle defended Barkley, while Barkley's fellow NBA superstar Karl Malone criticized him in *Sports Illustrated*. Leading news magazines, including *Time* and *Newsweek*, published articles exploring the controversy. Newspaper columnists from coast to coast—on and off the sports pages—also weighed in. The topic still sparks debate today.

Of the many phrases and concepts Merton coined—including "self-fulfilling prophecy" and "unintended consequences"—"role model" has had the most impact. On the surface, the argument that young people tend to model their behavior after high-profile, successful adults is harmless. However, in retrospect, the elevation of athletes and other celebrities as primary figures in the formation of behavioral norms for young people helped create the conditions that are powering the destructive Black Lives Matter movement today.

Merton's role model concept undercuts the importance of parents and nuclear families. That was the point of Barkley's criticism. Feminists and other progressive critics of America's "patriarchal" society—including the Black Lives Matter movement, whose Marxist-influenced statement of purpose opposes "the Western-prescribed nuclear family structure"—have used Merton's concept to great effect. Muhammad Ali, Pete Rose, Farrah Fawcett, Barbara Streisand, Mick Jagger, Marvin Gaye, and Burt Reynolds infringed on territory primarily reserved for mom, dad, aunts, uncles, grandparents, and teachers.

Technology has helped advance the process, diminishing the influence of traditional authority figures and strengthening the reach of celebrities. Kids shut their bedroom doors, turn on their televisions, laptops, and game consoles, plug in earbuds, open social media apps, and disappear into a world far removed from mom and dad. With a mere push of a button they tune out the worldview of their families and tune in the worldview of athlete LeBron James, actress Lena Dunham, rapper Snoop Dogg, social media race-baiter Shaun King, and others like them.

On top of all this, we now see America's enemies, particularly China, using these modern role models to promote racial division and destabilize our country—with those on the political Left as their accomplices. Today, they have coalesced around the Black Lives Matter movement to push America toward a level of racial dysfunction and animus not experienced since the Civil War.

It's fitting that Charles Barkley fired the first shot against this trend, because American sports have become the Gettysburg of what some have called our "cold civil war." And if China and the Left complete their radicalization of sports, our nation may never recover.

———

Sport has the power to change the world. It has the power to inspire. It has the power to unite people in a way that little else does. It speaks to youth in a language they understand. Sport can create hope, where once there was only despair. It is more powerful than governments in breaking down racial barriers. It laughs in the face of all types of discrimination.

Nelson Mandela, the South African freedom fighter-turned-statesman, spoke those words in an effort to heal the country he came to lead after spending a quarter century incarcerated for opposing apartheid. Mandela embraced sports' power to bridge racial divides, looking on athletic competition as a kind of antibiotic for racial animus and discrimination. South Africa's victory in the 1995 Rugby World Cup and Mandela's presentation of the Webb Ellis Cup to team captain Francois Pienaar stand as an iconic symbol of unity in post-apartheid South Africa. Clint Eastwood directed a movie, *Invictus*, starring Morgan Freeman and Matt Damon, that memorialized the importance of the moment. It bears re-watching today.

Since sprinter Jesse Owens won four gold medals at the 1936 Berlin Olympics and boxer Joe Louis scored a first-round knockout over German heavyweight Max Schmeling in 1938, sports have served as a powerful racial unifier in America as well. The victories earned by Owens and Louis punctured Hitler's Aryan superiority myth, unified black and white Americans in celebration, and established Owens and Louis as this country's first black national heroes.

Owens and Louis laid the foundation for Brooklyn Dodgers General Manager Branch Rickey's partnership with Jackie Robinson to integrate our national pastime, Major League Baseball, a decade later. Robinson's successful integration of baseball, in turn, inspired Dr. Martin Luther King Jr., Rosa Parks, and the Civil Rights Movement of the 1950s.

Indeed, Barack Obama, America's first black president—the world's first black leader of a predominantly white country—credited Robinson's career for his own political rise. "There's a direct line between Jackie Robinson and me standing here," Obama said in January 2017, while hosting the world champion Chicago Cubs at the White House. He continued:

There's a direct line between people loving Ernie Banks, and then the city being able to come together and work together in one spirit.... Sometimes it's just a matter of us being able to escape and relax from the difficulties of our days, but sometimes it also speaks to something better in us. And when you see this group of folks of different shades and different backgrounds, and coming from different communities and neighborhoods all across the country, and then playing as one team and playing the right way, and celebrating each other and being joyous in that, that tells us a little something about what America is and what America can be.

Yes, America is a shining example of sports' transformative power. The games we play, the games at the center of our social behavior, combine with our founding principles to enhance the American experience. America's enemies know this, which is why the culture war has moved to our arenas and stadiums. Sports are now in the same crosshairs as our Founding Fathers, under attack for past racial sins and unappreciated for their vital role in cultivating racial unity. Thomas Jefferson owned slaves, but by writing the Declaration of Independence he made the emancipation of slaves inevitable. American sports were once segregated, but no American industry can match sports' empowerment of black men.

The black-player-dominated National Football League is the most powerful force in American popular culture. It provides the number one television show on five different networks—CBS, FOX, NBC, ESPN, and the NFL Network. In this era of have-it-your-way TV, where consumers record and watch shows when they want while fast-forwarding through advertisements, only live sporting events can be consistently counted on to deliver audiences that sit through commercials.

But while American sports have never been more influential, they've also never been more vulnerable to foreign influence. Their partnership with global brands and their desire to build global audiences have given foreign countries a pathway to manipulate American sports and culture.

Look at how China, with its 1.4 billion consumers, rules the National Basketball Association and its *de facto* parent company, Nike, the same way it rules Hollywood. Access to China's consumers and Asia's cheap labor (even sometimes slave labor) is the key to Nike's economic growth. The Portland-based shoe and apparel manufacturer generates $40 billion a year in revenue. Its global reach, agenda, and revenue streams dictate the strategy of the $8-billion-a-year NBA. Many are unaware that Nike, and not the NBA, controls basketball. One could make a fair argument that the NBA is nothing more than the in-house marketing department of Nike.

Both Nike and the NBA kowtow to China, which explains their silence on the horrific human rights abuses inside China and the suppression of Hong Kong freedom fighters by China's communist government. More important, Nike and the NBA's China agenda helps explain why Nike pitchmen LeBron James and Colin Kaepernick enthusiastically smear the United States as inherently racist and evil. From Joseph Stalin to Fidel Castro to our own time, the communists' favorite propaganda tactic has been to paint the West, and the U.S. in particular, as racist.

The militant social justice messaging of James and Kaepernick serves the interests of not only the Chinese Communist Party and globalist corporations like Nike, but also our political Left. Kaepernick's National Anthem defiance in 2016 gave the Left an opportunity to politicize football, America's new national pastime, and force it into the kind of "progressive" posturing already commonplace in the NBA and Hollywood. Arrogance, lack of foresight, and the advice of an inner circle that included former Clinton administration press secretary Joe Lockhart as the NFL's vice president of communications, explain commissioner Roger Goodell's laissez-faire approach to Kaepernick's protest. Underestimating the determination of the Left and the power of social media to intimidate corporate America, Goodell and the NFL's TV partners wrongly thought that the Kaepernick controversy would fade over time.

Instead, four years after Kaepernick first knelt, the Leftist mob has forced the National Football League, Major League Baseball, the National Hockey League, and the National Basketball Association to take their own knees and pay homage to the dishonest Black Lives Matter narrative on police brutality. The NFL plans to paint social justice messages across its end zones this season and to allow players to wear helmet decals with the names of alleged police victims. The San Francisco 49ers fly a BLM flag next to an American flag at Levi's Stadium. MLB opened its COVID-shortened season with "BLM" carved into pitcher's mounds, and the Boston Red Sox put up a 254-foot BLM billboard outside Fenway Park. NHL players are now regularly kneeling during the National Anthem. The NBA's basketball bubble at Disney World is a virtual shrine to BLM: "Black Lives Matter" is painted on the court, players wear social justice messages on the back of their jerseys, and it's major news when a player *stands* during the National Anthem.

The entire American sports world—a culture that traditionally celebrates victors, meritocracy, colorblindness, and patriotism—has suddenly immersed itself in black victimization and left-wing radicalism. This immersion threatens to do permanent damage to American culture as a whole. It has certainly undermined national pride. A country that no longer believes in its founding ideals cannot prosper and survive.

If our sports stadiums and arenas have become the Gettysburg of the culture war, Lebron James and Colin Kaepernick are playing the roles of Robert E. Lee and Stonewall Jackson, fighting to divide the nation even further than it is. The mainstream media is only half right in casting them as modern-day equivalents of Muhammad Ali. Ali's religious sect, the Nation of Islam, was certainly divisive: it championed black secession. But unlike the BLM movement, it also rejected victimhood. Its founder Elijah Muhammad and its spokesman Malcolm X promoted bootstrap self-reliance and were disdainful of liberal politics. "The worst enemy that the Negro [has]," said Malcolm X,

> is this white man that runs around here drooling at the mouth professing to love Negros and calling himself a liberal. It is following these white liberals that has perpetuated problems that Negros have. If the Negro wasn't taken, tricked or deceived by the white liberal, then Negros would get together and solve our own problems. I only cite these things to show you that in America, the history of the white liberal has been nothing but a series of trickery designed to make Negros think that the white liberal was going to solve our problems.

Pro-BLM athletes today have moved beyond the idea of a role model that was debated in 1993—the idea of modeling behavior to be imitated, such as self-reliance, hard work, responsibility, and good parenthood. Through the power of social media, to which they are addicted, these modern role models exert influence by promoting commercial products and political causes. In the case of NBA athletes like Lebron James, this means turning their backs not only on the oppressed people of China and Hong Kong, but also on the poor and underprivileged in America among whom so many of these wealthy athletes grew up, and who they now condemn to victimhood and dependency with their political activism.

Charles Barkley was right 30 years ago. Parents, not athletes, should be role models. Today the situation is even worse, with sports further dividing an already dangerously divided nation, rather than providing the unifying and even healing force Nelson Mandela described. Predictably, there are now calls to boycott sports, and it seems inevitable that the TV ratings of the pro sports leagues will decline. This is unlikely to matter, however, to the suddenly-woke billionaire team owners and their handpicked commissioners.

As fans, we can only hope and pray that these feckless leaders will reconsider their embrace of the BLM cult—a necessary first step to returning American sports to what it has been in the past: a force for unity and a model of a diverse and colorblind meritocracy.

Gender Ideology Run Amok

Abigail Shrier

June/July 2021

In 2007, America had one pediatric gender clinic; today there are hundreds. Testosterone is readily available to adolescents from places like Planned Parenthood and Kaiser, often on a first visit—without even a therapist's note.

How did we get to this point? How is it that we are all supposed to pretend that the only way you can know I'm a woman is if I tell you my pronouns? How did we get to an America in which a 13-year-old in the State of Washington can begin "gender affirming" therapy without her parents' consent? How did we get to an America in which a 15-year-old in Oregon can undergo "top surgery"—elective double mastectomy—without her parents' permission? And what can we do about it?

To understand how we got to this point, it is useful to begin by considering gender dysphoria—the feeling of severe discomfort in a person's biological sex. Gender dysphoria is certainly real. It is also exceedingly rare. It afflicts about 0.01 percent of the population, most of whom are male.

For nearly 100 years of diagnostic history, gender dysphoria typically began in early childhood, between the ages of two and four, and usually involved a boy who insisted that he was not a boy but a girl. Children afflicted are insistent, consistent, and persistent in the feeling that they are in the wrong body. It is by all accounts excruciating—I've talked to many transgender adults, most of them biological males, who describe the relentless chafe of a body that feels all wrong.

Historically, this has been the classic presentation of gender dysphoria. When these children were left alone—when no one intervened medically or encouraged what we today call "social transition"—over 70 percent of them naturally outgrew their gender dysphoria. Most of those who outgrew it became gay men. Those who did not outgrow it became what used to be known as transsexuals. They did not believe they were women, but they felt most comfortable presenting themselves as females.

Today, however, we don't leave these children alone. Instead, the moment children seem not to be perfectly feminine or perfectly masculine, we label them as "trans kids." Teachers encourage them to reintroduce themselves to their classes with new names and new pronouns. We take them to therapists or doctors, nearly all of whom practice so-called affirmative care—meaning they think it is their job to affirm the diagnosis of gender dysphoria and help the children medically transition.

The typical first step in treatment administered to these kids is puberty blockers, which shut down the part of the pituitary gland that directs the release of hormones catalyzing puberty. The most common of these drugs is Lupron, whose original purpose was the chemical castration of sex offenders. To this day, the FDA has never approved this drug for halting healthy puberty.

One has to wonder why a parent or a doctor would take measures to stop a child's puberty, given that even a child with genuine gender dysphoria would most likely outgrow that condition if left alone. Some argue that it is traumatizing to let children go through the puberty of the sex to which they do not wish to belong. But in many cases, puberty seems to have helped children overcome gender dysphoria. The truth is that there is no satisfying answer, given that scientists have no way of predicting which children will outgrow the dysphoria on their own and which won't.

Proponents of "affirmative care" also argue that allowing puberty to occur is dangerous, because suicide rates for trans-identified youth and trans adults are very high. Therefore, they say, we need to start treating children with gender dysphoria as soon and as dramatically as possible.

Yet there are no good long-term studies indicating that puberty blockers cure suicidality or even improve mental health. Nor are there studies that show puberty blockers are safe or reversible when used in this manner.

What we do know is that puberty blockers prevent the development of secondary sex characteristics, sexual maturation, and bone density. Indeed, because of the inhibition of bone density and other risks, doctors don't like to keep children on puberty blockers for more than two years.

We also know that in almost every case when a child's healthy puberty is medically arrested, placing the child out of step with his or her peers, that child proceeds to cross-sex hormones. And when puberty blockers *and* cross-sex hormones are administered to a girl, she becomes infertile. She may also have permanent sexual dysfunction given that her sex organs never reach adult maturity.

Given this, the claims made by so many doctors and gender activists today that these medical transition measures for children are safe and reversible—that they are a "pause button," without serious downsides—are not only dishonest, but destructive. We would not accept this sort of glib salesmanship in any other area of medicine.

Trans Identification among Teenage Girls

As I mentioned, for the nearly 100-year history of scientific study of gender dysphoria, it has been diagnosed almost exclusively in young children, and mostly in boys. But over the last decade, large numbers of teenage girls have begun to claim they have gender dysphoria.

Prior to 2012, in fact, there was no scientific literature on gender dysphoria arising in teenage girls. Dr. Lisa Littman, then a Brown University public health researcher, used the phrase "rapid onset gender dysphoria" to refer to the subsequent sudden spike in transgender identification among teenage girls with no childhood history of gender dysphoria.

This spike is not unique to America—we see it across the Western world. To offer just one statistic, there has been a decade-to-decade increase of over

4,400 percent in the number of teenage girls seeking treatment at the United-Kingdom's national gender clinic. Across the West, teen girls are now the leading demographic claiming to have gender dysphoria.

What is behind this is social contagion—the spread of ideas, emotions, and behaviors through peer influence, one more instance of teenage girls sharing and spreading their pain. There is a long history of social contagion with this demographic—anorexia and bulimia are also spread this way. And we know that teen girls today are in the midst of the worst mental health crisis on record, with the highest rates of anxiety, self-harm, and clinical depression.

The teen girls susceptible to this social contagion are the same high-anxiety, depressive girls who struggle socially in adolescence and tend to hate their bodies. Add to that a school environment where you can achieve status and popularity by declaring a trans identity. Add to that the teenage temptation to stick it to mom. Also add the intoxicating influence of social media, where trans activists push the idea that identifying as trans and starting a course of testosterone will cure a girl's problems. Put those together, and you have a fast-spreading social phenomenon.

I've spoken to families at top girls' schools who attest that 15, 20, or in one case 30 percent of the girls in their daughter's seventh grade class identify as trans. When you see figures like that, you're witnessing a social contagion in action. There is no other reasonable explanation.

These teen girls are in a great deal of pain. Almost all of them have at some point dealt with an eating disorder, engaged in cutting, or been diagnosed with other mental health comorbidities. And now they're being allowed to self-diagnose gender dysphoria by a medical establishment that has decided that its job is to affirm and agree with trans-identified adolescents.

Turning a Blind Eye

You may not know the name Keira Bell. She is a young woman in the U.K., very troubled in adolescence, who was rushed to transition in her teen years and came to regret it. She underwent double mastectomy and spent years on testosterone, only to realize that her problem had never been gender dysphoria. She sued the U.K.'s national gender clinic, and last December, after the High Court of Justice examined her case and the claims of similarly situated plaintiffs, she won.

The Court examined the medical protocols applied to Keira Bell—*protocols identical to the ones we have in the United States*—and was horrified that a young girl had been allowed to consent to begin a process of eliminating her future fertility and sexual function at an age, 15, when she could not possibly have gauged that loss.

Hailed as a "landmark case" by *The Times* of London, *The Economist*, and even *The Guardian*, Bell's victory was widely viewed as a serious condemnation of the effort to fast-track teen girls to gender transition. One of the appalling things the Court noted was that the national gender clinic had been unable to show any psychological improvement in the adolescents it had treated with transitioning hormones.

If, as I suspect, you haven't read or heard about the Keira Bell case, that's because America's legacy media decided to pretend the case didn't happen. Similarly, they continue to ignore or dismiss the stories of the thousands of "detransitioners"—young women who underwent medical transition, later regretted it, and attempt to reverse course. A lot of the treatments these girls have undergone are permanent, but they do what they can to try to reverse some of the effects.

Thus it is that in the United States, this crisis among teenage girls gets treated as a political issue—a conservative issue—rather than a medical one. And so perhaps the greatest medical scandal of our time is dismissed as a conservative preoccupation.

The Assault on Women's Sports and Safe Spaces

No discussion of gender ideology can ignore the ongoing movement to eradicate girls' and women's sports and protective spaces. Many or most of the people pushing this are not transgender themselves. But they are activists, they are energized, and they seem to be winning.

This movement promotes dangerous bills like the Equality Act, which would make it illegal ever to distinguish between biological men and women—and thus to exclude a biological male from a girls' sports team or a women's protective space, whether it be a restroom, locker room, or prison. We have these laws now in California and in the State of Washington—and as you might imagine, one result is that hundreds of biological male prisoners, many of them violent felons, have applied to transfer to women's units.

For activists pushing this, it is not enough to create unisex bathrooms, a separate category for trans-identified athletes, or separate safe zones in prisons for trans-identified biological men. No, they are working to abolish all women's-only spaces and they want to abolish them now.

———

The common thread running through these topics is that the truth is being obscured by gender ideology. Lies are told about the risks of the transition treatments administered to young children, both to play down the dangers of those treatments and to exaggerate the degree to which those treatments are known to be helpful. Lies are told about the researchers and journalists who attempt to report on the crisis of social contagion among teenage girls undergoing transition treatments. And lies are told about the movement to eradicate women's protective spaces.

The gender ideology behind these lies is a sibling of critical race theory. While critical race activists are teaching kids that they are largely defined by their skin color, gender activists are teaching kids that there are a great many genders, and that only they know their true gender. And just as families who object to racial indoctrination in schools are told that their denials of racism are proof of racism, young women who object to biological males participating in girls' sports are told that their objections are proof of transphobic bigotry.

These mendacious dogmas have corrupted our K-12 schools, our universities, and our legacy media, as well as our scientific journals and our medical accrediting organizations—the American Academy of Pediatrics, the American Medical Association, the American Psychiatric Association, etc. To give you a sense of how far things have gone, I was informed late last year by a member of the National Association of Science Writers—an association of journalists with scientific backgrounds—that a member of the association's online forum had been expelled for mentioning my book on the transgender social contagion among teenage girls. He hadn't even read my book. He just mentioned that it sounded interesting, and for that he was banned as transphobic.

Similarly, endocrinologists, psychiatrists, pediatricians, and researchers who are concerned about the risks of gender interventions report that they struggle today to get their research published. And public and private funding of research is almost entirely restricted to researchers who promote gender transition and downplay the risks.

There are phalanxes of young doctors now, many of them in pediatrics or child psychiatry, who are open about their belief that their primary job is "social justice." They unreservedly celebrate the increase in transitioning treatment of young people and are inexcusably complacent about the risks of those treatments. *The Washington Post* recently quoted some of these doctors to the effect that puberty blockers are fully reversible—which is not something that any honest doctor can claim to know. We simply don't have the data to know whether puberty blockers are fully physically reversible when applied to halt healthy puberty—and they are certainly not psychologically reversible. We're seeing a startling politicization of medicine and science, which is symptomatic of a larger woke corruption of American society.

———

Now, there's something I make a point of saying whenever I speak, and I say it for the simple reason that it is true: transgender adults are some of the soberest and kindest people I have met in my work as a journalist. Many of them seem to have been helped by transition, and they are leading admirable and productive lives. They have no desire to harm women or to push transition on children. The gender ideology activists do not represent them.

My understanding of freedom includes a belief that society should allow adults to make consequential decisions about their lives, which includes choosing to undergo sex reassignment surgery. And whenever I am asked by a transgender adult, I use his or her chosen name and pronouns. This seems to me the courteous and the right thing to do. But—and this is a big but—I never lie. This means I never say, and I will never say, that trans women are women. I think reciting this lie leads, as we are seeing, to unjust and dangerous consequences for women and girls. It is not courteous or right to parrot these lies. It is the cowardly surrender of women's welfare to the woke gods. And it is wrong.

I'm also often asked why it is that the gender ideology activists are doing what they are doing. What possible justification could there be, for instance, for telling small boys that they might be girls and small girls that they might be boys? My best guess at an answer occurred to me while talking to detransitioners. I heard repeatedly from these young women that while they were transitioning, they were angry and politically radical. They often cut off relations with their families, having been coached to do so online by gender activists. Related to this, if you look, you'll notice a disproportionate number of gender-confused people among the ranks of Antifa in cities like Portland.

In other words, chaos is the point, and these troubled girls become prey for those who seek to recruit revolutionaries. Just as the destructive objective of critical race theory is to divide Americans racially, that of gender ideology is to disrupt the formation of stable families, the building blocks of American life.

So what do we do about it? How do we push back? First and foremost, we must oppose the indoctrination of children in gender ideology. There is no good reason for it, and it does real harm. We can absolutely insist that all children treat each other kindly without indoctrinating an entire generation in gender confusion.

Second, we must overcome our squeamishness and speak the truth in public. Wherever we find ourselves, we must refuse to recite lies. And we must always clearly distinguish between transgender Americans, generally wonderful people, and the ideological transgender movement, which seeks to warp children and weaken families.

This is a movement that would turn our children against themselves because its advocates know there is no greater harm—no quicker way to bring America to its knees—than by driving our children to do themselves irreversible damage. The people pushing this ideology have gotten a head start on us by perhaps a decade. But now I think they have awakened a sleeping giant. The success of my book is one indication. The many state legislatures that are now debating these issues is another.

These are our kids and grandkids. Our future depends on our winning this fight.

NATIONAL DEFENSE

Exit Communism, Cold War and the Status Quo

Jeane Kirkpatrick

January 1991

I t is exciting to be here at Hillsdale College. I was pleased and honored when Hillsdale presented me with the Freedom Leadership Award in 1984. As a speaker for the College's off-campus programs for some years, I was also happy to share some of my views about the importance of Hillsdale on the College's recently released FreedomQuest campaign video, but this is my first visit to campus and, like Charlton Heston, who preceded me during this program, I'm impressed with what I see. I'm impressed with the hundreds of loyal and interested supporters who are here too, who share the sense that what goes on here—indeed, the very idea of this college—is important to our country, our values, and our culture. So I congratulate you, Hillsdale, and I thank you for inviting me.

How 1989 Changed the World

I'm here to talk a little bit about the world of the late 1980s and early 1990s. The year 1989, in particular, was one of the most extraordinary periods in modem history. The most important lessons this year has taught are, first, that we must expect the unexpected, and second, that we must stand firm for what we believe. The old adage that if we have patience and persist, things will get better turned out to be true.

There was a very direct relationship between the patient and persistent policies from President Truman to President Reagan. With his rebuilding of American strength in the 1980s, and his unembarrassed defense of democratic ideals at home and abroad, Reagan encouraged the remarkable changes that have occurred in Eastern Europe and in the Soviet Union and are indeed still occurring.

In truth, 1989 changed the world. At the beginning of that year, the world was much as it had been for the previous four decades. It was the post-World War II status quo: Europe was divided by a cold war created by a real Soviet threat, as evidenced by the brutal occupation of Eastern Europe and by continuing Soviet expansion into five continents. Soviet dominance extended into our own backyard, not only in Nicaragua, but by the threat of its attempted expansion into El Salvador, Guatemala, Columbia, Peru, Grenada, and Jamaica.

It is difficult today even to recall the situation of the world in 1980, which remained nearly unchanged up until 1989, when there was what the Soviets call a "change of the world correlation of forces." This change had been brought about by the resurgence and renaissance of American strength, and by the continuing decline of the Soviet Union. The Soviet Union was and still is the only industrial power in the world whose living standards are declining rather than increasing, whose average life expectancy is declining (from 74 years for Soviet males to 71 years over a period of about five years in the last decade) while infant mortality rates are rising.

A "Crisis of the Soul"

By 1989, it was undeniable that the Soviet Union was in a decline that was incredible by any standards, and it was equally evident that such a decline had created a kind of "crisis of conscience," or, perhaps, that the crisis of conscience had created the decline. We don't usually talk about conscience when we talk about Soviet leaders and Soviet policy. I've been discovering of late some fascinating facets reading the speeches of some of Mikhail Gorbachev's principal advisors. Let me share with you a few words from the text of Aleksandr Yakovlev, for example.

Yakovlev is the man whom almost everyone thinks is Mikhail Gorbachev's closest advisor. Yakovlev has emphasized intellectual and spiritual factors in Soviet changes. One of his statements about the Soviet people that has been widely quoted is: "we have suffered not only a crisis in economics but a crisis of the soul." This is Aleksandr Yakovlev on July 2, 1990:

> I am convinced that the time has come for truth. To speak of nobility, charity, honor, and conscience, even at a Congress of Communists, shaking from our feet the mud of enmity and suspicion that has built up over the decades. It is the very time for the party to take the initiative in the moral cleansing of our existence and our consciousness. This is why I am convinced of the historic correctness of the choice that was made in 1985 to establish perestroika.

He went on to remark on his activities in the years since 1985, which went beyond advising Mikhail Gorbachev:

> A special sphere of my work in recent years has been the Commission study of materials relating to the repressions visited on our country in the past. I will tell you honestly; it is heavy, spiritually exhausting work when the ashes of millions of people constantly haunt you. The good names of almost a million people have been returned. But there has been falsification of such a scale. Repressions could not have been a matter of chance and could not have been the consequence of an evil will alone. [By] whom and how is the mechanism of repression created and set in motion? How did it function? Why did nothing stand in its path?

Yakovlev then went on to discuss the Stalinist period. He paused over the collectivization in the Ukraine, that horror about which Robert Conquest has written movingly and accurately in books like *The Great Terror* and *The Genocide of the Ukraine*, in which a manmade famine was visited upon the people of the Ukraine. Starving men, women, and children were driven off their land, scattered, and killed.

Yakovlev says, "In my view that was the most monstrous crime when hundreds of thousands of peasant families were driven out of the villages, not understanding why such a fate befell them. They were driven out by the authorities they themselves had established. The dead cannot be brought back but their good names may be restored in history." And then Yakovlev added a line that has since become famous among his countrymen: "Let us remember not the empty shelves but the empty souls who have brought a change to our country which demands revolutionary change."

The reaction of Yakovlev, one of the most well-known public figures in the Soviet Union, is worth our serious attention. Unfortunately, his comments and those of others like him are being largely ignored or discounted in the West.

Yakovlev quoted Kant in early September: "Long ago, the great philosopher Kant wrote that there are two prejudices: 'to believe everything and to believe nothing.' But then again, he wrote there are also mysteries, the scarlet sky above us, and the moral law within us."

Imagine the second most powerful man in the Soviet Union talking about the moral law within us—and then imagine virtually all the major media outlets in the West ignoring his extraordinary pronouncement! Both are remarkable.

Yakovlev added, "according to the moral law, our society that is transforming itself into a free society has yet…in the process of transforming itself to overcome the obstructions of falsehood." He goes on to charge that the confidence of the people had been abused in the old communist system, and that "the people wished us merely good and the State responded with the evil of prisons and camps."

Yakovlev ends this comment with an extraordinary appeal, "Preserve me, Almighty, from calls for vengeance, from a new round of intolerance, that our society must know the names of the people who committed these deeds in order to assess them according to moral criteria."

Soviet Reprisals: The Dog That Didn't Bark

I share these words of Aleksandr Yakovlev with you that I've been reading with growing surprise myself. I also want to share with you a sense of the depth of change that is taking place in the Soviet Union today. That change has, of course, already transformed the post-World War II world in which we had lived for over 40 years. It was an uncomfortable world, because we were faced by continuous challenges, and because it imposed very heavy burdens on our country. Yet it was comfortable, because we knew it and were accustomed to it, and we knew what we should do—help defend the frontiers of freedom.

What happened in 1989 that was most remarkable was like the dog that didn't bark in Sherlock Holmes's famous mystery tale. What didn't happen was that the Soviet troops did not intervene to crush the liberation movements in Hungary, Poland, Czechoslovakia, and East Germany. I was in Poland in late August of that year. The first elected government since World War II had been installed. It was, naturally, largely Solidarity government, although you will recall that it included two communist ministers (who have only recently been fired). Those two communist ministers were in the Defense ministry and in the Interior. The newly-elected Polish Solidarity government had agreed to give the communists, who had been clobbered in the elections, the control over the armed forces and the police. Why? Because they thought they had to; because they feared that Soviet troops would crush their democratic movement.

At the time I was there last August, Solidarity's victory was still uncertain. No one knew what to expect; every step toward independence was taken courageously enough, but was attended by great misgivings. Two Solidarity leaders, ministers in the new government, confessed privately to me: "None of us forgets our years in prison." After all, they had been in prison less than five years before when Poland was under martial law and no one's rights were protected. And it had been less than a decade since Father Popieluszko had been beaten to death for daring to speak about independence for his country.

The uncertainty existed for all Eastern Europe. No one knew what was going to happen in Hungary when its citizens announced that they were going to change the national constitution and open the border with Austria. Even though it was rumored that they had the approval of Mikhail Gorbachev, no one, not even Gorbachev, could predict the results of such unprecedented reform. We know now that when the border did open, East Germans began to surge through in a kind of human tidal wave. We also know that this mass exodus began the process of the reunification of Germany.

No one knew what would happen when the citizens of Czechoslovakia went into the streets for the first time since 1968. Miraculously, they did not encounter tanks—just each other—and there, too, freedom at last was realizable.

The Challenge of Normal Times

The most important event of 1989 was really a non-event: the tanks that did not roll and the Soviet troops that stayed in their barracks. This was the end of the Soviet empire, and it disintegrated faster than any other empire in modern history. Obviously, the danger is not yet over—there are still Soviet tanks and troops in Eastern Europe, and there are tens of thousands of Soviet missiles. But the "will to empire" has disappeared. We can say of the year 1989 that history's most bold, daring, and ruthless experiment in social engineering was effectively abandoned by the heirs of the men who began it.

Now, the question is, what will replace that experiment? Some Soviets like Yakovlev, who lived in the West for nearly a decade, talk of building a free society. Gorbachev often says the same thing, and although I am not sure that he understands what such freedom really means, he is a very pragmatic man who understands that reform is in his and the Soviet Union's best interest. In the last few years he has begun to ask questions that the Soviet people were, to say the least, unaccustomed to hearing. For example, he asked if it were true old Bolsheviks were guilty of the crimes they had been executed for, and even went to the trouble of establishing two investigative commissions that discovered that some were wrongly accused.

"Is it true?"—that is not a Bolshevik question, as anyone knows who recalls the infamous Moscow show trials of the 1930s. And Gorbachev followed up with another uncharacteristic question about the Soviet economy. He asked, simply, "Does it work?" When Bolsheviks before him asked if the economy worked, what they really meant was, "Does it serve the Revolution?" To his credit, Gorbachev meant something quite different. He pointed to Soviet agriculture as an unworkable system and advocated following the practice of Hungary and China in leasing land to farmers. The state is still in control, of course, but once even half-measures of private ownership are introduced, the pressure for complete reform begins to build momentum.

Watching Soviet leaders like Gorbachev let go of power is a fascinating experience. The stops and starts, the infighting with other Soviets like Ligachev, the retrenchments and advances—these are all part of a historical drama. There has never been a totalitarian state quite like the Soviet Union, and there has never been one that was dismantled without great violence. Yet we seem to be witnessing a relatively peaceful transformation to a democratic political structure and a market economy in the USSR.

Ironically enough, our libraries are filled with books on the transformation from capitalism to socialism, but practically no books have been written about how to bring about the reverse. There are only one or two like the brilliant Peruvian Hernando de Soto's book about his country called *The Other Path*. They desperately need such books in Eastern Europe and the Soviet Union.

In the West, we need books that will remind us that it has been democratic capitalism, not socialism, that has won the Cold War, lest we allow the former's few remaining adherents to convince us that socialism is the wave of the future. We also need to be aware, as we have been vividly reminded by the Persian Gulf crisis, that the post-Cold War world is not necessarily a more peaceful world. Military power and national resolve still count. In this less predictable, less "connected" world, there are many centers of power, and international politics has become much more complicated. The challenge ahead is not the same as it was during the Cold War; it is, rather, the challenge of "normal times," times in which the future is still uncertain. Let us hope that we will see more years like 1989.

Classics and War

Victor Davis Hanson

February 2002

T he study of Classics—of Greece and Rome—can offer us moral lessons as well as a superb grounding in art, literature, history, and language. In our present crisis after September 11, it also offers practical guidance—and the absence of familiarity with the foundations of Western culture in part may explain many of the disturbing reactions to the war that we have seen on American campuses.

If more in our universities really understood the Greeks and Romans and their legacy in the West, then they would not see this present conflict through either therapeutic or apologetic lenses. As Classics teaches us, war in classical antiquity—and for most of the past 2,500 years of Western Civilization—was seen as a tragedy innate to the human condition—a time of human plague when, as the historian Herodotus said, fathers bury sons rather than sons fathers. In others words, killing humans over disagreements should not happen among civilized people. But it does happen. So war, the poet Hesiod concluded, was "a curse from Zeus."

Tragically, the Greeks tell us, conflict will always break out—and very frequently so—because we are human and thus not always rational. War is "the father, the king of us all," the philosopher Heraclitus lamented. Even the utopian Plato agreed: "War is always existing by nature between every

Greek city-state." How galling and hurtful to us moderns that Plato, of all people, once called peace, not war, the real "parenthesis" in human affairs. Warfare could be terrifying—"a thing of fear," the poet Pindar summed up—but not therein unnatural or necessarily evil.

No, the rub was particular wars, not war itself. While all tragic, wars could be good or evil depending on their cause, the nature of the fighting, and the ultimate costs and results. The Greek defense against Persian attack in 480 B.C., in the eyes of the playwright Aeschylus (who chose as his epitaph mention of his service at the battle of Marathon, not his dramas), was "glorious." Yet the theme of Thucydides' history of the internecine Peloponnesian wars was folly and sometimes senseless butchery. Likewise, there is language of freedom and liberty associated with the Greeks' naval victory at Salamis, but not with the slaughter at the battle of Gaugamela—Alexander the Great's destruction of the Persian army in Mesopotamia that wrecked Darius III's empire and replaced eastern despots with Macedonian autocrats.

The Roots of War

If war was innate, and its morality defined by particular circumstances, fighting was also not necessarily explained by prior exploitation or legitimate grievance. Nor did aggression have to arise from poverty or inequality. States, like people, the historian Thucydides tells us, can be envious—and even rude and pushy. And if they can get away with things, they most surely will. Thucydides later says states battle out of "honor, fear, and self-interest." How odd to think that the Japanese and Germans were not starving in 1941, but rather were proud peoples who wanted those whom they deemed inferior and weak to serve them.

To the Greeks, such rotten peoples also fought mostly over tangible things—more land, more subjects, more loot. Wars were a sort of acquisition, Aristotle said. Bullies, whether out of vanity or a desire for power and recognition, will take things from other people unless they are stopped. And if they are to be stopped, citizens—among them good, kind, and well-read men like Socrates, Sophocles, Thucydides, and Demosthenes—must fight to protect their freedom and save the innocent.

To a student of the Classics who trusts Thucydides or Plato more than Marx, Freud, or Michel Foucault, the present crisis, I think, looks something like this: The United States, being a strong and wealthy society, invites envy because of the success of its restless culture of freedom, constitutional democracy, self-critique, secular rationalism, and open markets that threaten both theocracy and autocracy alike. That we are often to be hated—and periodically to be challenged by those who want our power, riches, or influence and yet simultaneously hate their own desire—is to be often regretted, but always expected. Our past indulgence of Osama bin Laden did not bring us respect, much less sympathy. Rather, human nature being what it is, our forbearance invited ever more contempt and audacity on his part—and more dead as the bitter wages of our self-righteous morality and tragic miscalculation.

The enemies of free speech and intolerance—German Nazis, Italian fascists, Japanese militarists, Stalinist communists, or Islamic fundamentalists—will always attack us for what we are, rather than what we have done, inasmuch as they must innately hate freedom and the liberality which is its twin. Only our moral response—not our status as belligerents per se—determines whether our war is just and necessary. If, like the Athenians, we butcher neutral Melians for no good cause, then our battle against the innocent is evil and we may not win. But if we fight to preserve freedom like the Greeks at Thermopylae and the GIs on the beaches of Normandy, then war is the right and indeed the only thing we can do. Caught in such a tragedy, where efforts at reason and humanity fall on the deaf ears of killers, we must go to war for our survival and to prove to our enemies that their defeat will serve as a harsh teacher—at least for a generation or two—that it is wrong and very dangerous to use two kilotons of explosives to blow up 5,000 civilians in the streets of our cities.

The Modern View of War

This depressing view of human nature and conflict is rarely any longer with us. It was not the advent of Christianity that ended it; Christian philosophers and theologians long ago developed the doctrine of "just war," having realized that nonresistance meant suicide. More likely, the twentieth century and the horror of the two World Wars—Verdun, the Somme, Hiroshima—put an end to the tragic view of war. Yet out of such numbing losses—and our arrogance—we missed the lesson of the World Wars. The calamity of 60 million dead was not only because we went to war, but rather because we were naïve and deemed weak by our enemies well before 1914 and 1939—at a time when real resolve could have stopped Prussian militarism and Nazism before millions of blameless perished.

The deviant offspring of the Enlightenment—Marxists and Freudians—gave birth to even more pernicious social sciences that sought to 'prove' to us that war was always evil and therefore—with help from Ph.D.s—surely preventable. Indeed, during the International Year of Peace in 1986, a global commission of experts concluded that war was unnatural and humans themselves unwarlike! Unfortunately, innocent people get killed because of that kind of thinking. Many, especially in our universities, now are convinced that war always results from real, rather than perceived, grievances, such as the poverty arising out of the usual list of sins: colonialism, imperialism, racism, and sexism. In response, dialogue and mediation have been elevated to the grand science of "conflict resolution theory," a sort of marriage counseling or small claims court taken to the global level.

Rich and conceited Westerners simply could not accept the idea that more people in the twentieth century were killed by Hitler, Stalin, and Mao off the battlefield than on it. How depressing to suggest that the Khmer Rouge, the Hutus, and the Serbians went on killing when left alone—and quit only when either satiated or stopped!

In the new moral calculus of the American university, bin Laden figures to be no Xerxes or Tojo. He is not even an inherently evil man who hates us for our clout and our influence. Far too few in the university understand that bin Laden wishes to strut over a united Middle Eastern caliphate under his brand of Medieval Islam, and to make decadent Westerners cower in fear. Instead, they insist that he is either confused (call in Freud) or has legitimate grievances (read Marx), and so we must find answers within us for what he does. Western importation of Arab oil? Stolen land from the Palestinians? Decadent democracy and capitalism? Jewish-American women walking in the land of Mecca? Puppet Arab governments? Take your pick—bin Laden has cited them all.

To stop the evil of Islamic fundamentalism, the tragic Greeks would make ready the 101st Airborne and the Rangers, while too many in academia would rather that we chit-chat with him, fathom him, or accommodate him as did the Clinton State Department. Seeing war as "Zeus's curse" in this age of our greatest learning and wealth—and pride—is to descend into "savagery," when our sophisticated elite promise that prayer, talk, or money can yet prevail. But if we deem ourselves too smart, too moral, or too soft to stop killers, then—as Socrates and Pericles alike remind us—we have become real accomplices to evil through inaction. Generations slaughtered in Europe, incinerated Jews, massacred Russians and Chinese, and the bleached bones of Cambodians are proof enough of what the Greeks once warned us.

Western Exceptionalism

Finally, Classics teaches how unique the Greeks and Romans were among the peoples of the ancient world; theirs was an anti-Mediterranean culture whose approach to politics, culture, literature, and religion was antithetical to almost every state in Africa, Asia, and the tribal confines of northern Europe. In our ignorance, too many Americans have made the fatal mistake of assuming that our enemies are simply different from us, rather than far worse than us—as if the current war in the Middle East is largely due to a misunderstanding among equals, rather than reflective of a vast faultline that goes back to the very origins of our civilization. Athens was a democracy; Sidon was not. Farmers owned their own property in Greece, voted, and formed the militia of the polis; not so in Persia and Egypt. Thucydides was able to criticize his mother country, Greece; Persian clerks who recorded Darius's res gestae on the walls of Persepolis were not. The Greek language and its European descendants have a rich vocabulary of words for "constitution," "citizen," "freedom," and "democracy"; this is true of neither old Persian or modern Arabic. Such differences are not perceived, but real and critical, for they affect the manner in which people conduct their daily lives—whether they live in fear or in safety, in want or in security.

If our students and professors today would study the Classics, they might rediscover the origins of their culture—and in doing so learn that we are not even remotely akin to the Taliban or the Saudis, but are in fact profoundly different in the manner we craft our government, treat women, earn our living, and set the parameters of our religion. Modern cultural anthropology, social linguistics, cross-cultural geography, sociology, and nearly any discipline with the suffix "studies" would lecture us that the Taliban's desecration of the graves of the infidel, clitorectomies of infants, torture of the accused, murder of the untried, and destruction of the non-Islamic is merely "different" or "problematic"—almost anything other than "evil." Yet a world under the Taliban or its supporters, like the satrapy that Xerxes envisioned for a conquered Greece, would mean no free expression, no voting, no protection from arbitrary and coercive government, but instead theocracy, censorship, and brutality in every facet of daily life. Such were the stakes at Salamis and so too is the contest now with the Islamic fundamentalists, who are as akin to ancient absolutists as we are to the Greeks.

Such ignorance of one's own past can weaken a powerful society such as ours that must project confidence, power, humanity—and hope—to those less fortunate abroad. This new species of upscale and pampered terrorist hates America for a variety of complex reasons. He despises, of course, his own attraction toward our ease and liberality. He recognizes that our freedom and affluence spur on his appetites more than Islam can repress them. But just as importantly, these terrorists realize that there is an aristocratic guilt within many comfortable Americans, who are too often ashamed of, or apologetic about, their culture. And in this hesitance, our enemies sense not merely our ignorance of our own foundations, but also both decadence and weakness. Rather than appreciating Americans' self-confidence or simple manners when we accept rebuke so politely, our enemies despise us all the more, simply because they can—and can so easily, and without rejoinder.

Classics, then, can teach us who we once were—and thus who we are now in the present war. The ancients not only teach us that life is spirited and tragic, but also that what was created in and followed from Greece and Rome was, and is, man's last and greatest hope on earth.

EMP: America's Achilles' Heel

Frank J. Gaffney, Jr.

June 2005

If Osama bin Laden—or the dictators of North Korea or Iran—could destroy America as a twenty-first century society and superpower, would they be tempted to try? Given their track records and stated hostility to the United States, we have to operate on the assumption that they would. That assumption would be especially frightening if this destruction could be accomplished with a *single attack* involving just one relatively small-yield nuclear weapon—and if the nature of the attack would mean that its perpetrator might not be immediately or easily identified.

Unfortunately, such a scenario is not far-fetched. According to a report issued last summer by a blue-ribbon, Congressionally-mandated commission, a single specialized nuclear weapon delivered to an altitude of a few hundred miles over the United States by a ballistic missile would be "capable of causing catastrophe for the nation." The source of such a cataclysm might be considered the ultimate "weapon of mass destruction"(WMD)—yet it is hardly ever mentioned in the litany of dangerous WMDs we face today. It is known as electromagnetic pulse (EMP).

How EMP Works

A nuclear weapon produces several different effects. The best known, of course, are the intense heat and overpressures associated with the fireball and accompanying blast. But a nuclear explosion also generates intense outputs of energy in the form of x- and gamma-rays. If the latter are unleashed outside the Earth's atmosphere, some portion of them will interact with the upper atmosphere's air molecules. This in turn will generate an enormous pulsed current of high-energy electrons that will interact with the Earth's magnetic field. The result is the instantaneous creation of an invisible radio-frequency wave of uniquely great intensity—roughly a million-fold greater than that of the most powerful radio station.

The energy of this pulse would reach everything in line-of-sight of the explosion's center point at the speed of light. The higher the altitude of the weapon's detonation, the larger the affected terrestrial area would be. For example, at a height of 300 miles, the entire continental United States, some of its offshore areas, and parts of Canada and Mexico would be affected. What is more, as the nuclear explosion's fireball expands in space, it would generate additional electrical currents in the Earth below and in extended electrical conductors, such as electricity transmission lines. If the electrical wiring of things like computers, microchips, and power grids is exposed to these effects, they may be temporarily or permanently disabled.

Estimates of the combined direct and indirect effects of an EMP attack prompted the Commission to Assess the Threat to the United States from Electromagnetic Pulse Attack to state the following in its report to Congress:

> The electromagnetic fields produced by weapons designed and deployed with the intent to produce EMP have a high likelihood of damaging electrical power systems, electronics, and information systems upon which American society depends. Their effects on dependent systems and infrastructures could be sufficient to qualify as catastrophic to the nation.

If it seems incredible that a single weapon could have such an extraordinarily destructive effect, consider the nature and repercussions of the three distinct components of an electromagnetic pulse: fast, medium, and slow. The "fast component" is essentially an "electromagnetic shock-wave" that can temporarily or permanently disrupt the functioning of electronic devices. In twenty-first century America, such devices are virtually everywhere, including in controls, sensors, communications equipment, protective systems, computers, cell phones, cars, and airplanes. The extent of the damage induced by this component of EMP, which occurs virtually simultaneously over a very large area, is determined by the altitude of the explosion.

The "medium-speed component" of EMP covers roughly the same geographic area as the "fast" one, although the peak power level of its electrical shock would be far lower. Since it follows the "fast component" by a small fraction of a second, however, the medium-speed component has the potential to do extensive damage to systems whose protective and control features have been impaired or destroyed by the first onslaught.

If the first two EMP components were not bad enough, there is a third one—a "slow component" resulting from the expansion of the explosion's fireball in the Earth's magnetic field. It is this "slow component"—a pulse that lasts tens of seconds to minutes—which creates disruptive currents in electricity transmission lines, resulting in damage to electrical supply and distribution systems connected to such lines. Just as the second component compounds the destructive impact of the first, the fact that the third follows on the first two ensures significantly greater damage to power grids and related infrastructure.

The EMP Threat Commission estimates that, all other things being equal, it may take "months to years" to bring such systems fully back online. Here is how it depicts the horrifying ripple effect of the sustained loss of electricity on contemporary American society:

Depending on the specific characteristics of the attacks, unprecedented cascading failures of our major infrastructures could result. In that event, a regional or national recovery would be long and difficult and would seriously degrade the safety and overall viability of our nation. The primary avenues for catastrophic damage to the nation are through our electric power infrastructure and thence into our telecommunications, energy, and other infrastructures. These, in turn, can seriously impact other important aspects of our nation's life, including the financial system; means of getting food, water, and medical care to the citizenry; trade; and production of goods and services.

The recovery of any one of the key national infrastructures is dependent on the recovery of others. The longer the outage, the more problematic and uncertain the recovery will be. It is possible for the functional outages to become mutually reinforcing until at some point the degradation of infrastructure could have irreversible effects on the country's ability to support its population.

The EMP Threat Today

The destructive power of electromagnetic pulses has been recognized by the United States national security community for some time. The EMP Threat Commission noted that

> EMP effects from nuclear bursts are not new threats to our nation.... Historically, [however,] this application of nuclear weaponry was mixed with a much larger population of nuclear devices that were the primary source of destruction, and thus EMP as a weapons effect was not the primary focus.

As long as the Cold War threat arose principally from the prospect of tens, hundreds or even thousands of nuclear weapons detonating on American soil, such attention as was given to protecting against EMP effects was confined to shielding critical components of our strategic forces. The military's conventional forces were generally not systematically "hardened" against such effects. And little, if any, effort was made even to assess—let alone to mitigate—the vulnerabilities of our civilian infrastructure. As the theory went, as long as our nuclear deterrent worked, there was no need to worry about everything else. If, on the other hand, deterrence failed, the disruptions caused by EMP would be pretty far down the list of things about which we would have to worry.

Unfortunately, today's strategic environment has changed dramatically from that of the Cold War, when only the Soviet Union and Communist China could realistically threaten an EMP attack on the United States. In particular, as the EMP Threat Commission put it:

> The emerging threat environment, characterized by a wide spectrum of actors that include near-peers, established nuclear powers, rogue nations, sub-national groups, and terrorist organizations that either now have access to nuclear weapons and ballistic missiles or may have such access over the next 15 years, have combined to raise the risk of EMP attack and adverse consequences on the U.S. to a level that is not acceptable.

Worse yet, the Commission observed that "some potential sources of EMP threats are difficult to deter." This is particularly true of "terrorist groups that have no state identity, have only one or a few weapons, and are motivated to attack the U.S. without regard for their own safety." The same might be said of rogue states, such as North Korea and Iran. They "may also be developing the capability to pose an EMP threat to the United States, and may also be unpredictable and difficult to deter." Indeed, professionals associated with the former Soviet nuclear weapons complex are said to have told the Commission that some of their ex-colleagues who worked on advanced nuclear weaponry programs for the USSR are now working in North Korea.

Even more troubling, the Iranian military has reportedly tested its Shahab-3 medium-range ballistic missile in a manner consistent with an EMP attack scenario. The launches are said to have taken place from aboard a ship—an approach that would enable even short-range missiles to be employed in a strike against "the Great Satan." Ship-launched ballistic missiles have another advantage: The "return address" of the attacker may not be confidently fixed, especially if the missile is a generic Scud-type weapon available in many arsenals around the world. As just one example, in December 2002, North Korea got away with delivering twelve such missiles to Osama bin Laden's native Yemen. And al-Qaeda is estimated to have a score or more of sea-going vessels, any of which could readily be fitted with a Scud launcher and could try to steam undetected within range of our shores.

The EMP Threat Commission found that even nations with whom the United States is supposed to have friendly relations, China and Russia, are said to have considered limited nuclear attack options that, unlike their Cold War plans, employ EMP as the primary or sole means of attack. Indeed, as recently as May 1999, during the NATO bombing of the former Yugoslavia, high-ranking members of the Russian Duma, meeting with a U.S. congressional delegation to discuss the Balkans conflict, raised the specter of a Russian EMP attack that would paralyze the United States.

America the Vulnerable

What makes the growing EMP attack capabilities of hostile (and potentially hostile) nations a particular problem for America is that, in the words of the EMP Threat Commission, "the U.S. has developed more than most other nations as a modern society heavily dependent on electronics, telecommunications, energy, information networks, and a rich set of financial and transportation systems that leverage modern technology." Given our acute national dependence on such technologies, it is astonishing—and alarming—to realize that:

- Very little redundancy has been built into America's critical infra-structure. There is, for example, no parallel "national security power grid" built to enjoy greater resiliency than the civilian grid.

- America's critical infrastructure has scarcely any capacity to spare in the event of disruption—even in one part of the country (recall the electrical blackout that crippled the northeastern U.S. for just a few days in 2003), let alone nationwide.

- America is generally ill-prepared to reconstitute damaged or destroyed electrical and electricity-dependent systems upon which we rely so heavily.

These conditions are not entirely surprising. America in peacetime has not traditionally given thought to military preparedness, given our highly efficient economy and its ability to respond quickly when a threat or attack arises. But EMP threatens to strip our economy of that ability, by rendering the infrastructure on which it relies impotent.

In short, the attributes that make us a military and economic superpower without peer are also our potential Achilles' heel. In today's world, wracked by terrorists and their state sponsors, it must be asked: Might not the opportunity to exploit the essence of America's strength—the managed flow of electrons and all they make possible—in order to undo that strength prove irresistible to our foes? This line of thinking seems especially likely among our Islamofascist enemies, who disdain such manmade sources of power and the sorts of democratic, humane, and secular societies which they help make possible. These enemies believe it to be their God-given responsibility to wage jihad against Western societies in general and the United States in particular.

Calculations that might lead some to contemplate an EMP attack on the United States can only be further encouraged by the fact that our ability to retaliate could be severely degraded by such a strike. In all likelihood, so would our ability to assess against whom to retaliate. Even if forward-deployed U.S. forces were unaffected by the devastation wrought on the homeland by such an attack, many of the systems that transmit their orders and the industrial base necessary to sustain their operations would almost certainly be seriously disrupted.

The impact on the American military's offensive operations would be even further diminished should units based outside the continental United States also be subjected to EMP. Particularly with the end of the Cold War, the Pentagon has been reluctant to pay the costs associated with shielding much of its equipment from electromagnetic pulses. Even if it had been more willing to do so, the end of underground nuclear testing in 1992 denied our armed forces their most reliable means of assessing and correcting the EMP vulnerabilities of weapon systems, sensors, telecommunications gear, and satellites.

The military should also be concerned that although the sorts of shielding it has done in the past may be sufficient to protect against the EMP effects of traditional nuclear weapons designs, weapons optimized for such effects may well be able to defeat those measures. Without a robust program for assessing and testing advanced designs, we are unlikely to be able to quantify such threats—let alone protect our military hardware and capabilities against them.

What is to be Done?

If the EMP Threat Commission is correct about the phenomenon of electromagnetic pulse attacks, the capabilities of our enemies to engage in these attacks and the effects of such attacks on our national security, cosmopolitan society and democratic way of life, we have no choice but to take urgent action to mitigate this danger. To do so, we must immediately engage in three focused efforts:

First, *we must do everything possible to deter EMP attacks against the United States.* The EMP Threat Commission described a comprehensive approach:

> We must make it difficult and dangerous to acquire the materials to make a nuclear weapon and the means to deliver them. We must hold at risk of capture or destruction anyone who has such weaponry, wherever they are in the world. Those who engage in or support these activities must be made to understand that they do so at the risk of everything they value. Those who harbor or help those who conspire to create these weapons must suffer serious consequences as well.

To be effective, these measures will require vastly improved intelligence, the capacity to perform clandestine operations the world over, and the assured means of retaliating with devastating effect. The latter, in turn, will require not only forces capable of carrying out such retaliation in the aftermath of an EMP attack, but also the certain ability to command and control those forces. It may also require the communication, at least through private if not public channels, of the targets that will be subjected to retaliation—irrespective of whether a definitive determination can be made of culpability.

Second, *we must protect to the best of our ability our critical military capabilities and civilian infrastructure from the effects of EMP attacks.* This will require a comprehensive assessment of our vulnerabilities and proof of the effectiveness of corrective measures. Both of these may require, among other things, periodic underground nuclear testing.

The EMP Threat Commission judged that, given the sorry state of EMP-preparedness on the part of the tactical forces of the United States and its coalition partners, "It is not possible to protect [all of them] from EMP in a regional conflict." But it recommended that priority be given to protecting "satellite navigation systems, satellite and airborne intelligence and targeting systems [and] an adequate communications infrastructure."

Particularly noteworthy was the Commission's recommendation that America build a ballistic missile defense system. Given that a catastrophic EMP attack can be mounted only by putting a nuclear weapon into space over the United States and that, as a practical matter, this can only be done via a ballistic missile, it is imperative that the United States deploy as quickly as possible a comprehensive defense against such delivery systems. In particular, every effort should be made to give the Navy's existing fleet of some 65 AEGIS air defense ships the capability to shoot down short- to medium-range missiles of the kind that might well be used to carry out ship-launched EMP strikes.

Third, *an aggressive and sustained effort must be made to plan and otherwise prepare for the consequences of an EMP attack in the event all else fails.* This will require close collaboration between government at all levels and the private sector, which owns, designs, builds, and operates most of the nation's critical infrastructure. Among other things, we will need to do a far better job of monitoring that infrastructure and remediating events that could ensue if EMP attacks are made on it. We must also ensure that we have on hand, and properly protected, the equipment and parts—especially those that are difficult or time-consuming to produce—needed to repair EMP-damaged systems. The EMP Threat Commission identified the latter as including "large turbines, generators, and high-voltage transformers in electrical power systems, and electronic switching systems in telecommunications systems."

Conclusion

We have been warned. The members of the EMP Threat Commission—who are among the nation's most eminent experts with respect to nuclear weapons designs and effects—have rendered a real and timely public service. In the aftermath of their report and in the face of the dire warnings they have issued, there is no excuse for our continued inaction. Yet this report and these warnings continue to receive inadequate attention from the executive branch, Congress and the media. If Americans remain ignorant of the EMP danger and the need for urgent and sustained effort to address it, the United States will continue to remain woefully unprepared for one of the most serious dangers we have ever faced. And by remaining unprepared for such an attack, we will invite it.

The good news is that steps can be taken to mitigate this danger—and perhaps to prevent an EMP attack altogether. The bad news is that there will be significant costs associated with those steps, in terms of controversial policy changes and considerable expenditures. We have no choice but to bear such costs, however. The price of continued inaction could be a disaster of infinitely greater cost and unimaginable hardship for our generation and generations of Americans to come.

Foreign Policy and
the Constitution

Tom Cotton

October 2015

In the last week, President Obama moved ahead with a nuclear-arms control agreement with a mortal and unrepentant enemy, having the support only of a rump, partisan minority in Congress. This dangerous turn of events offers an occasion to reflect on the state of American foreign policy today and on the Constitution's place in our foreign policy.

Over the past 25 years, a major preoccupation of foreign-policy elites has been to forge a new grand strategy for the United States. Scholars and practitioners tend to see a foreign policy adrift after the fall of the Soviet Union, when containment of Soviet expansion became obsolete overnight. Seeing no major ideological or military rival, some believed the Owl of Minerva had taken flight, and that the end of history had reduced the need for strategic thinking. Alas, that fantasy came crashing down along with two big towers 14 years ago this month. Again, foreign-policy elites searched for a new strategy, this time for the age of Islamic terror.

Circumstances do change, and foreign policy, often a matter of prudence, must change with them to achieve the same ends. Too often, however, the search for a new strategy simply becomes the search for something *new*. This way of thinking carries a hint of disdain for the principles and foreign policy traditions of our past—and disdaining those principles and traditions is a mistake. When the makers of breakfast cereals roll out a new product, after all, they say it's "new *and* improved," because the former doesn't necessarily imply the latter.

Likewise, every new and fashionable idea in foreign policy isn't necessarily an improvement. To the contrary, we ought to pay some respect to older foreign policy ideas—the ideas that took us from a small and weak colonial outpost to the greatest superpower in history in just 170 years. With that track record, common sense would suggest there's something special we can learn from the Constitution—and the strategies that arose from it—to help us chart our way in the world.

———

Our Founders gave us a constitutional democracy, a system of government that informs our foreign policy just as it does our domestic policy. For many foreign-policy elites, especially those abroad, this is a serious problem for U.S. foreign policy. The Constitution empowers the people, these critics say, and the people, they believe, can be ignorant, emotional, and fickle, swinging wildly from war mongering to isolationism, from moralism to callousness. Far better, they say, is what Walter Mead has called the "auteur theory of foreign policy"—a foreign policy guided by a brilliant strategist, insulated from the unruly masses.

One hears an echo of this viewpoint in the praise for what these critics see as the coherent and decisive strategic thinking of Russia's Vladimir Putin and China's Xi Jinping. Putin is praised as a brilliant strategist who is redefining 21st-century warfare. Xi has been called a game-changer in China's rise, one whose ambitions and power rival those of Mao Zedong and Deng Xiaoping.

I'll admit that Putin and Xi may have stolen a march on our president here and there. But that's an indictment of President Obama's particular abilities and policies, not of our system. By the traditional measures of international influence—economic might, per capita measures of wellbeing, military and trade cooperation agreements, cultural weight—the United States far outpaces both Russia and China, as well as the rest of the world.

And while a brooding auteur may in fact have strategic foresight, intellect, and prudence, no man is infallible, no matter how talented. Napoleon, brilliant general that he was, still marched the Grand Armée across the Nieman River into Russia. Otto von Bismarck toiled for decades to unify the German states, only to see his fragile work undone a few years later by Wilhelm II's militarism and adventurism. In the same way, I believe that over time Putin and Xi—to say nothing of North Korea's Kim Jong Un or the ayatollahs in Tehran—will also miscalculate and suffer strategic setbacks.

But the United States is different from these regimes. Our constitutional system doesn't depend on brilliant leaders. "Enlightened statesmen," as Madison wrote in *Federalist* 10, "will not always be at the helm." Our system is based on individual rights, safeguarded by well crafted, ultimately democratic institutions. While we always hope for wise leaders, our Constitution works in their absence by filtering the wisdom of the people through those institutions.

This approach couldn't be more at odds with the auteur theory of foreign policy. From that perspective, our system looks like some kind of policymaking Frankenstein. Authority is divided between the executive and the legislature, and the executive itself is divided among competing departments. The president and secretary of state serve short tenures compared to the kings and ministers of the Old World. Equal representation of states in the Senate gives considerable influence to regional interests. The arcane rules of the Senate, along with the separation of powers itself, slow the whole process down. How could this ever work?

Yet it does, again and again. The talent of a single leader or a small group with outsized control over foreign policy can never match the moderation, prudence, and self-correcting capability of our constitutional democracy over the long term. And in international relations, it's the long term that counts.

In the realm of domestic policy, these ideas are familiar. Our constitutional system works to ensure that all the individuals, interests, factions, lobbies, and others who influence and are influenced by domestic policy are more or less satisfied—or perhaps minimally dissatisfied. And the same thing plays out in foreign policy. America's foreign policy tradition is flexible, agile, and multifaceted, and it therefore tends to produce positive results for us in a complicated world.

Again, I cannot stress enough how alien and unfashionable this way of thinking is in Foggy Bottom and in the West Wing, not to mention European ministries. Among many foreign-policy elites, these democratic influences are something to be suffered and overcome—as we've seen most recently in the debate about the Iran nuclear deal. In the end, though, we usually survive mistakes by particular leaders because leaders are not the foundation of our system. The foundation of U.S. foreign policy is the views and values of the American people, filtered by elected representatives through democratic institutions, proven by time.

This foreign policy tradition is not an accident. When designing the Constitution, the Founders were very conscious of the need to invest the federal government with strong foreign affairs powers, while accounting for the interests of the states and the people.

A driving force behind the Constitutional Convention was the failure of the Continental Congress to manage the foreign affairs of the young republic. This imperative was clear in the ratification debates. The first five papers of *The Federalist* are devoted to the necessity of blunting the influence of foreign powers and to the organization of U.S. military power. Fifteen additional papers focus on international relations and civilian control of the military.

Against this background, the Constitution could be understood not only as a national charter, but also as a strategic document. The institutions established by the Constitution to channel the conduct of foreign policy imply certain principles of foreign policy. We ought to keep these timeless principles in mind as we craft strategy for today's world.

One principle we find in the Constitution is so simple it's usually overlooked: the states are stronger as a Union than as separate powers. A Union of the states overcame divisions of culture, economic interest, and military capacity—divisions that would have been exploited by foreign powers to turn one state against another, and to weaken and cow the American continent into submitting to their designs.

A Union strengthened the collective power of the states in their foreign relations. It allowed them to pool their various resources to create advantages of scale and scope in military and economic power. As *Federalist* 4 states, "The people of America . . . consider union and a good national government as necessary to put and keep them in such a situation as, instead of inviting war, will tend to repress and discourage it." Further, "If [foreign powers] see that our national government is efficient . . . our trade prudently regulated, our militia properly organized and disciplined, our resources and finances discreetly managed, our credit re-established, our people free, contented, and united, they will be much more disposed to cultivate our friendship than provoke our resentment." Conversely, if the states remained divided, the U.S. would earn not only the "contempt" of foreign nations, but their "outrage."

This principle came under threat— but survived—during the Civil War. In his First Annual Message to Congress, President Lincoln sent a clear warning to foreign powers to refrain from interfering in the war. At the same time, he acknowledged that "factious domestic division" exposed the nation to "disrespect abroad."

We may take this principle for granted today, but it's very much in play around the world. The European Union, for example, has a greater combined population and economy than the U.S. But political division greatly reduces the EU's role in world affairs. The smaller nation-states of Central and Eastern Europe, in particular, find themselves at risk from—or perhaps at the mercy of—Russia. Likewise, the countries of the Asia-Pacific region, from South Korea to India, worry about China's aggressive drive for regional hegemony. Yet they struggle, due to their own enmity and rivalries, to form a united strategy to counter China.

The primacy of Union gives rise to a second, subsidiary principle: treaties with foreign powers are very serious business, ought not be entered into lightly, and must be widely supported across the country.

The Founders believed the violation of major foreign commitments was a chief source of friction and war in international relations. In fact, *Federalist 3* recognized only two sources of war: direct violence and the breach of treaties. Thus the Constitution requires that a major foreign commitment that binds our nation have a broad consensus among the people, and not result from the parochial interests of a minority or even a narrow majority. As matters of war and peace, treaties should reflect a strong Union, not a divided nation.

This principle led to the Treaty Clause, which empowers the president to negotiate treaties, but requires two-thirds of the Senate to approve them and—if necessary—to demand changes. This extraordinary requirement is really just an ongoing expression of the original decision to form a Union. And it has produced a system in which treaties routinely go through many iterations and rounds of negotiations, even after initial signature by the president. Treaties throughout our history carry scores of conditions, reservations, and amendments added by Congress, precisely to ensure widespread acceptance among the people.

This was in fact how the first treaty ratified under the Treaty Clause played out. The Jay Treaty with Britain— negotiated by a co-author of *The Federalist*—only gained Senate approval on the condition that Jay rework the treaty to add a clause regarding trade between the United States and the British West Indies.

Another principle of foreign policy rooted in the Constitution is that the Union must have a strong military, but one that is at the same time restrained and subject to the control of the people.

At the time of the Founding, a powerful and restrained military was something of an oxymoron. *Federalist* 11, for instance, states that a strong military—and in particular a strong navy—is vital not only to deter aggression, but also to secure and expand international trade. Yet *Federalist* 26 recognizes that military might has historically posed a grave threat to individual liberty. This presented what seemed to be a Hobson's choice between a strong military and a weak military, both of which would threaten liberty over time.

But our Founders charted a way out of this dilemma. The Constitution empowered the president, as commander-in-chief, to defend against attack and take decisive military action where necessary. At the same time, it entrusted the people's representatives in Congress with a wide range of foreign affairs powers as a means of fostering prudence, democratic control, and protection against tyranny. Thus only Congress can raise and support armies; only Congress may declare war and invoke the legal obligations and protections that this state of international relations confers; only Congress regulates foreign commerce, and with it control over important levers of influence with foreign nations in order to better relations, exact costs, and prevent war.

Under President Obama, there has been considerable drift away from all three of these principles. And that drift has contributed to the general drift of U.S. foreign policy. Even former President Carter has said, "I can't think of many nations in the world where we have a better relationship now than when he took over." Our interests are threatened, our alliances are stressed, our honor is stained, and our adversaries are increasingly tempted into new episodes of adventurism and aggression.

The most recent example of this drift is the Iran nuclear deal. This is a major arms-control agreement with a mortal enemy—an enemy with the blood of thousands of Americans on its hands, and for whom "death to America" is a foreign-policy bedrock. And the agreement goes to the heart of the gravest threat facing the world: a terror-sponsoring state armed with nuclear weapons. It is precisely the type of agreement that the Founders intended to be tested and refined by the treaty process. It is precisely the type of agreement implicating matters of war and peace that must be supported by a widespread consensus of the American people.

But the President didn't submit the Iran nuclear deal as a treaty. From the beginning, his intention was to circumvent the people's representatives and obligate the U.S. to the ayatollahs by a mere executive agreement. Instead of rallying two-thirds of the Senate to support the deal, he relied on a tiny, partisan minority to protect his executive agreement from the judgment of the American people.

This is dangerous and nearly unprecedented. Executive agreements are and should be reserved for technical matters. Among the first executive agreements in our history were the 1792 agreements between the United States and other nations to coordinate mail delivery. Executive agreements have also traditionally been used to assign claims and debts between nations. These issues are low-stakes, and are not breeding grounds for armed conflict. They are akin to deciding whether cars will drive on the right or left side of the road. That's why they do not need to be tested by a supermajority vote.

Nuclear weapons agreements are different. The dividing line between subjects reserved for treaties and subjects reserved for less formal scrutiny is not precise at the margins. But this isn't anywhere near the margins. Historically, major arms control agreements that bind the U.S. have almost invariably been reached through treaty. One notable exception was the Agreed Framework with North Korea negotiated under President Clinton in 1994, which aimed at keeping North Korea from becoming a nuclear power. I doubt President Obama would like to cite the North Korea case as precedent—although it surely is a precedent in its contempt for Congress, and likely in its failure as well.

Why did President Obama ignore the Treaty Clause? The answer is stunning. Secretary of State Kerry lamented in testimony to Congress that it is "physically impossible" to get a treaty through the Senate in these polarized times. Of course, this logic could apply to any politically inconvenient part of the Constitution. Moreover, Secretary Kerry must have forgotten that, as chairman of the Senate Foreign Relations Committee, he guided a nuclear arms control treaty with Russia to ratification less than five years ago.

The simple fact is that the President ignored the Constitution because he knew the Senate would reject his deal. This disregard for the Treaty Clause is the height of hubris. It mistakes tunnel vision for principle, closed-mindedness for superior wisdom, and personal legacy for the vital national interest. The nuclear deal with Iran is a travesty, one that betrays our close friend Israel, provides billions for Iran's campaign of terror, and paves the way for Iran to obtain nuclear weapons capability.

Besides the immediate damage to our national security, the deal also damages the foundational principle that major foreign commitments should be backed by a broad consensus of the people as reflected by Congress. This episode, added to the North Korea example, will make it extremely tempting for future presidents to avoid the expenditure of political capital required to pass a treaty. Presidents will be tempted to reach expedient deals on momentous issues, deals that divide rather than unite the nation.

———

While the Iran deal is the latest blow to our foreign policy tradition, a long-festering wound is the decline of our military might. Our military has endured 15 years of war and six years of repeated budget cuts. It is now breaking under the burden of a mindless sequestration that indiscriminately cuts across the board and treats every dollar of federal spending equally—whether for defense or for pork. As a consequence, our military is facing a crisis. The Navy has 260 ships— the smallest number since the end of the Cold War. Our Air Force is the smallest and oldest force in our history. The Army and the Marine Corps are on track to drop below 450,000 and 190,000 personnel, respectively—the bare minimum levels our commanders say we need to fulfill our missions.

These unwise cuts to our military call into question U.S. resolve and security commitments. It's not a coincidence that, in the span of a few years, we have seen a revisionist Russia exert its will in Ukraine and in the Middle East, radical Jihadism metastasize across the Middle East and North Africa, China project power over more and more aerial and maritime territories, and Iran out-negotiate us while it spreads chaos across the Middle East through its proxies and clients.

This picture isn't pretty, but as I said earlier, the American foreign policy tradition has a knack for self-correction, for turning the ship around and reversing past mistakes. To make that happen, however, we need to look back to the foundational principles of our Constitution. To restore respect for the Treaty Clause, we must make every effort over the next year to isolate and impugn the President's nuclear deal with Iran as a singular, one-off agreement that ought never to be repeated. We must put every nation and every business on notice that this deal is temporary and unique. They must understand that U.S. sanctions on Iran—either through new legislation or through a new president—will return. We must work to elect a new president who will rescind the Iran nuclear deal—and who will restore the credible threat of force.

Put simply, our allies and our adversaries must understand that this nuclear arms control deal reached by executive agreement is not secure. They have to understand that it is in our interest and in their interest to conclude stable and long-lasting agreements by way of treaties. And all future presidents should see that building consensus through the constitutionally mandated advice and consent of the Senate will afford them a genuine, lasting legacy.

A restoration of the Treaty Clause must be accompanied by a restoration of our military might. Frederick the Great said, "Diplomacy without arms is like music without instruments"—in other words, inert, inaudible, and ineffective. If we want our diplomacy to be effective and our agreements to be strong, we must rebuild our military.

The American tradition has never been to seek war, or to seek it first in a dispute. Lincoln, again in his First Annual Message to Congress, prized diplomacy as a means of defusing tensions with foreign powers and maintaining our "rights and honor." But he also called for a military build-up. "Aggressions," said his Secretary of War Simon Cameron, "are seldom made upon a nation ever ready to defend its honor and to repel insults."

To ensure that we are ready to defend our national honor today, we will need significantly more defense spending than Congress and the President have managed to agree upon in recent years. Our current defense budget is little more than a political compromise, which may be appropriate for highway funding or tax policy, but which is no way to fund a military or to counter rising threats. Congress and the President must return to the foundational principle that our military edge must not be challenged. We must give our fighting men and women the resources they need to deter, fight, and win wars.

The Founders and generations of statesmen since have recognized the unique advantages with which the United States is blessed. We are a continental nation, and we enjoy the protection of two oceans that separate us from the historic cauldrons of conflict in Europe and Asia. We have abundant natural resources and an industrious society, making us a powerful trading partner. Ours is a people slow to anger, but imbued with a martial tradition and a fighting spirit. Our democratic culture is vigorous, resilient, and cherished by the people. These strengths are channeled by the Constitution into our foreign policy tradition. U.S. strategy abroad—while not successful in every instance—has brought us from being a world-affairs backwater to being the world's superpower.

As we think about our future and new strategies, it would serve us well to look back at old truths. We must hold fast to foundational principles. We must continue our rich foreign policy tradition, and vigorously fight any efforts to undermine it. While each Congress and president will have particular differences, we should all share the same goal: a world of peace and freedom, of prosperity and opportunity, of hope. We have a duty to be true to our beliefs, to use our great power wisely on behalf of freedom, guided by constitutional principle. As Ronald Reagan admonished in his speech to the British Parliament in 1982, "Let us go to our strength. Let us offer hope. Let us tell the world that a new age is not only possible but probable."

How to Meet the Strategic Challenge Posed by China

David P. Goldman

March 2018

China poses a formidable strategic challenge to America, but we should keep in mind that it is in large part motivated by insecurity and fear. America has inherent strengths that China does not. And the greatest danger to America is not a lack of strength, but complacency.

China is a phenomenon unlike anything in economic history. The average Chinese consumes 17 times more today than in 1987. This is like the difference between driving a car and riding a bicycle or between indoor plumbing and an outhouse. In an incredibly short period of time, this formerly backward country has lifted itself into the very first rank of world economies.

Over the same period, China has moved approximately 600 million people from the countryside to the cities—the equivalent of moving the entire population of Europe from the Ural Mountains to the Atlantic Ocean. To accommodate those people, it built the equivalent of a new London, plus a new Berlin, Rome, Glasgow, Helsinki, Naples, and Lyons. And of course, moving people whose ancestors spent millennia in the monotony of traditional village life and bringing them into the industrial world led to an explosion of productivity.

Where does America stand in respect to China? By a measure economists call purchasing power parity, you can buy a lot more with $100 in China than you can in the United States. Adjusted for that measure, the Chinese economy is already bigger than ours. In terms of dollars, our economy is still bigger. But the Chinese are gaining on us, and in the next eight to ten years their economy—unlike the economies of our previous competitors—will catch up.

China, on the other hand, is an empire based on the coercion of unwilling people. Whereas the United States became a great nation populated by people who chose to be part of it, China conquered peoples of different ethnicities and with different languages and has kept them together by force. Whereas our principle is *E Pluribus Unum*, the Chinese reality is *E Pluribus Pluribus* with a dictator at the top.

China once covered a relatively small geographic area. It took about 1,500 years for it to reach its current borders in the ninth century. These borders are natural frontiers. China can't expand over the Himalayas to India, while to its extreme west is desert and to its east is the ocean. So China is not an inherently expansionist power.

Nor is China unified. It has a written system of several thousand characters that takes seven years of elementary education to learn, working four hours a day with an ink brush, ink pot, and paper. Learning these characters well enough to read a school textbook or a newspaper is how the Chinese are socialized. The current generation is the first where the majority of Chinese understand the common language, due to the centralization of the state and the mass media. But the Chinese still *speak* very different languages. Cantonese and Mandarin are as different as Finnish and French. In Hong Kong, you'll see two Chinese screaming at each other in broken English because one speaks Mandarin and the other speaks Cantonese and they don't have a word in common.

China is inherently unstable because all that holds it together is an imperial culture and the tax collector in Beijing. It is like a collection of very powerful, oppositely charged magnets held together by super glue—it looks stable, but it isn't.

Within the living memory of older Chinese, China underwent an era of national division, warlordism, civil war, starvation, and degradation. The

Century of Humiliation, as the Chinese call it—which began with the opium wars in 1848 and ended with the success of the Communist Revolution in 1949—was a century in which civil war claimed untold millions of lives, and the terror of a return to those conditions is a specter that haunts the Chinese leadership.

China, like Russia, responds to its past humiliation by challenging American power. It would be naïve to expect the Chinese or the Russians to be our friends; the best we can hope for is peaceful competition and occasional cooperation in matters of mutual concern. But it is also important to recognize that American policy errors exacerbate their suspicion and distrust. For example, our decision to impose majority rule in Iraq created a Shi'ite sectarian state now allied to Iran, and it left Iraq's Sunni minority without a state to protect them. This drove the Sunnis into the hands of non-state actors and unintentionally helped al-Qaeda and ISIS. Sunni jihad is a serious security threat to Russia and China, and Russia's intervention in Syria is, in part, a response to our mistakes.

The Chinese live a double life. If you walk down the street in Beijing, you see people who dress very drably, who show little emotion and do their best not to draw attention to themselves. But if you go to a Chinese wedding or a restaurant where families gather, the same people are loud and bumptious. Their real existence is a family existence. During the Lunar New Year, the Chinese have the largest migration in history—three billion long-distance journeys are undertaken—because all Chinese will travel long distances to be with their family.

Here in the West, we have a concept of rights and privileges that traces back to the Roman Republic—we serve in the army, we pay taxes, and the state has certain obligations in return. There is no such concept in China. Beijing rules by whim. The Chinese do whatever the emperor—or today, the Communist Party—asks, hoping they will be rewarded. But there is no sense of anything deserved. The idea of the state held together by a common interest as in Cicero, or by a common love as in St. Augustine, is unknown in China. The imperial power is looked on as a necessary evil. The Chinese had an emperor for 3,000 years, and when they didn't have an emperor they killed one another. It's all very well to lecture the Chinese about the benefits of Western democracy, but most Chinese believe they need the equivalent of an emperor to prevent a reprise of the Century of Humiliation.

From the standpoint of most Chinese, the Communist Party dynasty that took charge in 1949 has brought about a golden age. It's the first time in Chinese history when no one is afraid of starving to death or of a warlord coming through and raping the women and burning the crops. So for the time being, the regime has a great deal of support, even though it is more comprehensively totalitarian than Hitler or Stalin could have imagined. As deplorable as the regime looks to us, the prospects for transforming China's way of governance are for now negligible.

China's Communist Party government is a merciless meritocracy, which is one reason the Chinese have difficulty understanding American politics. If you're in the Chinese leadership, you made it there by scoring high on a long series of exams, starting at age twelve—which means you haven't met a stupid person since you were in junior high school. The fact that democracies can frequently advance stupid people—we are entitled to do that if we wish—doesn't make sense to the Chinese. The one thing President Xi Jinping cannot do is get his child into Peking University unless that child scores high on his exams. Here in America, you can buy your way into Harvard. You can't do that in China. So while the Chinese Communist Party is not a particularly efficient organization, and is certainly not a moral one, it has a lot of incredibly smart people in it.

Along with ensuring internal stability at all costs, China's leaders are determined to make China impregnable from the outside. We hardly hear the term South China Sea these days, because that sea has become a Chinese lake. It has become a Chinese lake because the Chinese have made it clear they will go to war over it. There's a Chinese proverb: "Kill the chicken for the instruction of the monkey." China has an even greater concern over Taiwan. The Chinese Communist Party is terrified that a rebel province like Taiwan can set in motion centrifugal forces that the Party will be unable to control. So the adhesion of Taiwan to the Chinese state—the imperial center—is for the Chinese government an existential matter. They will go to war over it. By demonstrating their willingness to fight over the South China Sea, they are demonstrating that they will fight all the more viciously over Taiwan.

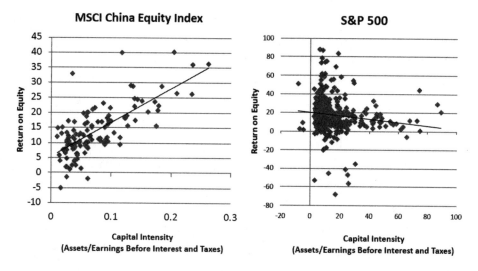

MSCI China Equity Index

Return on Equity

Capital Intensity
(Assets/Earnings Before Interest and Taxes)

S&P 500

Return on Equity

Capital Intensity
(Assets/Earnings Before Interest and Taxes)

Source: Bloomberg

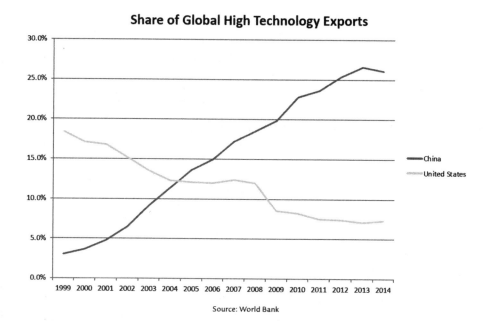

Share of Global High Technology Exports

China
United States

Source: World Bank

Turning back to our two economies, consider the three graphs above. China does something that Japan, Korea, and other Asian nations do—it massively subsidizes capital investment in heavy industry. From the Chinese standpoint, a steel mill or a semiconductor fabrication plant are public goods—the Chinese look at these things the way we look at highways and airports. And as a result of Chinese subsidies for heavy industry, America has been pushed out of any major capital-intensive manufacturing. Thirty years ago the Japanese were doing this, which is why the Reagan administration took steps to force the Japanese to build car plants in the U.S. But Japan's economy was very small compared to ours. Because China's economy is roughly the same size as ours, the impact of Chinese subsidies is huge.

The first graph shows the capital intensity of the companies in the major Chinese stock index (MSCI) versus their return on equity. The more capital-intensive, the higher the return. In the United States, on the other hand, if you look at the S&P 500 on the second graph, the slope is in the other direction. More capital-intensive industries are less profitable. This distortion of global investment by Chinese subsidies for heavy industry has led to a stripping out of capital from American heavy industry. It's not that Americans prefer financial assets to real assets—it's that the Chinese have pushed us out. That's why we've lost so much ground in terms of industry.

As the third graph shows, China's share of high tech exports has risen from about five percent in 1999 to about 25 percent at present, while America's has plummeted from about 20 percent to about seven percent. That's not a sustainable situation. What it means in practical terms is that America can't build a military aircraft without Chinese chips. That's a national security issue.

China's "One Belt, One Road" policy, announced by President Xi in 2013, is a plan to dominate industry throughout Eurasia—both by land (belt) and by sea (road).

As a rule, so-called developing economies *don't* develop, because 40 percent of the people are outside of the formal economy—they're in the "underground" economy, mostly in small villages, and they live relatively unproductive lives. What the Chinese have done is to rip out the social structure of village life.

China's economy is nothing like Japan's, because Japan wanted to maintain its social structure. The Japanese protected agriculture, small retail, and small business. So in Japan we see a few great companies with global capacity sitting on top of a protected, inefficient economy. In China, which moved the mass of people from the villages to the cities, their equivalent of Amazon—Alibaba—will manage labor back in the villages. The Chinese have broadband everywhere, so as entrepreneurs figure out what villages can make, the villages will work for them.

The Chinese intentionally dismantled their social structure to avoid Japan's constraints. And what they propose to do with "One Belt, One Road" is repeat that experiment throughout all of Asia—to Sinofy every country from Turkey to Southeast Asia.

A couple years ago, I visited the headquarters of Huawei, China's telecommunications company—the biggest in the world—which hardly existed a dozen years ago. It has a campus that makes Stanford look like a swamp. Today it has 70 percent of the world market in telecommunications. How did Huawei do that? It cut prices and got massive subsidies from the government. After a three-hour tour, the Chinese sat the Latin Americans I was with down in a little amphitheater and said, "If you turn your economy over to us, we will make you like China. We'll put in telecommunications. We'll put in broadband. We'll bring in e-commerce. We'll bring in e-finance. You'll be advanced like we are." The Latin Americans didn't take the deal, but the Turks have taken it.

Turkey plans to be a cash-free society in five years. Chinese telecommunications companies are rebuilding the Turkish broadband network. Turkey has given up on the West and is becoming the western economic province of China.

The impact of what China is doing is felt all over the world. Former allies of the U.S., including former NATO members, are orienting towards China. Russia—which has become totally dependent on China—has quadrupled its energy exports to China, providing China with land-based energy imports in case the U.S. tries interfering with seaborne energy traffic.

China has an extensive high-speed rail network, with trains going 200 miles an hour. This has had huge productivity effects, and the Chinese are proposing to build these trains all over Southeast Asia. Thailand, an agricultural country, sees that with high-speed trains built by China, it can become the source of fresh fruits and vegetables for China. So Thailand—which used to be an American ally—is being absorbed into the Chinese economy. And so on.

One of the most dangerous misconceptions Americans have about the Chinese is that they can't innovate. Who do you think invented gunpowder, the magnetic compass, the clock, and movable type? Yes, China's culture is much more conformist than ours. And on average, Chinese are less likely than Americans to be innovators. But there are 1.38 billion Chinese, and their research and development (R&D) spending is quickly catching up with ours. They're producing four times as many science, technology, engineering, and mathematics (STEM) bachelor's degrees and twice as many STEM Ph.D.s as the United States. Granted, some of them are of low quality—but many are excellent.

The single most troublesome deficiency we have in the United States is not the industrial base, which is relatively easy to deal with. It is the lack of scientific and engineering education. Six or seven percent of U.S. college students major in engineering. In China that number is 30-40 percent. That's our biggest problem. Second to that is the fact, already mentioned, that there is a massive distortion of the global economic system caused by Chinese industrial policy.

The Chinese play very dirty. One of the issues raised in the Trump administration's recent National Security Strategy is forced technology transfer. That is, if Intel wants to get access to the Chinese market—the biggest chip market in the world—China requires Intel to divulge everything it knows. From the standpoint of Intel stock price over the next five to ten years, that's a pretty good deal. But it is bad from the standpoint of America's national interest. If the U.S. government prohibits the transfer of technology to China, the Intels and the Texas Instruments of the world will scream, because it will hurt their stock prices. I'm a free trader, but national security sometimes supersedes the free market. This would be such a case.

Virtually all of American investment in R&D today goes to software. This means that we've conceded to Asia, and especially China, the actual manufacturing, to the point that—this bears repeating—we can't put a warplane in the air without Chinese chips.

So what do we do about China? The answer is not to adopt an industrial policy. As Americans, we believe in individual liberty. We are not good at being collectivists. China and Germany have industrial policies. Culturally they can deal with it. We cannot. If we're going to compete with China, we've got to do it the American way. And what we are best at is innovation.

In the 1970s, all the smart people thought Russia was going to win the Cold War. Economists at the CIA and in the universities believed that Russia had a great economy. But by 1989, we realized that the Russian economy was a piece of junk. It actually had a negative worth, because the cost of environmental cleanup exceeded the value of whatever Russia was producing.

What happened in the interim was the greatest wave of industrial innovation in American history. We invented fast, light, small, inexpensive microchips. We invented sensors that didn't exist before. We invented the semiconductor laser. And we did virtually all of this through the Defense Advanced Research Projects Agency and NASA, in cooperation with the great corporate laboratories.

The U.S. turned the Russian economy into junk by creating an economy that hadn't existed before. That was the Reagan economy. During this creation, the Fortune 500 lost employment. The monopolies were all ruined. New companies no one ever heard of sprang up to commercialize the new technologies, and corruption declined because we had challengers taking market share away from the entrenched interests.

In 1983, I wrote a memo for the National Security Council arguing that the Strategic Defense Initiative would pay for itself—that the impact of the new technologies we were researching, once they were commercialized, would generate more tax revenue than we'd spent on R&D. When you do R&D, you don't know the outcome. Manufacturing using CMOS chip technology came about because the Pentagon thought it would be great for fighter pilots to have a weather forecasting module in the cockpit. The semiconductor laser came about because the Pentagon wanted to light up the battlefield during nighttime warfare. These technologies produced unforeseen consequences that rippled in unimaginable ways through our economy.

We have failed to continue this innovation in recent decades. Starting with the Clinton administration, we came to believe we were so powerful that we didn't have to invest in national defense and new technologies. Investment went into the Internet bubble of the 1990s, as if downloading movies was going to be the economy of the future.

I'm a free marketer. But the one thing markets cannot do is divorce themselves from culture. It is when we have a national security requirement, forcing us to the frontier of physics to develop weapons that are better than those of our rivals, that we get the best kind of innovation. So the government has a role—a critical role—in meeting the Chinese challenge.

If the Chinese are spending tens of billions of dollars to build chip fabrication plants and we come up with a better way of doing it, suddenly they'll have a hundred billion dollars' worth of worthless chip manufacturing plants on their hands. But you can't predict the outcome in advance. You have to make the commitment and take a leap of faith in American ingenuity and science. We can meet the strategic challenge of China, but we have to meet it as Americans in the American way.

Facing Up to the China Threat

Brian T. Kennedy

September 2020

We are at risk of losing a war today because too few of us know that we are engaged with an enemy, the Chinese Communist Party (CCP), that means to destroy us. The forces of globalism that have dominated our government (until recently) and our media for the better part of half a century have blinded too many Americans to the threat we face. If we do not wake up to the danger soon, we will find ourselves helpless.

That is a worst-case scenario. I do not think we Americans will let that happen. But the forces arrayed against us are many. We need to understand what we are up against and what steps must be taken to ensure our victory.

Our modern understanding of Communist China begins during the Cold War, with President Nixon's strategic belief that China could serve as a counterweight to the Soviet Union. This belief seemed to carry with it two great benefits. First, the U.S. wouldn't have to take on the Soviet Union by itself: Communist China was a populous country that bordered the Soviet Union and shared our interest, or so we thought, in checking its global ambitions. Second, by engaging with China—especially in terms of trade, but also by helping it develop technologically—we would help to end communism as a guiding force in China. This second notion might be called the China dream: economic liberalism would lead to political liberalism, and China's communist dictatorship would fade away.

At the end of the Cold War, pursuing the China dream appeared a safe course of action, given that the U.S. was then the world's preeminent military power. The 9/11 Islamic terrorist attacks reinforced the notion that superpower conflict was a thing of the past—that our major enemy was now radical Islam, widely diffused but centered in the Middle East. Later that same year, China was granted "Most Favored Nation" trading status and membership in the World Trade Organization. Little changed when the Bush administration gave way to the Obama administration. The latter's "pivot to Asia" was mostly rhetorical—a justification to degrade our military capabilities vis-à-vis China, integrate even further the U.S. and Chinese economies, and prioritize the Middle East above all else.

Under both administrations, the U.S. failed to build a military that could challenge Communist China's aggression in the Pacific—specifically its building of a modern navy and its construction of military installations on artificial islands in the South China Sea—and acquiesced in the export of much of the U.S. manufacturing base to China and elsewhere.

History will record that America's China policy from the 1970s until recently was very costly because it involved a great deal of self-deception about the nature of the Chinese regime and the men who were running it.

Communist China Today

The People's Republic of China (PRC) has a population of 1.4 billion. They are governed by the Chinese Communist Party, which has 90 million members, and by an elite class of approximately 300 million additional Chinese who are deeply invested in the regime's success. Not all of them may believe in every aspect of what the party calls "socialism with Chinese characteristics"—an admixture of Maoist, Marxist, and Leninist communism—but they actively support the regime. The system benefits these elites, whose businesses, mostly state-owned enterprises, are privately run with active participation by the CCP. Once a business reaches a certain size, it will take on board a cadre of party members who serve as a direct liaison between the business and the government.

However inefficient this may sound, understand that the CCP operates a massive global intelligence network through its Ministry of State Security. This network does its part to assist Chinese business and industry through industrial espionage, cyber warfare, and economic coercion. This type of state capitalism or neo-mercantilism has led to the creation of a modern economy that rivals that of the U.S. We might like to believe that communism in China cannot be sustained and will lead to the collapse of the regime. And it well may someday. But the CCP has proven extremely capable in building an empire that can govern 1.4 billion people. This required the conquest of a large number of peoples who were not willingly subjugated, as well as the physical mastery of a territory not easily managed. Doing this in such a short period of time and in such a ruthless and determined way is an achievement unparalleled in the known history of the world.

Today the PRC has a military of two million men, including the world's largest navy. This military may not be qualitatively on par with the U.S. military, but quantity has a quality of its own. In the last five years of U.S. naval war game simulations, in which the U.S. is pitted against China, the U.S. has failed to come out victorious. We do not have enough ships and munitions to defeat China's navy absent the use of nuclear weapons. And while it is often said that the Chinese do not have a nuclear arsenal to challenge the U.S., the fact is we don't know what the Chinese possess. We know they are capable of building nuclear weapons and advanced missiles and rocketry. We know they stole or otherwise obtained advanced U.S. technology involving warhead miniaturization and guidance systems and that they have had the industrial capacity to build these for nearly two decades.

On our side, we know that the U.S. has not tested a nuclear warhead since 1992 and has not built the kind of advanced arsenal that might be required to deter China. And we know that Chinese President and CCP General Secretary Xi Jinping adheres to the beliefs of Mao Tse-tung, who held that the U.S. was a "paper tiger" that possessed nuclear weapons but would not use them. There is also the rather disturbing belief, also a favorite of Mao, that even if we did use our nuclear weapons, we could not kill all of them. Such is the way a nation at war thinks.

As for China's air force, it possesses and is building today advanced fighter aircraft that rival anything the U.S has built. They may not yet have the quantity, but that will come with time. As for proficiency in war fighting, that is something that likewise can be acquired. For all of our nation's military superiority, we have not been in combat with a peer competitor for half a century. As good as we may be, history contains many examples of militarily inferior nations developing military superiority. If we think that this is not what Communist China is seeking to do today, we are mistaken.

Unrestricted Warfare

There is a famous book, *Unrestricted Warfare*, written in 1999 by two People's Liberation Army colonels. It argues that war between the PRC and the U.S. is inevitable, and that when it occurs China must be prepared to use whatever means are necessary to achieve victory. This includes economic warfare, cyber warfare, information warfare, political warfare, terrorism, and biological warfare, in addition to conventional and nuclear warfare. The book's purpose was not only to shape Chinese policy, but also to plant the idea in the minds of U.S. policymakers that China will consider nothing out of bounds. The book itself is an act of information warfare. Understanding the lengths to which the PRC is willing to go, might the U.S. prefer some kind of accommodation in lieu of building a military capable of challenging China's strategic designs?

In thinking about the implications of the word *unrestricted*, it is useful to look at the CCP's treatment of its own people.

Estimates put the number of those killed at the hands of the CCP—whether through war, starvation, or execution—at roughly 100 million. The mass murder committed by the party and its Red Guards during the Great Leap Forward (1958-1962) and the Cultural Revolution (1966-1976) alone resulted in some 70 million dead. And these numbers do not even take into account the forced abortions stemming from China's one-child policy. That number is conservatively estimated to be 500 million—500 million children murdered in the womb.

The Chinese government today is perfecting a system of social credit scoring that relies on constant monitoring of its people using the tools of social media, with the aim of grading each individual based on his or her support of the regime. This exerts a chilling effect on the people, who seem to have decided to go along with their communist masters lest they be excluded from whatever benefits they might enjoy from China's economic modernization.

Many of us have heard of the CCP's imprisonment in concentration camps of one to two million Muslim Uyghurs in Xinjiang province. Fewer of us are aware of how the Chinese government facilitates the abduction of Uyghur women for sexual use by Chinese soldiers—or even worse, if that were possible, how the government harvests the organs of the Uyghur population for sale both in China and abroad. This latter atrocity has become a multi-billion dollar industry: the Uyghur organs, since they are uncorrupted by alcohol or pork, are especially desirable to wealthy Muslims in the Middle East and elsewhere.

The ability of Westerners to avert their eyes from such abject horrors is clearly illustrated by the new Disney movie *Mulan*, parts of which were filmed mere miles from some of these camps. Disney went so far as to thank the Turpan Municipal Bureau of Public Security, responsible for imprisoning the Uyghurs, for its help during filming.

As an indication of the CCP's treatment of Christianity, Chinese school textbooks are now promoting a false account of Christianity and of Jesus's life and teaching. In the Chinese version of the story from the Gospel of John about the adulteress threatened with stoning, for example, Jesus explains that he too is a sinner and then stones the woman to death after the crowd disperses. Despite this and the CCP's long history of persecuting Christians, Pope Francis will be renewing his agreement with the CCP that gives it effective control over how the Catholic Church, or what passes for it, is run in China.

The CCP operates a vast intelligence network in the U.S as well. It is made up not merely of intelligence operatives working for the Ministry of State Security, but also a myriad of business and industry officials, Chinese scholar associations, Confucius Institutes operating on American campuses, and 370,000 Chinese students attending American universities. Every one of these Chinese citizens is subject to Article 7 of the PRC's National Intelligence Law of 2017, which requires that "any organization or citizen shall support, assist, and cooperate with state intelligence work." Students and others must report to handlers in Chinese consulates and embassies about who they meet, the research they're working on, and whatever else is demanded.

It should not be surprising that a combination of the efforts of this network and of China-based cyber criminals yields $500 to $600 billion of intellectual property theft annually. Also aiding the effort is China's Thousand Talents Program, which seeks to recruit the brightest Chinese and American professionals to support Chinese science and industry. This has proved to be a real problem for the U.S.—consider the recent arrest of Harvard chemist Charles Lieber for not disclosing his ties to the Chinese government and the firing of the Chinese-American CIO of the California Public Employees' Retirement System, who had invested CalPERS funds in Chinese corporations tied to the People's Liberation Army.

Perhaps the greatest threat to the U.S. posed by the CCP is its corruption of America's business and financial elites, who view the economic benefits of dealing with China as more important than America's national interests. If there is a single group committed to the globalist project and the delusory China dream, it is Wall Street. Our great investment banks are now selling trillions of dollars in debt and equity in Chinese corporations to American investors and retirees. They are literally betting on the success of China at the expense of the U.S.

The People's War

Over the past decade alone, the PRC has stolen almost $6 trillion of U.S. intellectual property, including tech innovations coming out of Silicon Valley and Seattle, entertainment coming out of Hollywood, and medical research and development coming out of New England and elsewhere. Properly understood, this is China stealing the wealth and future wealth of the American people. It is only recently that our government began trying to combat this theft in a serious way. At the same time, the U.S. has begun a strategic military buildup—including the creation of a new branch of our armed services, the U.S. Space Force, sending a signal that the U.S. would not cede the strategic high ground of space to China, which is already active in militarizing space.

In response, on May 13, 2019, the PRC, through the Xinhua News Agency—which is controlled by the CCP—declared a "People's War" against the U.S. This was specifically in response to U.S. tariffs on Chinese goods, which themselves were a response to restrictions of access to Chinese markets and China's failure to negotiate in good faith on the theft of intellectual property.

What was meant by this declaration of a People's War? Was the phrase essentially rhetorical or did it signal a fundamental shift or escalation in Chinese thinking?

I would not go so far as to say that the COVID-19 virus that originated in the Wuhan Institute of Virology was part of this People's War. But the virus did set into motion a radical reorientation of American society that had grave economic and political consequences.

We know with certainty that after the virus began spreading in Wuhan in the fall of 2019, the Chinese government closed down flights from Wuhan, which is in Hubei province, to the rest of China. At the same time, it allowed flights from Wuhan to continue to go to Europe and to the U.S.—where the Chinese knew with certainty that the virus would spread. And when President Trump closed the U.S. to flights from China, its foreign ministry and one of the CCP's propaganda arms, the *Global Times*, pushed for a reversal of this policy—again, knowing full well how contagious the virus was. Indeed, the Chinese government locked down Wuhan and released videos of men in hazmat suits welding doors shut so that people could not leave their homes.

The U.S. government and its Centers for Disease Control, which has offices in China, asked to be let into Wuhan to investigate. To this day China has denied us access. The initial gene sequencing for the virus that we received from China—evidence that led the now famous public health bureaucrat Anthony Fauci to say that China was being open and cooperative—was incorrect, a fact that made testing Americans for the virus all the more difficult. Were these decisions by the Chinese government part of the People's War?

When challenged on its dishonesty regarding the virus's origins, the CCP's Xinhua News Agency threatened that China could plunge America into a "mighty sea of coronavirus," pointing out that China controlled the supply chain for the active pharmaceutical ingredients used in the production of 90 percent of our medicines. This fact alone—the result of the loss of the

U.S. manufacturing base to China and other nations, an explicit policy of our government until recently—is a scandal of immense proportions that our government is now working to correct.

Regardless of whether the COVID-19 virus was a by-product of biological weapons research or resulted from inadequate safeguards in a virology lab, it is the CCP that is to blame for its spread throughout the world, and it was criminal for the Chinese government to keep the world in the dark about the nature of the pathogen.

Nor has COVID-19 been the only line of attack in this People's War. It should come as no surprise that the PRC uses its diplomatic missions around the world as a base for industrial espionage and to conduct political and information warfare. Thus it was that on July 24 of this year, the U.S. State Department closed down the Chinese consulate in Houston, saying that it was serving as a hub for CCP operatives who were engaging in theft of America's research into, among other things, the development of a COVID-19 vaccine.

To quote a State Department official:

> Consulates are also bases of operations for Fox Hunt teams. These are teams of agents sent from China here to coerce economic fugitives—meaning political rivals of President Xi, the Communist Party critics, and refugees—coercing them, that is, to return to the PRC. Consulates enabled the activities of those teams. Consulates also enabled direct lobbying of state and local officials, as well as business people, to favor Chinese interests. And while that's to be expected by diplomats, when it takes a turn towards the coercive or the covert, that becomes a national security problem.

It is also believed that Chinese operatives in the Houston consulate provided intelligence to Black Lives Matter and Antifa rioters in Houston as a way of demonstrating their solidarity. Indeed, there is growing evidence that the CCP's United Front includes these groups, and that some of the funding for BLM and Antifa is coming from CCP-sponsored or affiliated groups: Liberation Road, the Freedom Road Socialist Organization, and the Chinese Progressive Association.

In conclusion, Americans are not looking for war with Communist China, but Communist China appears to be at war with us. As a first order of business, we must continue what we have at long last begun: building a military designed to deter Chinese aggression and pursuing trade and other policies that put our own national interests first.

Equally important—especially given the violence in our cities that our foreign enemies cheer—is defending our American way of life and teaching our countrymen why America deserves our love and devotion, now and in the days ahead.

THE CONSTITUTION

The Liberal Assault on Freedom of Speech

Thomas G. West

January 2004

America has less freedom of speech today than it has ever had in its history. Yet it is widely believed that it has more. Liberal law professor Archibald Cox has written: "The body of law presently defining First Amendment liberties" grew out of a "continual expansion of individual freedom of expression." Conservative constitutional scholar Walter Berns agrees: "Legally we enjoy a greater liberty [of speech] than ever before in our history." Both are wrong.

Liberals and libertarians applaud what Cox, Berns, and others perceive as an expansion of free speech. Conservatives sometimes deplore it, because they rightly assume that the expansion in question leads to greater scope for nude dancers, pornographers, and flag burners. But from the point of view of the original meaning of free speech, our speech today is much less free than it was in the early republic.

Campaign Finance Regulation

In 1974, for the first time in American history, amendments to the Federal Elections Campaign Act (FECA) made it illegal in some circumstances for Americans to publish their opinions about candidates for election. Citizens and organizations who "coordinate" with a candidate for public office were prohibited from spending more than a set amount of money to publish arguments for or against a candidate. Those who "coordinate" with a candidate are his friends and supporters. In other words, publication was forbidden to those with the greatest interest in campaigns and those most likely to want to spend money publishing on behalf of candidates.

The Bipartisan Campaign Reform Act of 2002 goes well beyond the 1974 law, imposing substantial limits on the right of political parties and nonprofit organizations to publicize their views on candidates during election campaigns. Imagine the shock of the Founders if they were here to see that government was heavily into the business of banning private citizens from pooling their fortunes to publicize their opinions about candidates for elections.

These laws do contain a notable exception. Newspaper owners may spend as much money as they wish publishing arguments in support of candidates with whom they "coordinate." This solitary exemption from restrictions on free speech is, of course, no mistake: The dominant newspapers in America are liberal, and the 1974 law was passed by a Democratic Congress on the day before Richard Nixon resigned in disgrace from the presidency.

Campaign finance regulation stands in direct opposition to the Founders' understanding of the First Amendment. For a large class of people, it effectively prohibits and punishes the most important thing that the right to free speech is supposed to guarantee: open discussion of candidates and issues at election time.

Those who favor campaign finance regulation sometimes claim that their primary concern is with "corruption and the appearance of corruption"—that is, what used to be called bribery or the appearance of bribery. But that is not the real agenda of the reformers. There is a good reason why the 2002 Act, like the 1974 law, was voted for by almost every House and Senate Democrat, and opposed by a large majority of Republicans: These laws are primarily about limiting the speech of conservatives.

Here are some quotations from the 2002 congressional debate:

Sen. Maria Cantwell (Dem.-Wash.): "This bill is about slowing the ad war.... It is about slowing political advertising and making sure the flow of negative ads by outside interest groups does not continue to permeate the airwaves."

Sen. Barbara Boxer (Dem.-Calif.): "These so-called issues ads are not regulated at all and mention candidates by name. They directly attack candidates without any accountability. It is brutal. . . . We have an opportunity in the McCain-Feingold bill to stop that."

Sen. Paul Wellstone (Dem.- Minn.): "I think these issue advocacy ads are a nightmare. I think all of us should hate them. . . . [By passing the legislation], [w]e could get some of this poison politics off television."

In other words, the law makes it harder for citizens to criticize liberal politicians when they disagree with their policy views.

Some congressmen were willing to be even more open about the fact that the new law would cut down on conservative criticism of candidates. Rep. Jan Schakowsky (Dem.-Ill.) said: "If my colleagues care about gun control, then campaign finance is their issue so that the NRA does not call the shots." Democratic Reps. Marty Meehan (Mass.) and Rosa DeLauro (Conn.), and Democratic Sens. Harry Reid (Nev.) and Dick Durbin (Ill.) also cited the National Rifle Association's political communications as a problem that the Act would solve. Several liberal Republicans chimed in.

What this means is that government is now in the business of silencing citizens who believe in the Second Amendment right to keep and bear arms.

Sen. Jim Jeffords (Ind.-Vt.) said that issue ads "are obviously pointed at positions that are taken by you, saying how horrible they are." "Negative advertising is the crack cocaine of politics," added Sen. Tom Daschle (Dem.-S.D.). What these quotations show—and there are many more like them—is that the purpose of campaign finance regulation is to make it harder for conservatives to present their views to the public about candidates and issues in elections.

In its shocking December 2003 decision in *McConnell v. Federal Election Commission*, the five most liberal members of the Supreme Court upheld this law and saw no conflict with the First Amendment guarantee of freedom of speech and of the press. Yet it is impossible to imagine a more obvious violation of the First Amendment, unless the government were explicitly to authorize the Federal Election Commission to close down conservative newspapers and magazines. In his powerful dissent in the *McConnell* case, Justice Clarence Thomas wrote:

> The chilling endpoint of the Court's reasoning is not difficult to foresee: outright regulation of the press. None...of the reasoning employed by the Court exempts the press.... What is to stop a future Congress from determining that the press is 'too influential,' and that the 'appearance of corruption' is significant when media organizations endorse candidates or run 'slanted' or 'biased' news stories in favor of candidates or parties? Or, even easier, what is to stop a future Congress from concluding that the availability of unregulated media corporations creates a loophole that allows for easy 'circumvention' of the limitations of the current campaign finance laws?

With the National Rifle Association announcement that it intends to acquire a media outlet in order to get around Congress's unconstitutional restrictions on issue ads during elections, Justice Thomas's nightmare might come true even sooner than he anticipated. We are already hearing statements suggesting that any media owned by the NRA will not count as "real" media. At some point, perhaps in the very near future, the Federal Election Commission may find itself deciding which newspapers and broadcast stations are "real" news media (and can therefore be permitted their First Amendment rights) and which ones are "slanted" or "biased" (and whose First Amendment rights must therefore be denied).

Censorship Through Broadcast Licensing

Reading today's scholarship on freedom of speech, one would hardly guess that government control over the content of speech through licensing requirements—supposedly outlawed long ago—is alive and well. The amazing ignorance with which this matter is usually discussed today may be seen in the following quote from legal scholar Benno Schmidt, the former president of Yale:

The First Amendment tolerates virtually no prior restraints [on speech or the press]. This doctrine is one of the central principles of our law of freedom of the press.... [T]he doctrine is presumably an absolute bar to any wholesale system of administrative licensing or censorship of the press, which is the most repellent form of government suppression of expression.

Schmidt fails to notice that every radio, television, and cable broadcaster in America is subject to a "wholesale system of administrative licensing," i.e., the "most repellent form of government suppression of expression."

Broadcasters have to obtain a license from the Federal Communications Commission. Stations receive licenses only when the FCC judges it to be "in the public interest, convenience, or necessity." Licenses are granted for a limited period, and the FCC may choose not to renew. The FCC has never defined what the "public interest" means. In the past, it preferred a case-by-case approach, which has been called "regulation by raised eyebrow."

During most of its history, the FCC consistently favored broadcasters who shared the views of government officials, and disfavored broadcasters who did not.

The first instance of serious and pervasive political censorship was initiated by Franklin Roosevelt's FCC in the 1930s. The Yankee Radio network in New England frequently editorialized against Roosevelt. The FCC asked Yankee to provide details about its programming. Sensing the drift, Yankee immediately stopped broadcasting editorials in 1938. In order to drive its point home, the FCC found Yankee deficient at license renewal time. They announced,

Radio can serve as an instrument of democracy only when devoted to the communication of information and exchange of ideas fairly and objectively presented.... It cannot be devoted to the support of principles he [the broadcaster] happens to regard most favorably.

In other words, if you want your broadcasting license renewed, stop criticizing Roosevelt.

The FCC soon afterwards made exclusion of "partisan" content a requirement for all broadcasters. It was understood, of course, that radio stations would continue to carry such supposedly "nonpartisan" fare as presidential speeches and "fireside chats" attacking Republicans and calling for expansions of the New Deal. In the name of "democracy," "fairness," and "objectivity," the FCC would no longer permit stations to engage in sustained criticism of Roosevelt's speeches and programs.

In 1949, the FCC announced its Fairness Doctrine. Broadcasters were required "to provide coverage of vitally important controversial issue...and...a reasonable opportunity for the presentation of contrasting viewpoints on such issues." In practice, the Fairness Doctrine only worked in one direction: against conservatives.

During the Republican Eisenhower years, the FCC paid little attention to broadcasting content, and a number of conservative radio stations emerged. After John Kennedy was elected in 1960, his administration went on the offensive against them. Kennedy's Assistant Secretary of Commerce, Bill Ruder, later admitted, "Our massive strategy was to use the Fairness Doctrine to challenge and harass right-wing broadcasters and hope that the challenges would be so costly to them that they would be inhibited and decide it was too expensive to continue."

This strategy was highly successful. Hundreds of radio stations cancelled conservative shows that they had been broadcasting. The FCC revoked the license of one radio station, WXUR of Media, Pennsylvania, a tiny conservative Christian broadcaster. When WXUR appealed to the courts, one dissenting judge noted "that the public has lost access to information and ideas...as a result of this doctrinal sledge-hammer [i.e., the Fairness Doctrine]." The Supreme Court refused to hear the appeal. It saw no free speech violation in the government shutdown of a radio station for broadcasting conservative ideas.

The government also revoked the license of a television station in Jackson, Mississippi. WLTB was unapologetically and openly opposed to federal civil rights policies at the time, and would introduce NBC's news reports with this warning: "What you are about to see is an example of biased, managed, Northern news. Be sure to stay tuned at 7:25 to hear your local newscast." The D.C. Circuit Court ordered the FCC to revoke WLTB's license. In an outrageous opinion authored by Warren Burger, who was shortly afterward appointed by President Nixon as Chief Justice of the Supreme Court, the Circuit Court demanded in indignant tones that WLTB's owner be silenced: "After nearly five decades of operation, the broadcast industry does not seem to have grasped the simple fact that a broadcast license is a public trust subject to termination for breach of duty." Again, the Supreme Court refused to hear the station's appeal.

Conservatives tried to use the Fairness Doctrine as well, but failed in every case. Liberal author Fred Friendly writes, "After virtually every controversial program [on the major TV networks]—'Harvest of Shame,'... 'Hunger in America' [1960s programs advocating liberal anti-poverty policies]—fairness complaints were filed, and the FCC rejected them all. As FCC general counsel Henry Geller explained, 'We just weren't going to get trapped into determining journalistic judgments.'" In other words, when liberals were on the air, the FCC called it journalism. When conservatives were on the air, the FCC called it partisan and political, and insisted that the liberal point of view be given equal time.

In the 1980s, President Reagan appointed a majority to the Federal Communications Commission, and it abolished the Fairness Doctrine in 1987. The effect was dramatic. Immediately, conservative talk radio blossomed. Rush Limbaugh was the biggest winner. He came along at just the moment, for the first time since the 1950s, when stations could be confident that conservative broadcasting would no longer lead to license renewal problems or Fairness Doctrine complaints and litigation.

The end of the Fairness Doctrine was a tremendous victory for the First Amendment. But it does not mean that broadcast media are now free. The authority of the FCC over broadcasters remains in place. It can be brought back with the full partisan force of the Roosevelt and Kennedy administrations as soon as one party gets control over all three branches of the federal government and chooses to do so.

Harassment Law

For about 25 years, government has required businesses and educational institutions to punish speech that can be characterized as "hostile environment" harassment. This standard is so vague that the question of what constitutes a "hostile working environment" is endlessly litigated. One court ordered employees to "refrain from any racial, religious, ethnic, or other remarks or slurs contrary to their fellow employees' religious beliefs." Another court banned "all offensive conduct and speech implicating considerations of race." Of course, there are some who find any criticism of affirmative action offensive, even racist. Others are offended when someone alludes to his own religious convictions. So this policy, in effect, makes it potentially illegal for employees to say anything about their own religious beliefs, or to defend the "wrong" kind of political opinions. UCLA law professor Eugene Volokh has cited a headline in a major business magazine that sums up the denial of free speech in the workplace: "Watch What You Say, or Be Ready to Pay."

The Founders' Approach

Let us turn to the original meaning of free speech in the Constitution to see how far we have abandoned the original meaning of that document.

The Declaration of Independence calls liberty an inalienable right with which we are "endowed by our Creator." As human beings are born free in all respects, they are also born free to speak, write, and publish.

Nevertheless, although all human beings possess the same natural right to liberty, the Founders believed that there is a law of nature that teaches us that no one has the right to injure another. The most obvious kind of injurious speech is personal libel. Here is a quotation from an early libel case:

> [T]he heart of the libeller...is more dark and base than...his who commits a midnight arson.... [T]he injuries which are done to character and reputation seldom can be cured, and the most innocent man may, in a moment, be deprived of his good name, upon which, perhaps, he depends for all the prosperity, and all the happiness of his life.

But the Founders knew very well that allowing government to punish abuses of speech is potentially dangerous to legitimate free speech. So they relied on three pillars to secure this right of free speech while setting limits on injurious speech:

First, no speech could be prohibited by government except that which is clearly injurious. Today, as we have seen, noninjurious political and religious speech is routinely prohibited and punished through campaign finance and other laws.

Second, there could be no prior restraint of speech. Government was not permitted to withhold permission to publish if it disapproved of a publisher or his views. Today, the media from which most Americans get their news is subject to a government licensing scheme that is strikingly similar to the system by which England's kings kept the press in line in the sixteenth and seventeenth centuries.

Third, injurious speech had to be defined in law, and punishment of it could only be accomplished by due process of law. Guilt or liability could be established only by juries—that is, by people who are not government officials. Today, clear legal standards, formal prosecutions, and juries are mostly avoided in the convoluted censorship schemes employed by government in broadcasting law, campaign finance law, harassment law, and the like.

As an aside, I mention one other area where the dominant view today is opposed to the older view. The Founders viewed prohibition of obscene or pornographic materials in the same light as the regulation of sexual behavior, public nudity, and the like. Sex is by its nature connected to children. The political community cannot be indifferent to *whether* and *how* children, its future citizens, are generated and raised. That is why the laws prohibited or discouraged nonmarital sex such as premarital sex, homosexuality, and adultery. Obscene words or pictures were banned because they tended to promote the idea of sex apart from marriage and children, dehumanizing sex by making men and women into "sex objects."

Today's Liberal View

Why have liberals rejected the Founders' idea of free speech?

The Founders looked toward a society in which each person's right to life, liberty, property, free exercise of religion, and pursuit of happiness would be protected by government. Except for sex, marriage, and other matters connected with the generation of children, and injuries to persons or property, government would be mostly indifferent to the manner in which citizens lived their private lives. Laws would protect everyone's rights equally, but it was understood that equal rights lead to unequal results, because of differences in talent, character, and luck. About a century ago, liberals began to argue that the Founders' view, which is embodied in the Constitution, is unjust in two ways.

First, they argued that by protecting everyone's property equally, government in effect sides with the rich against the poor. It protects the rich, and leaves the poor open to oppression. It is not enough, in the liberal view, for government to be neutral between business and labor, between men and women, between whites and racial minorities, and so on. In each case, liberals say, justice requires that government must put burdens on the rich and powerful and give special advantages to the weak and vulnerable.

Applied to free speech, the liberal view leads to the conclusion that government must limit spending by those who can afford to publish or broadcast their views. As University of Chicago law professor Cass Sunstein writes, the traditional autonomy of newspapers "may itself be an abridgment of the free speech right." Government interference with broadcasting content through FCC licensing is from this standpoint a positive good for free speech. Without it, rich white males will dominate, and the poor, women, and minorities will be marginalized and silenced. Therefore, in the liberal view, speech rights must be redistributed from the rich and privileged to the poor and excluded.

University of Maryland professor Mark Graber endorses this view: "Affluent Americans," he writes, "have no First Amendment right that permits them to achieve political success through constant repetition of relatively unwanted ideas." In other words, if you publish or broadcast "too much," government has the right, and the duty, to silence you. Yale law professor Stephen Carter agrees: "Left unregulated, the modern media could present serious threats to democracy." Sunstein calls for a "New Deal for Speech," in which government will treat speech in exactly the same way as it already treats property, namely, as something that is really owned by government, and which citizens are only permitted to use or engage in when they meet conditions established by government to promote fairness and justice.

Arguments like these are the deepest reason that liberals no longer follow the Constitution, and why Americans today no longer know what the free speech clause really means.

One might raise the objection that these are only law professors. But their view turns out to be squarely in the mainstream. Several candidates for the presidency in 2000 from both political parties (but not George W. Bush) called for much more stringent limitations on free speech in the name of campaign finance reform. One of those candidates, Bill Bradley, proposed a constitutional amendment in 1996 that would have repealed the free speech clause of the First Amendment. Dick Gephardt, the former minority leader of the House of Representatives, has made the same proposal. In the end, even President Bush signed the Bipartisan Campaign Reform Act of 2002.

I am reminded by this of Abraham Lincoln's remark in the 1850s about those who would read blacks out of the Constitution and the Declaration of Independence: If that view is to prevail, why not move to Russia, he asked, where we can take our despotism unalloyed? Liberals today are on the verge of throwing off all pretense and admitting openly that what they mean by *equality* is the abolition of *liberty*.

There is a second reason that today's liberals see the Founders' view of free speech as oppressive. The Founders' regulation of sexually explicit and obscene pictures and words, they believe—like any interference in the sex lives of citizens—stands in the way of the most important meaning of liberty. People must be permitted, in this view, to establish their own way of life and engage in whatever kind of sex they please. A famous passage from a Supreme Court pro-abortion decision sums up this liberal view. It reads, "At the heart of liberty is the right to define one's own concept of existence, of meaning, of the universe, and of the mystery of human life."

The Founders would have replied that we are precisely *not* free to define our own concept of existence and meaning. God and nature have established the "laws of nature and of nature's God," which have already defined it for us. Human beings, Jefferson wrote, are "inherently independent of all but moral law." If men defy that law, they are not free. They are slaves, at first to their own passions, eventually to political tyranny. For men who cannot govern their own passions cannot sustain a democratic government.

Our task today is to recover the cause of constitutionalism. In doing so, the recovery of a proper understanding and respect for free speech must be a high priority.

The History and Danger of Administrative Law

Philip Hamburger

September 2014

There are many complaints about administrative law—including that it is arbitrary, that it is a burden on the economy, and that it is an intrusion on freedom. The question I will address here is whether administrative law is unlawful, and I will focus on constitutional history. Those who forget history, it is often said, are doomed to repeat it. And this is what has happened in the United States with the rise of administrative law—or, more accurately, administrative power.

Administrative law is commonly defended as a new sort of power, a product of the 19th and the 20th centuries that developed to deal with the problems of modern society in all its complexity. From this perspective, the Framers of the Constitution could not have anticipated it and the Constitution could not have barred it. What I will suggest, in contrast, is that administrative power is actually very old. It revives what used to be called prerogative or absolute power, and it is thus something that the Constitution centrally prohibited.

But first, what exactly do I mean by administrative law or administrative power? Put simply, administrative acts are binding or constraining edicts that come, not through law, but through other mechanisms or pathways. For example, when an executive agency issues a rule constraining Americans—barring an activity that results in pollution, for instance, or restricting how citizens can use their land—it is an attempt to exercise binding legislative power not through an act of Congress, but through an administrative edict. Similarly, when an executive agency adjudicates a violation of one of these edicts—in order to impose a fine or some other penalty—it is an attempt to exercise binding judicial power not through a judicial act, but again through an administrative act.

In a way we can think of administrative law as a form of off-road driving. The Constitution offers two avenues of binding power—acts of Congress and acts of the courts. Administrative acts by executive agencies are a way of driving off-road, exercising power through other pathways. For those in the driver's seat, this can be quite exhilarating. For the rest of us, it's a little unnerving.

The Constitution authorizes three types of power, as we all learned in school—the legislative power is located in Congress, executive power is located in the president and his subordinates, and the judicial power is located in the courts. How does administrative power fit into that arrangement?

The conventional answer to this question is based on the claim of the modernity of administrative law. Administrative law, this argument usually goes, began in 1887 when Congress created the Interstate Commerce Commission, and it expanded decade by decade as Congress created more such agencies. A variant of this account suggests that administrative law is actually a little bit older—that it began to develop in the early practices of the federal government of the United States. But whether it began in the 1790s or in the 1880s, administrative law according to this account is a post-1789 development and—this is the key point—it arose as a pragmatic and necessary response to new and complex practical problems in American life. The pragmatic and necessitous character of this development is almost a mantra—and of course if looked at that way, opposition to administrative law is anti-modern and quixotic.

But there are problems with this conventional history of administrative law. Rather than being a modern, post-constitutional American development, I argue that the rise of administrative law is essentially a re-emergence of the absolute power practiced by pre-modern kings. Rather than a modern necessity, it is a latter-day version of a recurring threat—a threat inherent in human nature and in the temptations of power.

The Prerogative Power of Kings

The constitutional history of the past thousand years in common law countries records the repeated ebb and flow of absolutism on the one side and law on the other. English kings were widely expected to rule through law. They had Parliament for making law and courts of law for adjudicating cases, and they were expected to govern through the acts of these bodies. But kings were discontent with governing through the law and often acted on their own. The personal power that kings exercised when evading the law was called prerogative power.

Whereas ordinarily kings bound their subjects through statutes passed by Parliament, when exercising prerogative power they bound subjects through proclamations or decrees—or what we today call rules or regulations. Whereas ordinarily kings would repeal old statutes by obtaining new statutes, when exercising prerogative power they issued dispensations and suspensions—or what we today call waivers. Whereas ordinarily kings enforced the law through the courts of law, when exercising prerogative power they enforced their commands through their prerogative courts—courts such as the King's Council, the Star Chamber, and the High Commission—or what we today call administrative courts. Ordinarily, English judges resolved legal disputes in accordance with their independent judgment regarding the law. But when kings exercised prerogative power, they expected deference from judges, both to their own decrees and to the holdings and interpretations of their extra-legal prerogative courts.

Although England did not have a full separation of powers of the sort written into the American Constitution, it did have a basic division of powers. Parliament had the power to make laws, the law courts had the power to adjudicate, and the king had the power to exercise force. But when kings acted through prerogative power, they or their prerogative courts exercised all government powers, overriding these divisions. For example, the Star Chamber could make regulations, as well as prosecute and adjudicate infractions. And defenders of this sort of prerogative power were not squeamish about describing it as absolute power. Absolutism was their justification.

Conceptually, there were three central elements of this absolutism: extra-legal power, supra-legal power, and the consolidation of power. It was extra-legal or outside the law in the sense that it bound the public not through laws or statutes, but through other means. It was supra-legal or above the law in the sense that kings expected judges to defer to it—notwithstanding their duty to exercise their own independent judgment. And it was consolidated in the sense that it united all government powers—legislative, executive, and judicial—in the king or in his prerogative courts. And underlying these three central elements was the usual conceptual justification for absolute power: necessity. Necessity, it was said, was not bound by law.

These claims on behalf of absolutism, of course, did not go unchallenged. When King John called Englishmen to account extralegally in his Council, England's barons demanded in Magna Carta in 1215 that no freeman shall be taken or imprisoned or even summoned except through the mechanisms of law. When 14th century English kings questioned men in the king's Council, Parliament in 1354 and 1368 enacted due process statutes. When King James I attempted to make law through proclamations, judges responded in 1610 with an opinion that royal proclamations were unlawful and void. When James subsequently demanded judicial deference to prerogative interpretations of statutes, the judges refused. Indeed, in 1641 Parliament abolished the Star Chamber and the High Commission, the bodies then engaging in extra-legal lawmaking and adjudication. And most profoundly, English constitutional law began to develop—and it made clear that there could be no extra-legal, supra-legal, or consolidated power.

The Rise of Absolutism in America

The United States Constitution echoes this. Early Americans were very familiar with absolute power. They feared this extra-legal, supra-legal, and consolidated power because they knew from English history that such power could evade the law and override all legal rights. It is no surprise, then, that the United States Constitution was framed to bar this sort of power. To be precise, Americans established the Constitution to be the source of all government power and to bar any absolute power. Nonetheless, absolute power has come back to life in common law nations, including America.

After absolute power was defeated in England and America, it circled back from the continent through Germany, and especially through Prussia. There, what once had been the personal prerogative power of kings became the bureaucratic administrative power of the states. The Prussians were the leaders of this development in the 17th and 18th centuries. In the 19th century they became the primary theorists of administrative power, and many of them celebrated its evasion of constitutional law and constitutional rights.

This German theory would become the intellectual source of American administrative law. Thousands upon thousands of Americans studied administrative power in Germany, and what they learned there about administrative power became standard fare in American universities. At the same time, in the political sphere, American Progressives were becoming increasingly discontent with elected legislatures, and they increasingly embraced German theories of administration and defended the imposition of administrative law in America in terms of pragmatism and necessity.

The Progressives, moreover, understood what they were doing. For example, in 1927, a leading Progressive theorist openly said that the question of whether an American administrative officer could issue regulations was similar to the question of whether pre-modern English kings could issue binding proclamations. By the 1920s, however, Progressives increasingly were silent about the continuity between absolute power and modern administrative power, as this undermined their claims about its modernity and lawfulness.

In this way, over the past 120 years, Americans have reestablished the very sort of power that the Constitution most centrally forbade. Administrative law is extra-legal in that it binds Americans not through law but through other mechanisms—not through statutes but through regulations—and not through the decisions of courts but through other adjudications. It is supra-legal in that it requires judges to put aside their independent judgment and defer to administrative power as if it were above the law—which our judges do far more systematically than even the worst of seventeenth-century English judges. And it is consolidated in that it combines the three powers of government—legislative, executive, and judicial—in administrative agencies.

Let me close by addressing just two of many constitutional problems illuminated by the re-emergence of absolutism in the form of administrative power: delegation and procedural rights.

One standard defense of administrative power is that Congress uses statutes to delegate its lawmaking power to administrative agencies. But this is a poor defense. The delegation of lawmaking has long been a familiar feature of absolute power. When kings exercised extra-legal power, they usually had at least some delegated authority from Parliament. Henry VIII, for example, issued binding proclamations under an authorizing statute called the Act of Proclamations. His binding proclamations were nonetheless understood to be exercises of absolute power. And in the 18th century the Act of Proclamations was condemned as unconstitutional.

Against this background, the United States Constitution expressly bars the delegation of legislative power. This may sound odd, given that the opposite is so commonly asserted by scholars and so routinely accepted by the courts. But read the Constitution. The Constitution's very first substantive words are, "All legislative Powers herein granted shall be vested in a Congress of the United States." The word "all" was not placed there by accident. The Framers understood that delegation had been a problem in English constitutional history, and the word "all" was placed there precisely to bar it.

As for procedural rights, the history is even more illuminating. Administrative adjudication evades almost all of the procedural rights guaranteed under the Constitution. It subjects Americans to adjudication without real judges, without juries, without grand juries, without full protection against self-incrimination, and so forth. Like the old prerogative courts, administrative courts substitute inquisitorial process for the due process of law—and that's not just an abstract accusation; much early administrative procedure appears to have been modelled on civilian-derived inquisitorial process. Administrative adjudication thus becomes an open avenue for evasion of the Bill of Rights.

The standard justification for the administrative evasion of procedural rights is that they apply centrally to the regular courts, but not entirely to administrative adjudication. But the history shows that procedural rights developed primarily to bar prerogative or administrative proceedings, not to regulate what the government does in regular courts of law. As I already mentioned, the principle of due process developed as early as the 14th century, when Parliament used it to prevent the exercise of extra-legal power by the King's Council. It then became a constitutional principle in the 17th century in opposition to the prerogative courts. Similarly, jury rights developed partly in opposition to administrative proceedings, and thus some of the earliest constitutional cases in America held administrative proceedings unconstitutional for depriving defendants of a jury trial.

———

In sum, the conventional understanding of administrative law is utterly mistaken. It is wrong on the history and oblivious to the danger. That danger is absolutism: extra-legal, supra-legal, and consolidated power. And the danger matters because administrative power revives this absolutism. The Constitution carefully barred this threat, but constitutional doctrine has since legitimized this dangerous sort of power. It therefore is necessary to go back to basics. Among other things, we should no longer settle for some vague notion of "rule of law," understood as something that allows the delegation of legislative and judicial powers to administrative agencies. We should demand rule *through* law and rule *under* law. Even more fundamentally, we need to reclaim the vocabulary of law: Rather than speak of administrative law, we should speak of administrative power—indeed, of absolute power or more concretely of extra-legal, supra-legal, and consolidated power. Then we at least can begin to recognize the danger.

Does Diversity Really Unite Us? Citizenship and Immigration

Edward J. Erler

July/August 2018

President Trump's zero-tolerance policy for illegal border crossers has provoked a hysterical reaction from Democrats, establishment Republicans, the progressive-liberal media, Hollywood radicals, and the deep state. What particularly motivated the ire of these Trump-haters was the fact that the zero-tolerance policy would require the separation of parents and children at the border. The hysteria was, of course, completely insincere and fabricated, given that the policy of separating children and parents was nothing new—it had been a policy of the Obama and Bush administrations as well.

Furthermore, where is the compassion for the thousands of American children who are separated from their parents every year as a result of arrests and convictions for non-violent crimes? Many of those arrested are single mothers whose infants become wards of the government until their mothers complete their sentences. No hysteria or effusive compassion is elicited by these separations, confirming that the object of the hysteria surrounding illegal border crossers is to force open borders on the nation under the guise of compassion for children.

President Trump's preferred solution for ending the influx of illegal immigrants and providing border security is a wall; it is also the preferred solution of the American people. Zero tolerance is an interim policy that—if enforced—will help deter illegal crossers. The hysteria provoked by zero tolerance could have been predicted, but its magnitude and sheer insanity are almost breathtaking. Some prominent constitutional scholars have gone so far as to argue that the government has no constitutional authority to control the border. And this, which seems almost beyond hysteria, from the elite intellectual class that should be most immune to hysteria!

In the meantime, a Federal District Court judge in Southern California has discovered a substantive due process right guaranteeing the right to "family integrity" lurking in the Due Process Clause of the Fifth Amendment and has ordered all children reunited with their illegal immigrant parents. Obviously the judge expects the parents to be released from incarceration to join their children, but the Trump administration seems determined to keep parents and children together in detention centers until legal proceedings determine their fate.

More than a century ago, the Supreme Court announced what was considered the settled sense of the matter when it remarked: "It is an accepted maxim of international law...and essential to self-preservation, to forbid the entrance of foreigners within [a sovereign nation's] dominions, or to admit them only in such cases and upon such conditions as it may see fit to prescribe." This view was reaffirmed in the recent Supreme Court decision, handed down on June 26, that upheld Trump's travel ban on foreign nationals from eight countries, six of which have majority Muslim populations.

Part of the complaint against the ban was that it violated the Establishment Clause of the First Amendment because Trump had displayed "animus" against Muslims in speeches before and after the 2016 election. The plaintiffs argued that the national security reasons for the ban were merely pretexts for Trump's thinly disguised contempt for the Muslim religion. Although the Court agreed that individual injury could be alleged under the Establishment Clause, the travel ban on its face was neutral with respect to religion, and it was therefore possible to decide the issue on statutory rather than constitutional grounds.

The dissenting opinion in this case would have invalidated the ban on constitutional grounds, based on the idea that the President's campaign statements and those of his advisers proved that animus against Islam was the real and pervasive motivation for the travel ban. Had this dissenting opinion prevailed, it would have created an anomaly in constitutional jurisprudence. Conceding that the plain language of the travel ban was neutral and therefore constitutional, what rendered the travel ban unconstitutional was Trump's purported display of animus in his public speeches. If signed by any president other than Trump, there would therefore be no constitutional objections. In other words, in the minds of the dissenters, psychoanalysis of Trump's motives held greater constitutional significance than the intent of the law expressed in its plain language.

In any case, the majority opinion held that "by its plain language" the Immigration and Naturalization Act "grants the President broad discretion to suspend the entry of aliens into the United States. The President lawfully exercised that discretion based on his findings... that entry of the covered aliens would be detrimental to the national interest." Few limits have ever been placed on the President's broad authority to act under the Immigration and Naturalization Act, especially when national security and foreign relations are involved.

In the 2016 presidential campaign, Donald Trump appealed to the importance of citizens and borders. In other words, Trump took his stand on behalf of the nation-state and citizenship against the idea of a homogeneous world-state populated by "universal persons." In appealing directly to the people, Trump succeeded in defeating *both* political parties, the media, political professionals, pollsters, academics, and the bureaucratic class. All these groups formed part of the bi-partisan cartel that had represented the entrenched interests of the Washington establishment for many years. Although defeated in the election, the cartel has not given up. It is fighting a desperate battle to maintain its power.

Historically, constitutional government has been found only in the nation-state, where the people share a common good and are dedicated to the same principles and purposes. The homogeneous world state—the European Union on a global scale—will not be a constitutional democracy; it will be the administration of "universal personhood" without the inconvenience of having to rely on the consent of the governed. It will be government by unelected and unaccountable bureaucrats, much like the burgeoning administrative state that is today expanding its reach and magnifying its power in the United States. "Universal persons" will not be citizens; they will be clients or subjects. Rights will be superfluous because the collective welfare of the community—determined by the bureaucrats—will have superseded the rights of individuals.

Progressive liberalism no longer views self-preservation as a rational goal of the nation-state. Rather, it insists that self-preservation and national security must be subordinate to openness and diversity. America's immigration policies, we are told, should demonstrate our commitment to diversity because an important part of the American character is openness, and our commitment to diversity is an affirmation of "who we are as Americans." If this carries a risk to our security, it is a small price to pay. Indeed, the willing assumption of risk adds authenticity to our commitment.

In support of all this, we are asked to believe something incredible: that the American character is defined only by its unlimited acceptance of diversity. A defined American character—devotion to republican principles, republican virtue, the habits and manners of free citizens, self-reliance—would, in that case, be impermissibly exclusive, and thus impermissibly American. The homogeneous world-state recognizes only openness, devotion to diversity, and acceptance as virtues. It must therefore condemn exclusivity as its greatest vice. It is the nation-state that insists on exclusive citizenship and immigration policies that impose various kinds of restrictions.

Our progressive politicians and opinion leaders proclaim their commitment to diversity almost daily, chanting the same refrain: "Diversity is our strength." This is the gospel according to political correctness. But how does diversity strengthen us? Is it a force for unity and cohesiveness? Or is it a source of division and contention? Does it promote the common good and the friendship that rests at the heart of citizenship? Or does it promote racial and ethnic division and something resembling the tribalism that prevents most of the world from making constitutional government a success? When is the last time we heard anyone in Washington talk about the common good? We are used to hearing talk about the various stakeholders and group interests, but not much about what the nation has in common.

This should not be surprising. Greater diversity means inevitably that we have less in common, and the more we encourage diversity the less we honor the common good. Any honest and clear-sighted observer should be able to see that diversity is a solvent that dissolves the unity and cohesiveness of a nation—and we should not be deceived into believing that its proponents do not understand the full impact of their advocacy!

Diversity, of course, marches under the banner of tolerance, but is a bastion of intolerance. It enforces its ideological liberalism with an iron fist that is driven by political correctness, the most ingenious (and insidious) device for suppressing freedom of speech and political dissent ever invented.

Political correctness could have been stopped dead in its tracks over three decades ago, but Republicans refused to kill it when they had the opportunity. In the presidential election campaign of 1980, Ronald Reagan promised to end affirmative action with the stroke of a pen by rescinding the executive order, issued by Lyndon Johnson, that created it. This promise was warmly received by the electorate in that election. But President Reagan failed to deliver his promised repeal. Too many Republicans had become convinced that they could use affirmative action to their advantage—that the largesse associated with racial class entitlements would attract minorities to the Republican Party. By signing on to this regime of political correctness, Republicans were never able to mount an effective opposition to its seemingly irresistible advance.

Today, any Republican charged or implicated with racism—however tendentious, outrageous, implausible, exaggerated, or false the charge or implication may be—will quickly surrender, often preemptively. This applies equally to other violations of political correctness: homophobia, Islamophobia, xenophobia, sexism, and a host of other so-called irrational prejudices. After all, there is no rational defense against an "irrational fear," which presumably is what the "phobias" are. Republicans have rendered themselves defenseless against political correctness, and the establishment wing of the party doesn't seem overly concerned, as they frequently join the chorus of Democrats in denouncing Trump's violations of political correctness. Only President Trump seems undeterred by the tyrannous threat that rests at the core of political correctness.

In addition to the Affirmative Action Executive Order in 1965, there were other actions taken during the Great Society that were meant to transform America. The Civil Rights Act of 1964 was sound legislation, authorized by the Fourteenth Amendment and designed to abolish racial discrimination in employment. But the administrative agencies, with the full cooperation of the courts, quickly transformed its laudable goals into mandates that required racial discrimination to achieve racial proportionality in hiring and promotion.

The Voting Rights Act of 1965 similarly sought to ban racial discrimination in voting. It too was transmogrified into an act that required racial discrimination in order to achieve proportional results in elections. Proportional results were touted by a palpable fiction as the only reliable evidence of free and fair elections.

The Immigration Act of 1965 was a kind of affirmative action plan to provide remedies for those races or ethnic groups that had been discriminated against in the past. Caucasian immigrants from European nations had been given preference in past years; now it was time to diversify the immigrant population by changing the focus to Third World nations, primarily nations in Latin America and Asia. The goal, as some scholars have slowly come to realize, was to diversify the demographic composition of the American population from majority white to a majority of people of color. There was also some anticipation that those coming from these Third World countries were more likely to need the ministrations of the welfare state and therefore more likely to be captured by the Democratic Party, the party promoting the welfare state.

White middle-class Americans in the 1960s and '70s were often referred to as selfish because their principal interests were improving their own lives, educating their own children, and contributing to their own communities. They showed no inclination to support diversity and the kind of authentic commitment to the new openness that was being advocated by progressive-liberalism. They stood as a constant roadblock to the administrative state, stubbornly resisting higher taxes, increased immigration, and expansion of the welfare state. Once they were no longer a majority, they would be powerless to resist. Demographers say that sometime around 2040 is the day of reckoning when whites will no longer be a majority and will sometime thereafter have to endure the fate they have inflicted on others for so many years. This radical demographic change will be due almost entirely to the immigration reform that was put into motion by the Immigration Act of 1965.

Of course, it is entirely a fiction that the American political system has produced monolithic white majorities that rule at the expense of so-called "discrete and insular minorities." Whites as a class have never constituted a majority faction in the nation, and the Constitution was explicitly written to prevent such majorities from forming. The fact that, among a host of other considerations, the Civil Rights Act of 1964 was passed by a supposed "monolithic white majority" to promote the equal protection rights of minorities belies the idea that it was a majority faction ruling in its own racial class interest.

President George W. Bush, no less than President Obama, was an advocate of a "borderless world." A supporter of amnesty and a path to citizenship for illegal aliens, he frequently stated that "family values don't stop at the border" and embraced the idea that "universal values" transcend a nation's sovereignty. He called himself a "compassionate conservative," and said on several occasions that we should be more compassionate to our less fortunate neighbors to the south.

President Reagan used this same kind of rhetoric when he signed the Immigration Reform and Control Act of 1986, which provided amnesty for three million illegal aliens. This was touted by Reagan as a way of "humanely" dealing with the issue of illegal immigration. In his signing statement, he said the Act "is both generous to the alien and fair to the countless thousands of people throughout the world who seek legally to come to America." The Act was supposed to be a one-time-only amnesty in exchange for stronger border control, but only the most naive in Washington believed that the promise of border control would be honored. In fact, illegal immigration continued unabated. The Act also fueled expectations—even demands—for additional amnesties, and delays in implementing new amnesties have been proffered as evidence by immigration activists (including Jeb Bush) that the American people lack compassion.

Any clear-thinking observer, however, can see that compassion is not a sound basis either for foreign policy or immigration policy. Compassion is more likely to lead to contempt than gratitude in both policy areas. The failure of the 1986 amnesty should be a clear reminder of the useful Machiavellian adage that in the world of *realpolitik*, it is better to be feared than loved.

Fear is more likely to engender respect, whereas love or compassion is more likely to be regarded as a contemptible sign of weakness. In 1984 Reagan received 37 percent of the Hispanic vote, but after the 1986 amnesty George H.W. Bush received a significantly lower 30 percent. Granted, Bush was no Reagan, but such ingratitude seemed to puzzle Republicans.

Republicans and Democrats alike are reluctant to consider serious measures to control illegal immigration. Republicans want to continue the steady supply of cheap and exploitable labor, and Democrats want future voters. Republicans are thinking only in the short term—they are not thinking politically; Democrats always think politically. President Trump wants to stop chain migration and the diversity lottery. Those who win in the diversity lottery also begin chain migration, as do all legal immigrants. Since 2005, more than nine million foreign nationals have arrived in the U.S. by chain migration, and when they become voting citizens, in all likelihood, two-thirds of them will vote Democrat. Trump knows how to think politically!

Birthright citizenship contributes to a borderless world. Any woman who comes to the United States as a legal or illegal alien and gives birth confers the boon of American citizenship on her child. In these instances, America has no control over who becomes a citizen. Constitutional law experts say it is a settled issue that the Constitution adopted the English common law of birthright citizenship. William Blackstone is cited as the authority for this proposition, having written the authoritative *Commentaries on the Laws of England*—a work that was well known to our nation's Founders. What the proponents of birthright citizenship seem to ignore is that Blackstone always refers to "birthright subjects" and "birthright subjectship," never mentioning citizens or citizenship in his four volume work. Under the common law, anyone born under the protection of the king owed "perpetual allegiance" to the king in return. Blackstone freely admitted that birthright subjectship was an inheritance from the feudal system, which defined the relations of master and servant. Under the English common law there were no citizens—only subjects.

The Declaration of Independence, however, proclaims that the American people "are Absolved from all Allegiance to the British Crown." Thus, it is clear that the American people rejected the common law as a basis for citizenship. What is substituted in place of "perpetual allegiance" to a king is "the consent of the governed," with the clear implication that no individual can be ruled without his consent. Consent—not the accident of birth—is the basis for American citizenship.

James Wilson, a signer of the Declaration and the Constitution and later a member of the Supreme Court, perfectly expressed the matter when he wrote: "In America there are citizens, but no subjects." Is it plausible—is it even remotely credible—that the Founders, after fighting a revolutionary war to reject the feudal relic of "perpetual allegiance," would have adopted that same feudal relic as the ground of citizenship for the new American regime?

The American people can, of course, consent to allow others to join the compact that created the American nation, but they have the sovereign right to specify the terms and conditions for granting entry and the qualifications for citizenship. Presumably the qualifications for entry and naturalization will be whether those who wish to enter demonstrate a capacity to adopt the habits, manners, independence, and self-reliance of republican citizens and devotion to the principles that unite the American people. Furthermore, it would be unreasonable not to expect that potential immigrants should possess useful skills that will ensure that they will not become victims of the welfare state.

Immigration policies should serve the interests of the American people and of the nation—they should not be viewed as acts of charity to the world. Putting America first is a rational goal. It is the essence of sovereignty. And the sovereign nation-state is the only home of citizenship—as it is the only home of constitutional government.

America's Cold Civil War

Charles R. Kesler

October 2018

Six years ago I wrote a book about Barack Obama in which I predicted that modern American liberalism, under pressures both fiscal and philosophical, would either go out of business or be forced to radicalize. If it chose the latter, I predicted, it could radicalize along two lines: towards socialism or towards an increasingly post-modern form of leadership. Today it is doing both. As we saw in Bernie Sanders' campaign, the youngest generation of liberals is embracing socialism openly—something that would have been unheard of during the Cold War. At the same time, identity politics is on the ascendant, with its quasi-Nietzschean faith in race, sex, and power as the keys to being and meaning. In the #MeToo movement, for example—as we saw recently in Justice Kavanaugh's confirmation battle—the credo is, "Believe the woman." In other words, truth will emerge not from an adversarial process weighing evidence and testimony before the bar of reason, but from yielding to the will of the more politically correct. "Her truth" is stronger than any objective or disinterested truth.

In the *Claremont Review of Books*, we have described our current political scene as a cold civil war. A cold civil war is better than a hot civil war, but it is not a good situation for a country to be in. Underlying our cold civil war is the fact that America is torn increasingly between two rival constitutions, two cultures, two ways of life.

Political scientists sometimes distinguish between normal politics and regime politics. Normal politics takes place within a political and constitutional order and concerns means, not ends. In other words, the ends or principles are agreed upon; debate is simply over means. By contrast, regime politics is about who rules and for what ends or principles. It questions the nature of the political system itself. Who has rights? Who gets to vote? What do we honor or revere together as a people? I fear America may be leaving the world of normal politics and entering the dangerous world of regime politics—a politics in which our political loyalties diverge more and more, as they did in the 1850s, between two contrary visions of the country.

One vision is based on the original Constitution as amended. This is the Constitution grounded in the natural rights of the Declaration of Independence, the Constitution written in 1787 and ratified in 1788. It has been transmitted to us with significant Amendments—some improvements and some not—but it is recognizable still as the original Constitution. To simplify matters we may call this "the conservative Constitution"—with the caveat that conservatives have never agreed perfectly on its meaning and that many non-conservatives remain loyal to it.

The other vision is based on what Progressives and liberals, for 100 years now, have called "the living Constitution." This term implies that the original Constitution is dead—or at least on life support—and that in order to remain relevant to our national life, the original Constitution must be infused with new meaning and new ends and therefore with new duties, rights, and powers. To cite an important example, new administrative agencies must be created to circumvent the structural limitations that the original Constitution imposed on government.

As a doctrine, the living Constitution originated in America's new departments of political and social science in the late nineteenth century—but it was soon at the very forefront of Progressive politics. One of the doctrine's prime formulators, Woodrow Wilson, had contemplated as a young scholar a series of constitutional amendments to reform America's national government into a kind of parliamentary system—a system able to facilitate faster political change. But he quickly realized that his plan to amend the Constitution was going nowhere. Plan B was the living Constitution. While keeping the outward forms of the old Constitution, the idea of a living Constitution would change utterly the spirit in which the Constitution was understood.

The resulting Constitution—let us call it "the liberal Constitution"—is not a constitution of natural rights or individual human rights, but of historical or evolutionary right. Wilson called the spirit of the old Constitution Newtonian, after Isaac Newton, and that of the new Constitution Darwinian, after Charles Darwin. By Darwinian, Wilson meant that instead of being difficult to amend, the liberal Constitution would be easily amenable to experimentation and adjustment. To paraphrase the late Walter Berns, the point of the old Constitution was to keep the times in tune with the Constitution; the purpose of the new is to keep the Constitution in tune with the times.

Until the 1960s, most liberals believed it was inevitable that their living Constitution would replace the conservative Constitution through a kind of slow-motion evolution. But during the sixties, the so-called New Left abandoned evolution for revolution, and partly in reaction to that, defenders of the old Constitution began not merely to fight back, but to call for a return to America's first principles. By seeking to revolve back to the starting point, conservatives proved to be Newtonians after all—and also, in a way, revolutionaries, since the original meaning of revolution is to return to where you began, as a celestial body revolves in the heavens.

The conservative campaign against the inevitable victory of the living Constitution gained steam as a campaign against the gradual or sudden disappearance of limited government and of republican virtue in our political life. And when it became clear, by the late 1970s and 1980s, that the conservatives weren't going away, the cold civil war was on.

———

Confronted by sharper, deeper, and more compelling accounts of the conservative Constitution, the liberals had to sharpen—that is, radicalize—their own alternative, following the paths paved by the New Left. As a result, the gap between the liberal and conservative Constitutions became a gulf, to the extent that today we are two countries—or we are fast on the road to becoming two countries—each constituted differently.

Consider a few of the contrasts. The prevailing liberal doctrine of rights traces individual rights to membership in various groups—racial, ethnic, gender, class-based, etc.—which are undergoing a continual process of consciousness-raising and empowerment. This was already a prominent feature of Progressivism well over a century ago, though the groups have changed since then. Before Woodrow Wilson became a politician, he wrote a political science textbook, and the book opened by asking which races should be studied. Wilson answered: we'll study the Aryan race, because the Aryan race is the one that has mastered the world. The countries of Europe and the Anglophone countries are the conquerors and colonizers of the other continents. They are the countries with the most advanced armaments, arts, and sciences.

Wilson was perhaps not a racist in the full sense of the term, because he expected the less advanced races over time to catch up with the Aryan race. But his emphasis was on group identity—an emphasis that liberals today retain, the only difference being that the winning and losing sides have been scrambled. Today the white race and European civilization are the enemy—"dead white males" is a favored pejorative on American campuses—and the races and groups that were oppressed in the past are the ones that today need compensation, privileges, and power.

Conservatives, by contrast, regard the individual as the quintessential endangered minority. They trace individual rights to human nature, which lacks a race. Human nature also lacks ethnicity, gender, and class. Conservatives trace the idea of rights to the essence of an individual as a human being. We have rights because we're human beings with souls, with reason, distinct from other animals and from God. We're not beasts, but we're not God—we're the in-between being. Conservatives seek to vindicate human equality and liberty—the basis for majority rule in politics—against the liberal Constitution's alternative, in which everything is increasingly based on group identity.

There is also today a vast divergence between the liberal and conservative understandings of the First Amendment. Liberals are interested in transforming free speech into what they call equal speech, ensuring that no one gets more than his fair share. They favor a redistribution of speech rights via limits on campaign contributions, repealing the Supreme Court's *Citizens United* decision, and narrowing the First Amendment for the sake of redistribution of speech rights from the rich to the poor. Not surprisingly, the Democratic Party's 2016 platform called for amending the First Amendment!

There is, of course, also a big difference between the liberal Constitution's freedom *from* religion and the conservative Constitution's freedom *of* religion. And needless to say, the liberal Constitution has no Second Amendment.

In terms of government structure, the liberal Constitution is designed to overcome the separation of powers and most other checks and balances. Liberals consistently support the increased ability to coordinate, concentrate, and enhance government power—as opposed to dividing, restricting, or checking it. This is to the detriment of popular control of government. In recent decades, government power has flowed mainly through the hands of unelected administrators and judges—to the point that elected members of Congress find themselves increasingly dispirited and unable to legislate. As the *Financial Times* put it recently, "Congress is a sausage factory that has forgotten how to make sausages."

If one thinks about how America's cold civil war could be resolved, there seem to be only five possibilities. One would be to change the political subject. Ronald Reagan used to say that when the little green men arrive from outer space, all of our political differences will be transcended and humanity will unite for the first time in human history. Similarly, if some jarring event intervenes—a major war or a huge natural calamity—it might reset our politics.

A second possibility, if we can't change the subject, is that we could change our minds. Persuasion, or some combination of persuasion and moderation, might allow us to end or endure our great political division. Perhaps one party or side will persuade a significant majority of the electorate to embrace its Constitution, and thus win at the polling booth and in the legislature. For generations, Republicans have longed for a realigning election that would turn the GOP into America's majority party. This remains possible, but seems unlikely. Only two presidents in the twentieth century were able to effect enduring changes in American public opinion and voting patterns—Franklin Roosevelt and Ronald Reagan. FDR inspired a political realignment that lasted for a generation or so and lifted the Democratic Party to majority status. Ronald Reagan inspired a realignment of public policy, but wasn't able to make the GOP the majority party.

Since 1968, the norm in America has been divided government: the people have more often preferred to split control of the national government between the Democrats and the Republicans rather than entrust it to one party. This had not previously been the pattern in American politics. Prior to 1968, Americans would almost always (the exceptions proved the rule) entrust the Senate, the House of Representatives, and the Presidency to the same party in each election. They would occasionally change the party, but still they would vote for a party to run the government. Not so for the last 50 years. And neither President Obama nor President Trump, so far, has persuaded the American electorate to embrace his party as their national representative, worthy of long-term patriotic allegiance.

Trump, of course, is new to this, and his party in Congress is basically pre-Trumpian. He did not win the 2016 election by a very large margin, and he was not able to bring many new Republicans into the House or the Senate. Nonetheless, he has the opportunity now to put his mark on the party. In trying to do so his populism—which is not a word he uses—will not be enough. He will have to reach out to the existing Republican Party as he has done, adopt some of its agenda, adopt its electoral supporters, and gradually bring them around to his "America first" conservatism if he is to have any chance of achieving a political realignment. And the odds remain against him at this point.

As for moderating our disagreements and learning to live with them more or less permanently, that too seems unlikely given their fundamental nature and the embittered trajectory of our politics over the last two decades.

So if we won't change our minds, and if we can't change the subject, we are left with only three other ways out of the cold civil war. The happiest of the three would be a vastly reinvigorated federalism. One of the original reasons for constitutional federalism was that the states had a variety of interests and views that clashed with one another and could not be pursued in common. If we had a re-flowering of federalism, some of the differences between blue states and red states could be handled discreetly by the states themselves. The most disruptive issues could be denationalized. The problem is, having abandoned so much of traditional federalism, it is hard to see how federalism could be revived at this late juncture.

That leaves two possibilities. One, alas, is secession, which is a danger to any federal system—something about which James Madison wrote at great length in *The Federalist Papers*. With any federal system, there is the possibility that some states will try to leave it. The Czech Republic and Slovakia have gone their separate ways peacefully, just within the last generation. But America is much better at expansion than contraction. And George Washington's admonitions to preserve the Union, I think, still miraculously somehow linger in our ears. So secession would be extremely difficult for many reasons, not the least of which is that it could lead, as we Americans know from experience, to the fifth and worst possibility: hot civil war.

Under present circumstances, the American constitutional future seems to be approaching some kind of crisis—a crisis of the two Constitutions. Let us pray that we and our countrymen will find a way to reason together and to compromise, allowing us to avoid the worst of these dire scenarios—that we will find, that is, the better angels of our nature.

Politics by Other Means: The Use and Abuse of Scandal

John Marini

March 2019

T he great difficulty of interpreting political scandals was summarized by a newspaper editor in the western film, *The Man Who Shot Liberty Valance.* Deciding not to publish the truth of an explosive political story, the editor justifies it by saying, "When the legend becomes fact, print the legend." We have certainly had many legends regarding political scandals foisted on us, especially since Watergate.

Nearly every political administration has potential scandal lying just below the surface. There are always those in government who seek to profit privately from public service, and there are always those who will abuse their power. All governments provide the occasion for scoundrels of both kinds. But the scandals they precipitate rarely erupt into full-blown crises of the political order. What differentiates the scandals that do?

To understand a political scandal fully, one must take into account all of the interests of those involved. The problem is that these interests are rarely revealed—which is precisely why it is so tempting for partisans, particularly if they are at a political disadvantage, to resort to scandal to attack their opponents. Many great scandals arise not as a means of exposing corruption, but as a means of attacking political foes while obscuring the political differences that are at issue. This is especially likely to occur in the aftermath of elections that threaten the authority of an established order. In such circumstances, scandal provides a way for defenders of the status quo to undermine the legitimacy of those who have been elected on a platform of challenging the status quo—diluting, as a consequence, the authority of the electorate.

The key to understanding how this works is to see that most political scandals, sooner or later, are transformed into legal dramas. As legal dramas, scandals become understood in non-partisan terms. The way in which they are resolved can have decisive political impacts, but those in charge of resolving them are the "neutral" prosecutors, judges, and bureaucrats who make up the permanent (and unelected) government, not the people's elected representatives. To resort to scandal in this way is thus a tacit admission that the scandalmongers no longer believe they are able to win politically. To paraphrase Clausewitz, scandal provides the occasion for politics by other means.

Richard Nixon won a landslide electoral victory in 1972 and was removed from office less than two years later. The Watergate scandal then became the model for subsequent political scandals, down to the current day. How and why did Watergate come about and what did it mean?

After the election of 1964, our two elected branches of government, each controlled by Democrats, worked together to expand power in Washington by centralizing administrative authority in the executive bureaucracy. This dramatic centralization of power created a political reaction in the electorate that began pushing back against the Great Society policies of the time. The Republican Party under Richard Nixon established itself as the partisan opponent of this centralized and powerful bureaucracy. Following his victory in 1968, Nixon's first term required political concessions that often expanded federal power—concessions aimed primarily at garnering support for the Vietnam War in a Democrat-controlled Congress. But Nixon's second term was not going to be a continuation of the first. Even *The New York Times* noted that the transformation of government demanded by Nixon after his 1972 re-election—his stated intention was to rein in the executive bureaucracy—was as extreme as if an opposition party had won.

As we all know, Nixon's intentions for his second term came to naught. American politics after Watergate were shaped by those who had engineered his downfall. As Henry Kissinger subsequently noted:

> Nixon in the final analysis had provoked a revolution. He had been re-elected by a landslide in 1972 in a contest as close to being fought on ideological issues as is possible in America.... The American people for once had chosen on philosophical grounds, not on personality.... For reasons unrelated to the issues and unforeseeable by the people who voted for what Nixon represented, this choice was now being annulled—with as-yet unpredictable consequences.

I recall being struck at the time of Watergate by the fact that there was a tremendous mobilization of partisan opinion against Nixon, but very little partisan mobilization in Nixon's defense. The reason for this, in retrospect, is that it is difficult—if not impossible—to mobilize partisan support once the contest is removed from the political arena and placed in the hands of prosecutors, grand juries, and judges. Nixon believed, correctly, that his partisan enemies were trying to destroy him. But even Republicans in Congress came to accept Watergate primarily in legal terms. The most remembered line from a Nixon defender was that of Senator Howard Baker: "What did the President know, and when did he know it?" Nixon quickly became boxed in; he was limited to making a legal, rather than political, defense of his office.

Also surprising at the time was how little disagreement there was about how to interpret Watergate. The political and intellectual elites of both parties came quickly to agree that executive abuse of power under Nixon posed a threat to democracy, and that Nixon's removal was required to meet that threat. Few noted the adverse effect on democratic or popular accountability: removing the elected chief executive further empowered the *unelected* executive bureaucracy, and further relegated Congress—which had created that bureaucracy—to serving as an executive oversight body rather than a legislative body.

Here is how the editors of the *Congressional Quarterly* summarized the situation at the time:

> When the 93rd [Congress] first convened in January 1973, President Nixon's sweeping assertions of executive authority posed a threat to the viability of the legislative branch. Even as Congress braced for confrontations with Nixon over spending, war powers, and other issues, its defiance was tempered by doubts as to whether it was indeed any match for the newly re-elected President. But by the time Congress adjourned [on] December 20, 1974, the balance of power had shifted dramatically. Both Nixon and . . . [Vice President] Agnew had been driven from office in disgrace—replaced by men whom Congress had a hand in selecting. Meanwhile, moving into a vacuum created by the disintegration of executive leadership, Congress had staked out a commanding role for itself.

The popular understanding of the Watergate scandal—that it was somehow rooted in Nixon's flawed personal character, and that it was essentially a legal matter—remains unshaken after more than 40 years. But I was not convinced then, nor am I convinced today, that Watergate can be properly understood in either personal or legal terms. By promising to use his executive power to bring the executive bureaucracy under his control, Nixon posed a danger to the political establishment after his landslide re-election. In response, the establishment struck back.

It wasn't until many years after Watergate that we learned the identity of the source of the leaks that led to Nixon's removal. Deep Throat, the source for the reporting of Bob Woodward and Carl Bernstein at *The Washington Post,* turned out to be Mark Felt, a high-level FBI official who had access to all of the classified information pertaining to the investigation. Felt leaked that information selectively over the course of a year or more, helping to shape public opinion in ways the prosecution could not. Although Woodward and Bernstein were lauded as investigative reporters, they merely served as a conduit by which the bureaucracy undermined the authority of the elected chief executive. Geoff Shepard, a young member of Nixon's defense team who has continued investigating Watergate using the Freedom of Information Act, has recently established as well that the prosecutors and judges involved in Watergate violated the procedural requirements that ensure impartiality, acting instead as partisans opposed to Nixon.

Our country was divided at the time of Watergate, as it remains divided today, over how we should be governed, and thus over what constitutes a good and just regime. Is the modern administrative state—the progressive innovation that took shape in the New Deal and was greatly expanded in the Great Society—the just and proper way to govern? Or is it just and proper to govern through the political structures established by the Constitution? Does the regulation of Americans' economic and social lives by a centralized bureaucracy establish the moral justification for government? Or does the underlying principle of American constitutionalism—the principle that the power of government must be limited and directed to the protection of its citizens' natural rights—remain valid?

Between these alternatives there can be no compromise. This division was not solely of Nixon's making, and it was the inability of the political parties and of the two elected branches of government to forge a consensus one way or the other that made the Watergate scandal possible, if not inevitable.

———

The Ethics in Government Act, passed by Congress in 1978, established the Independent Counsel statute. This legislation was justified on the ground that executive discretion must be subordinate to law. But that masked its political purpose, which was to insulate the permanent, unelected government from political control. The Independent Counsel statute was devised to stand as a bulwark against any president or senior executive branch official who dared threaten the centralized executive bureaucracy put in place by the Democratic Party majorities of the 1960s and '70s. It weakened the president's political control of that sprawling bureaucracy and strengthened Congress's hand in managing it. Ultimately, it had the effect of transforming political and policy disputes—adjudicated by the elected branches of government, and thus by the people—into legal disputes in which the people have no part. As former prosecutor Cliff Nichols has written:

The [Department of Justice] is an institution vested with formidable resources, including its authority over the FBI. It is also often the beneficiary of a thinly veiled, yet presumed, allegiance with most of the federal courts in which its attorneys operate. As a result, and given enough time, in most cases, the DOJ is empowered—via favorable rulings and otherwise—to access, manipulate, and maneuver the federal laws, rules, regulations, and procedures—not to mention witness testimony—in whatever ways it may deem necessary to ultimately bring most of those it targets to heel, . . . perhaps, even including a President.

For nearly two centuries of our nation's history, prior to passage of the Ethics in Government Act, there existed no legal mechanism of government outside the political and legal authority granted by the Constitution to the legislative, executive, and judicial branches. The Constitution established the separation of powers as the ground of adjudicating all political disputes. Members of the elected branches would defend their institutional interests, motivated by self-interest and by differing opinions regarding the public good. In the most serious political disputes, the legislature had the constitutional power to impeach the president—in which case both sides could make their case to the public and the people could decide.

Today, by contrast, the political branches, rather than defending their institutional interests, tend to accommodate the administrative state. The centralized executive bureaucracy has become the central feature of government, administrative rulemaking has replaced general lawmaking, and rule by bureaucrats has replaced rule by elected officials. Not only both political branches of government, but in some ways both parties, have accommodated themselves to this new way of governing. But given that this transformation of how we are governed was accomplished administratively, through the bureaucracy and the courts, rather than politically—with Congress passing legislation supported by a majority of the American people—it is not clear that the American people are on board. Certainly there is no public consensus on the question.

Nationally organized interests were well equipped to adjust to this new way of governing, and they continue to have access to, and be well served by, the Washington establishment. Citizens who exist outside those organized interests, on the other hand, seem to sense that they have been disenfranchised and that government no longer operates on behalf of a public or a common good. This explains the deep social and cultural division underlying the 2016 election results that shocked and awed the Washington establishment.

We see today, in the two-year Mueller investigation and its aftermath, yet another attempt to destroy an anti-establishment president using a legal rather than political process of adjudication. The most notable difference between this scandal and Watergate is that President Trump has so far succeeded—largely through his relentless characterization of most of those in the media as dishonest partisans rather than objective reporters—in preventing the scandals surrounding him from being defined, by his enemies, in legal rather than political terms.

The guardians of the status quo in the permanent government and the media have defined past political scandals so successfully that a full and proper understanding of Watergate, for instance, is likely impossible now. It remains to be seen whether, in the end, they will succeed again today—whether the legend will again become fact, and they will print the legend.

Orwell's *1984* and Today

Larry P. Arnn

December 2020

O n September 17, Constitution Day, I chaired a panel organized by the White House. It was an extraordinary thing. The panel's purpose was to identify what has gone wrong in the teaching of American history and to lay forth a plan for recovering the truth. It took place in the National Archives—we were sitting in front of the originals of the Declaration of Independence and the Constitution—a very beautiful place. When we were done, President Trump came and gave a speech about the beauty of the American Founding and the importance of teaching American history to the preservation of freedom.

This remarkable event reminded me of an essay by a teacher of mine, Harry Jaffa, called "On the Necessity of a Scholarship of the Politics of Freedom." Its point was that a certain kind of scholarship is needed to support the principles of a nation such as ours. America is the most deliberate nation in history—it was built for reasons that are stated in the legal documents that form its founding. The reasons are given in abstract and universal terms, and without good scholarship they can be turned astray. I was reminded of that essay because this event was the greatest exhibition in my experience of the combination of the scholarship and the politics of freedom.

The panel was part of an initiative of President Trump, mostly ignored by the media, to counter the *New York Times*' 1619 Project. The 1619 Project promotes the teaching that slavery, not freedom, is the defining fact of American history. President Trump's 1776 Commission aims to restore truth and honesty to the teaching of American history. It is an initiative we must work tirelessly to carry on, regardless of whether we have a president in the White House who is on our side in the fight.

We must carry on the fight because our country is at stake. Indeed, in a larger sense, civilization itself is at stake, because the forces arrayed against the scholarship and the politics of freedom today have more radical aims than just destroying America.

———

I taught a course this fall semester on totalitarian novels. We read four of them: George Orwell's *1984*, Arthur Koestler's *Darkness at Noon*, Aldous Huxley's *Brave New World*, and C.S. Lewis's *That Hideous Strength*.

The totalitarian novel is a relatively new genre. In fact, the word "totalitarian" did not exist before the 20th century. The older word for the worst possible form of government is "tyranny"—a word Aristotle defined as the rule of one person, or of a small group of people, in their own interests and according to their will. Totalitarianism was unknown to Aristotle, because it is a form of government that only became possible after the emergence of modern science and technology.

The old word "science" comes from a Latin word meaning "to know." The new word "technology" comes from a Greek word meaning "to make." The transition from traditional to modern science means that we are not so much seeking *to know* when we study nature as seeking *to make* things—and ultimately, to remake nature itself. That spirit of remaking nature—including human nature—greatly emboldens both human beings and governments. Imbued with that spirit, and employing the tools of modern science, totalitarianism is a form of government that reaches farther than tyranny and attempts to control the totality of things.

In the beginning of his history of the Persian War, Herodotus recounts that in Persia it was considered illegal even to think about something that was illegal to do—in other words, the law sought to control people's thoughts. Herodotus makes plain that the Persians were not able to do this. We today are able to get closer through the use of modern technology. In Orwell's *1984*, there are telescreens everywhere, as well as hidden cameras and microphones. Nearly everything you do is watched and heard. It even emerges that the watchers have become expert at reading people's faces. The organization that oversees all this is called the Thought Police.

If it sounds far-fetched, look at China today: there are cameras everywhere watching the people, and everything they do on the Internet is monitored. Algorithms are run and experiments are underway to assign each individual a social score. If you don't act or think in the politically correct way, things happen to you—you lose the ability to travel, for instance, or you lose your job. It's a very comprehensive system. And by the way, you can also look at how big tech companies here in the U.S. are tracking people's movements and activities to the extent that they are often able to know in advance what people will be doing. Even more alarming, these companies are increasingly able and willing to use the information they compile to manipulate people's thoughts and decisions.

The protagonist of *1984* is a man named Winston Smith. He works for the state, and his job is to rewrite history. He sits at a table with a telescreen in front of him that watches everything he does. To one side is something called a memory hole—when Winston puts things in it, he assumes they are burned and lost forever. Tasks are delivered to him in cylinders through a pneumatic tube. The task might involve something big, like a change in what country the state is at war with: when the enemy changes, all references to the previous war with a different enemy need to be expunged. Or the task might be something small: if an individual falls out of favor with the state, photographs of him being honored need to be altered or erased altogether from the records. Winston's job is to fix every book, periodical, newspaper, etc. that reveals or refers to what used to be the truth, in order that it conform to the new truth.

One man, of course, can't do this alone. There's a film based on *1984* starring John Hurt as Winston Smith. In the film they depict the room where he works, and there are people in cubicles like his as far as the eye can see. There would have to be millions of workers involved in constantly re-writing the past. One of the chief questions raised by the book is, what makes this worth the effort? Why does the regime do it?

Winston's awareness of this endless, mighty effort to alter reality makes him cynical and disaffected. He comes to see that he knows nothing of the past, of real history: "Every record has been destroyed or falsified," he says at one point, "every book has been rewritten, every picture has been repainted, every statue and street and building has been renamed, every date has been altered. And that process is continuing day by day and minute by minute....Nothing exists except an endless present in which the Party is always right." Does any of this sound familiar?

In his disaffection, Winston commits two unlawful acts: he begins writing in a diary and he begins meeting a woman in secret, outside the sanction of the state. The family is important to the state, because the state needs babies. But the women are raised by the state in a way that they are not to enjoy relations with their husbands. And the children—as in China today, and as it was in the Soviet Union—are indoctrinated and taught to spy and inform on their parents. Parents love their children but live in terror of them all the time. Think of the control that comes from that—and the misery.

There are three stratums in the society of *1984*. There is the Inner Party, whose members hold all the power. There is the Outer Party, to which Winston belongs, whose members work for—and are watched and controlled by—the Inner Party. And there are the proles, who live and do the blue collar work in a relatively unregulated area. Winston ventures out into that area from time to time. He finds a little shop there where he buys things. And it is in a room upstairs from this shop where he and Julia, the woman he falls in love with, set up a kind of household as if they are married. They create something like a private world in that room, although it is a world with limitations—they can't even think about having children, for instance, because if they did, they would be discovered and killed.

In the end, it turns out that the shopkeeper, who had seemed to be a kindly old man, is in fact a member of the Thought Police. Winston and Julia's room contained a hidden telescreen all along, so everything they have said and done has been observed. In fact, it emerges that the Thought Police have known that Winston has been having deviant thoughts for twelve years and have been watching him carefully. When the couple are arrested, they have made pledges that they will never betray each other. They know the authorities will be able to make them say whatever they want them to say—but in their hearts, they pledge, they will be true to their love. It is a promise that neither is finally able to keep.

After months of torture, Winston thinks that what awaits him is a bullet in the back of the head, the preferred method of execution of both the Nazis and the Soviet Communists. In Koestler's *Darkness at Noon*, the protagonist walks down a basement hallway after confessing to crimes that he didn't commit, and without any ceremony he is shot in the back of the head—eradicated as if he were vermin. Winston doesn't get off so easy. He will instead undergo an education, or more accurately a re-education. His final stages of torture are depicted as a kind of totalitarian seminar. The seminar is conducted by a man named O'Brien, who is portrayed marvelously in the film by Richard Burton. As he alternately raises and lowers the level of Winston's pain, O'Brien leads him to knowledge regarding the full meaning of the totalitarian regime.

As the first essential step of his education, Winston has to learn doublethink—a way of thinking that defies the law of contradiction. In Aristotle, the law of contradiction is the basis of all reasoning, the means of making sense of the world. It is the law that says that X and Y cannot be true at the same time if they're mutually exclusive. For instance, if A is taller than B and B is taller than C, C cannot be taller than A. The law of contradiction means things like that.

In our time, the law of contradiction would mean that a governor, say, could not simultaneously hold that the COVID pandemic renders church services too dangerous to allow, and also that massive protest marches are fine. It would preclude a man from declaring himself a woman, or a woman declaring herself a man, as if one's sex is simply a matter of what one wills it to be—and it would preclude others from viewing such claims as anything other than preposterous.

The law of contradiction also means that we can't change the past. What we can know of the truth all resides in the past, because the present is fleeting and confusing and tomorrow has yet to come. The past, on the other hand, is complete. Aristotle and Thomas Aquinas go so far as to say that changing the past—making what has been not to have been—is denied even to God. Because if something both happened and didn't happen, no human understanding is possible. And God created us with the capacity for understanding.

That's the law of contradiction, which the art of doublethink denies and violates. Doublethink is manifest in the fact that the state ministry in which Winston is tortured is called the Ministry of Love. It is manifest in the three slogans displayed on the state's Ministry of Truth: "War is peace. Freedom is slavery. Ignorance is strength." And as we have seen, the regime in *1984* exists precisely to repeal the past. If the past can be changed, anything can be changed—man can surpass even the power of God. But still, to what end?

Why do you think you are being tortured? O'Brien asks Winston. The Party is not trying to improve you, he says—the Party cares nothing about you. Winston is brought to see that he is where he is simply as the subject of the state's power. Understanding having been rendered meaningless, the only competence that has meaning is power.

"Already we are breaking down the habits of thought which have survived from before the Revolution," O'Brien says.

> We have cut the links between child and parent, and between man and man, and between man and woman. No one dares trust a wife or a child or a friend any longer. But in the future there will be no wives and no friends. Children will be taken from their mothers at birth, as one takes eggs from a hen. The sex instinct will be eradicated. Procreation will be an annual formality like the renewal of a ration card.... There will be no loyalty, except loyalty toward the Party. There will be no love, except the love of Big Brother. There will be no laughter, except the laugh of triumph over a defeated enemy....All competing pleasures will be destroyed. But always—do not forget this Winston—always there will be the intoxication of power, constantly increasing and constantly growing subtler. Always, at every moment, there will be the thrill of victory, the sensation of trampling on an enemy who is helpless. If you want a picture of the future, imagine a boot stamping on a human face—forever.

Nature is ultimately unchangeable, of course, and humans are not God. Totalitarianism will never win in the end—but it can win long enough to destroy a civilization. That is what is ultimately at stake in the fight we are in. We can see today the totalitarian impulse among powerful forces in our politics and culture. We can see it in the rise and imposition of doublethink, and we can see it in the increasing attempt to rewrite our history.

———

"An informed patriotism is what we want," Ronald Reagan said toward the end of his Farewell Address as president in January 1989. "Are we doing a good enough job teaching our children what America is and what she represents in the long history of the world?"

Then he issued a warning.

Those of us who are over 35 or so years of age grew up in a different America. We were taught, very directly, what it means to be an American. And we absorbed, almost in the air, a love of country and an appreciation of its institutions. If you didn't get these things from your family you got them from the neighborhood, from the father down the street who fought in Korea or the family who lost someone at Anzio. Or you could get a sense of patriotism from school. And if all else failed you could get a sense of patriotism from the popular culture. The movies celebrated democratic values and implicitly reinforced the idea that America was special. TV was like that, too, through the mid-sixties.

But now, we're about to enter the [1990s], and some things have changed. Younger parents aren't sure that an unambivalent appreciation of America is the right thing to teach modern children. And as for those who create the popular culture, well-grounded patriotism is no longer the style.... We've got to do a better job of getting across that America is freedom—freedom of speech, freedom of religion, freedom of enterprise. And freedom is special and rare. It's fragile; it needs protection.

So, we've got to teach history based not on what's in fashion but what's important—why the Pilgrims came here, who Jimmy Doolittle was, and what those 30 seconds over Tokyo meant. You know, four years ago on the 40th anniversary of D-Day, I read a letter from a young woman writing to her late father, who'd fought on Omaha Beach.... [S]he said, "we will always remember, we will never forget what the boys of Normandy did." Well, let's help her keep her word. If we forget what we did, we won't know who we are. *I'm warning of an eradication of the American memory that could result, ultimately, in an erosion of the American spirit.*

American schoolchildren today learn two things about Thomas Jefferson: that he wrote the Declaration of Independence and that he was a slaveholder. This is a stunted and dishonest teaching about Jefferson.

What do our schoolchildren not learn? They don't learn what Jefferson wrote in *Notes on the State of Virginia*: "I tremble for my country when I reflect that God is just," he wrote in that book regarding the contest between the master and the slave. "The Almighty has no attribute which can take side with us in such a contest." If schoolchildren learned that, they would see that Jefferson was a complicated man, like most of us.

They don't learn that when our nation first expanded, it was into the Northwest Territory, and that slavery was forbidden in that territory. They don't learn that the land in that territory was ceded to the federal government from Virginia, or that it was on the motion of Thomas Jefferson that the condition of the gift was that slavery in that land be eternally forbidden. If schoolchildren learned that, they would come to see Jefferson as a human being who inherited things and did things himself that were terrible, but who regretted those things and fought against them. And they would learn, by the way, that on the scale of human achievement, Jefferson ranks very high. There's just no question about that, if for no other reason than that he was a prime agent in founding the first republic dedicated to the proposition that all men are created equal.

The astounding thing, after all, is not that some of our Founders were slaveholders. There was a lot of slavery back then, as there had been for all of recorded time. The astounding thing—the miracle, even, one might say—is that these slaveholders founded a republic based on principles designed to abnegate slavery.

To present young people with a full and honest account of our nation's history is to invest them with the spirit of freedom. It is to teach them something more than why our country deserves their love, although that is a good in itself. It is to teach them that the people in the past, even the great ones, were human and had to struggle. And by teaching them that, we prepare *them* to struggle with the problems and evils in and around them. Teaching them instead that the past was simply wicked and that now they are able to see so perfectly the right, we do them a disservice and fit them to be slavish, incapable of developing sympathy for others or undergoing trials on their own.

Depriving the young of the spirit of freedom will deprive us all of our country. It could deprive us, finally, of our humanity itself. This cannot be allowed to continue. It must be stopped.